A fascinating and well-argued book that adds a vital, missing component to understanding Churchill. As a lifelong admirer who as a boy met Churchill and who has read widely on his life, I was curious to know what Sandys and Henley would present as evidence. I was not only convinced but delighted at the realism and relevance of their portrayal of Churchill. He emerges as anything but ardently religious, but he was more personally aware of his destiny and more biblically literate and attuned to the Christian worldview and Christian civilization than many Christians today.

OS GUINNESS
Author of *A Free People's Suicide*

I have known four generations of the Churchill family. Jonathan Sandys has both the vision and the voice to carry forth the legacy of his great-grandfather and is well worthy to offer this account of Churchill's life and faith. *God and Churchill* has earned a place next to the greatest of books ever written on the master statesman.

JAMES C. HUMES
Author and former presidential speech writer

What a wonderfully enthusiastic book, written with the insights of a great-grandson of Winston Churchill who understands his great ancestor in unique and special ways. Jonathan grasps the spiritual dimensions of Churchill's life and the struggle against the pure evil of Nazi tyranny. And there is no doubt: It was Churchill as prime minister in 1940 who not only saved Britain from defeat but saved Christian civilization itself, as Jonathan and Wallace make so very clear. This is a book for Christians as well as for Churchill enthusiasts.

DR. CHRISTOPHER CATHERWOOD
Fellow of the Royal Historical Society, Churchill Archives By-Fellow emeritus, historian of twentieth-century history, and evangelical writer

A graphic portrayal of the life and legacy of Winston Churchill, with emphasis on his guiding belief in divine providence. Long before "the clash of civilizations" had become a common term, Churchill knew what it meant and spent his life defending the civilization so decisively shaped by the Christian faith. A fascinating study!

TIMOTHY GEORGE
Founding dean of Beeson Divinity School at Samford University and general editor of the *Reformation Commentary on Scripture*

Having witnessed firsthand how God moves to influence major events in the world for the good of his people, I cannot imagine anyone better suited to tell the story of God's work in the life and times of Churchill than Churchill's own flesh and blood. Jonathan Sandys brings an unparalleled vibrancy and perspective on the great man and his times. He and Wallace Henley have artfully woven together the best-known and most obscure pieces of history to present the beautiful and compelling tapestry that is *God and Churchill*. An absolute must-read.

JOANNE KING HERRING
International diplomat, author, and president/CEO of the Marshall Plan Charities

Great leaders, and the times and circumstances in which they served, have long fascinated me. Winston Churchill has been of special interest to me for many years. I have read books about the British wartime leader, but they always seem to leave out a critical element. But Jonathan Sandys and Wallace Henley have captured it in this book. At last we have a detailed presentation not only of Churchill's legendary exploits but also of the inner dynamic that compelled him with a vision for "Christian civilization" and an iron will to defend it at all costs. Sandys and Henley, to use a Churchillian idea, have brought the inspiration and lessons of the past into our present for the sake of the future. This is a must-read for our critical times.

ED YOUNG
Senior pastor, Second Baptist Church, Houston

GOD & CHURCHILL

GOD & CHURCHILL

HOW THE GREAT

LEADER'S SENSE OF

DIVINE DESTINY

CHANGED HIS TROUBLED

WORLD AND OFFERS

HOPE FOR OURS

JONATHAN SANDYS
&WALLACE HENLEY

**TYNDALE®
MOMENTUM**

*An Imprint of
Tyndale House Publishers, Inc.*

Visit Tyndale online at www.tyndale.com.

Visit Tyndale Momentum online at www.tyndalemomentum.com.

Tyndale Momentum and the Tyndale Momentum logo are registered trademarks of Tyndale House Publishers, Inc. Tyndale Momentum is an imprint of Tyndale House Publishers, Inc.

God and Churchill: How the Great Leader's Sense of Divine Destiny Changed His Troubled World and Offers Hope for Ours

Designed by Stephen Vosloo

Published in association with the literary agency of WordServe Literary Group, www.wordserveliterary.com.

Library of Congress Cataloging-in-Publication Data

Sandys, Jonathan, author.
  God and Churchill : how the great leader's sense of divine destiny changed his troubled world and offers hope for ours / Jonathan Sandys, Wallace Henley.
      pages cm
  Includes bibliographical references.
  ISBN 978-1-4964-0602-6 (hc)
1. Churchill, Winston, 1874-1965—Religion. 2. Prime ministers—Great Britain—Biography. 3. Prime ministers—Religious life—Great Britain. 4. World War, 1939-1945—Religious aspects. I. Title.
  DA566.9.C5S267 2015
  941.084092—dc23
  [B]   2015021631

Printed in the United States of America

21	20	19	18	17	16	15
7	6	5	4	3	2	1

Soli Deo Gloria

FROM JONATHAN SANDYS

To my darling wife, Sara, without whose tireless help
and encouragement during my own "Black Dog"
times this project wouldn't have been possible.
To our beautiful son, Jesse, who despite kicking and
screaming throughout the editing process, gave smiles and
cooings that brought humor and welcomed respites.
To Sir Martin Gilbert, my great-grandfather's official biographer,
whose incredible life's work on Churchill has always provided
me with an accurate and in-depth map to follow.

FROM WALLACE HENLEY

To Irene, after fifty-three years, still my
golden princess and destiny-sharer.
To our dynamic, engaging, adventurous, never-
dull, ever-expanding family.
To the pastors and teachers who, many years ago,
helped me appreciate history and look for the
hand of God guiding it to its purpose.

CONTENTS

Foreword by James A. Baker III *xi*

Preface by Cal Thomas *xv*

Introduction *xxi*

Part I: The Remarkable Preparation

1 : A Vision of Destiny *3*

2 : Surviving Destiny's Perilous Paths *19*

3 : From the Admiralty to the Trenches *43*

Part II: Destiny

4 : Hitler's Vision *61*

5 : Prime Minister at Last *75*

Part III: Saving "Christian Civilization"

6 : Churchill and the Sermon on the Mount *91*

7 : Preserving "A Certain Way of Life" *115*

8 : Hitler and "Perverted Science" *133*

9 : Hitler and the Corruption of the Church *153*

10 : Nazism and the German Disaster *165*

11 : Churchill's Urgent Concern—and Ours *179*

Part IV: Hope for Our Time

12 : How Churchill Kept Calm and Carried On *191*

13 : Churchill and the Character of Leadership *211*

14 : Help and Hope for Our Times *227*

Notes *241*

Acknowledgments *263*

Index *265*

About the Authors *267*

But thou knowest it is difficult, things pressing upon
every sense, to believe that the informing power of them is
the unseen; that out of it they come; that, where we can
descry no hand directing, a will, nearer than any hand, is
moving from within, causing them to fulfill his word.

GEORGE MACDONALD, *UNSPOKEN SERMONS*

FOREWORD

By James A. Baker III

On September 22, 2010, I was honored to speak at Westminster College in Fulton, Missouri, where, sixty-four years earlier, Winston Churchill delivered the "Iron Curtain" speech that did so much to define American diplomacy for most of the second half of the twentieth century. The great question of Churchill's period focused on how the Cold War, and the ominous arms race between the West and the Communist bloc, would eventually end.

At Fulton in 1946, Churchill described the dangers ahead. "From Stettin in the Baltic to Trieste in the Adriatic, an iron curtain has descended across the [European] Continent," he said. As he contemplated the new military threats and oppressive Communist regimes, Churchill lamented that "this is certainly not the Liberated Europe we fought [the Second World War] to build up."

History, as we know, has a way of repeating itself. As I write this foreword in 2015, we are again on the precipice of crisis as international terror threatens civilization. Once again, we are asking: How will it all end? As Jonathan Sandys and Wallace Henley detail in these pages, we have much to learn from Churchill's leadership in his chaotic times.

As I noted in my Westminster speech in 2010, the Cold War ended—after forty-four years of tension, stress, and terrifying moments at the brink—with a whimper rather than the nuclear bang that so many had feared. I was in my teens in 1946 and could not have imagined then that I would be directly involved in the process that brought the conflict to resolution.

When discussions between President George H. W. Bush, under whom I served as secretary of state at the time; Soviet leader Mikhail Gorbachev; and German chancellor Helmut Kohl focused on the alignments of the new, unified Germany, there were seemingly unbridgeable disagreements, even as an accord seemed tantalizingly close.

Years later, in September 2009, I described the situation for the German magazine *Der Spiegel.* I told their two reporters how Kohl, Bush, and I had met at Camp David in February 1990 to talk specifically about German unification and the implications for NATO.

"Germany doesn't want neutrality in any way," Chancellor Kohl had told us. "A united Germany will be a member of NATO."

With that, he gave us a binding commitment.

The concern of many was that Gorbachev would insist on German neutrality, not wanting the new Germany to be aligned with the West, especially in a military alliance. Already the British and French were concerned about the unification of Communist East Germany (the German Democratic Republic, or GDR) with free West Germany, and neutrality might have stymied the negotiations. Gorbachev, however, had committed from the outset not to use military force. Because the East German population would not have accepted the survival of the GDR, Gorbachev could only have stopped the course of events by force of arms. So he had little choice.

As I described this situation to *Der Spiegel,* one of the interviewers said, "This retreat of the Soviets, who had for decades tried to hold the West in check with proxy wars and sharp rhetoric, even now seems like a miracle."

A *miracle*? The reporter likely had no spiritual implications in mind in choosing that term. Yet perhaps he was more insightful than he realized. I recalled a visit by Gorbachev to the White House in May 1990. We were in the Cabinet Room when he acknowledged that any country should have the right to choose any alliance it wanted to join.

When he said that, it was done.

Sitting there, I thought, *Wow!* What had seemed impossible had become a reality with Gorbachev's words.

Though Winston Churchill was not alive to see it, he may not have been surprised that the Cold War ended in what some would regard as a miraculous fashion. After all, as Sandys and Henley note in this book, Churchill's entire life and destiny seemed to have been miraculous. Though not a religious man, he nevertheless had a sense of divine destiny. As you will read in *God and Churchill*, his very survival sometimes was nothing short of miraculous. Likewise, both Britain's survival during the horrid summer of the 1940 Blitz and the near-impossible evacuation at Dunkirk have been characterized by some as miraculous.

But were these marvelous outcomes the result of divine intervention? The authors, and I, leave that to the reader's own conclusion. Such a question, however, raises the possibility of God's intervention in history and the interaction between the spiritual and material realms.

There was a time in my own life when there seemed to be no need for spiritual intervention. I thought that a successful professional never admitted to pain or problems. Then I walked through a personal crisis. My wife, Susan, helped me pray through it and understand that I really needed to stop trying to play God. Instead, I needed to turn the matter over to him.

We all have those critical moments when we are tempted to cry out to God—or actually do, as Churchill did one night while hiding in a ditch in South Africa as the enemy pursued him. As you will read, though he was struggling with his own faith, he prayed earnestly in that moment for God's help.

During my own years in Washington, DC, prayer became an important part of my routine. I met on Wednesdays to pray with a small group of very normal guys who just happened to hold positions of power and influence, as I phrased it in a speech at the National Prayer Breakfast in 1990. My prayer partners came from both major political parties and different religious traditions. But we all shared an understanding that I had come to recognize: Inner security and true fulfillment come by faith, not by wielding power in a town where power is king. Such fulfillment and inner security come only by developing a personal relationship with God, a relationship that for me is made possible by Jesus Christ.

In fact, there were three things that kept me grounded during my years under the searing national spotlight: my family, my friends, and my faith. Many people believe that faith is more difficult for those in public life. For me, at least—and apparently for Winston Churchill—the opposite was true. Living in the centrifuge of politics encouraged—even demanded—spiritual growth.

I concur with Lech Wałęsa, the great Polish leader who played a vital role in helping end the Cold War, who said: "Sooner or later we will have to go back to our fundamental values, back to God, the truth, the truth which is in God."

Winston Churchill saw this in his own times, and such vision compelled his great concern for what he repeatedly called *Christian civilization*. I hope *God and Churchill* will inspire such a perspective and urgency in all who read it.

James A. Baker III was White House chief of staff and secretary of the treasury under President Ronald Reagan, and White House chief of staff and secretary of state under President George H. W. Bush. He is now honorary chair of the James A. Baker III Institute for Public Policy at Rice University.

WHAT MADE WINSTON CHURCHILL?

Both Churchill's great-grandson Jonathan Sandys and Wallace Henley—a veteran of politics, journalism, and the church—have dug deeply to find the less exposed answers to this question. In a sense, they provide what may be the first "spiritual biography" of Winston Churchill.

The quest to understand the lives and motives of those who affect our times usually hinges on an old debating point: Do the times make the man, or does the man make the times?

Certainly the times in which Winston Churchill lived and worked had much to do with forming his global image. His service in the First World War as a battalion commander—after his departure from leadership of the Admiralty in a manner that some would find embarrassing—showed his pluck and commitment to duty. And Churchill of course was indispensable to Britain and America's victory in the Second World War.

By the standard he set, all political leaders since have been mere pygmies—with the possible exception of Margaret Thatcher and Ronald Reagan. Yet even they pale in his shadow. No one else can touch Churchill for his vision, leadership, and persistence.

Churchill reminds us of Babe Ruth, the great twentieth-century ballplayer. The Babe struck out a lot, but he also hit many home runs. So, too, Churchill, as Sandys and Henley remind us, experienced many failures, but history remembers him primarily for his huge successes. Not only did Churchill make history; he also bent it to his will and even today embodies the classic definition of a leader.

Churchill had many contemporary enemies, and there are still those in Britain who believe that he was too full of himself and that many of his ideas were ill-conceived. Yet his achievements were so momentous that these voices get little attention outside of academic circles or critics whose philosophies are put off by Churchill's beliefs.

Momentous is a word befitting of Churchill. His prescience as a teenager about his future leadership role for his nation, and his early experiences and relationships, would all be part of what prepared him for his life's mission. When he became prime minister on May 10, 1940, he declared it to be the destiny for which his previous life had been the groundwork.

As for relationships, Churchill had a far less than ideal upbringing. His father, Lord Randolph, mostly rejected him and gave him not love but criticism; his mother, Jennie, pushed him, but she was often preoccupied with a series of men who were not her husband. Churchill was small and often the object of bullying, but he overcame it all through the force of his ego, strong will, and persistence.

Such struggles shaped in Churchill the attitude that he would articulate one day: "Never give in, never give in, never, never, never—in nothing, great or small, large or petty—never give in except to convictions of honour and good sense. Never yield to force; never yield to the apparently overwhelming might of the enemy."

But who put such moral steel in Churchill's heart and spine?

If his parents were not strong spiritual and ethical guides, who gave Churchill such principles? Though he did not have accessible, engaged parents, there was one relationship that has been too little considered and written about. Elizabeth Everest, young Winston's nanny, was much more than a caregiver. She was a spiritual mentor, whose simple and resolute faith would anchor a little boy who could be a troublemaker and a disappointment to his teachers. Her influence would prove to be lifelong.

One of the great services that Sandys and Henley have rendered to us is in bringing Mrs. Everest more into focus. Among the unique factors that made Churchill who he was, Mrs. Everest's role is major. Sandys and Henley do not pretend that she made him a deeply religious man. However, she gave Churchill a love for the King James Bible and an understanding of the ways in which Christianity formed a "certain way of life" (in Churchill's own words) that he spoke of again and again as "Christian civilization." He was passionate in its defense, as the many references to it in his speeches demonstrates.

It was not just his times that made Churchill, but in many ways he shaped his times. Sandys and Henley end this book with hope. They discuss how Churchill "kept calm and carried on" in his day, demonstrating personally that, although the times were hard, they were endurable. The authors show how Churchill spoke with frankness about the "blood, toil, tears, and sweat" that lay ahead, but he always led his nation and its allies to maintain a positive outlook through the grim task of defeating Hitler and the Nazis.

Sandys and Henley note the opinion of Lord Moran, Churchill's personal physician, that a secret to Churchill's health and strength was his "buoyancy." True, he could fall into the deep depressions that he called his "black dog," but he always came up again into light—and hope.

This was more than psychology; it was the outcome of a deep

faith. Recent writers have tried to present Churchill as an agnostic or even an atheist. However, they seek to freeze him forever in his youthful doubts while he was serving in India. Churchill was not an active churchman, but as Sandys and Henley show, he was a person of deep faith and biblical knowledge who grew far beyond the skepticism of his younger days.

God and Churchill is intensely relevant to our own times. Beliefs, worldviews, religion, and spirituality are at the heart of contemporary conflicts. To ignore this is to misunderstand the nature of our times. Worse, it is to be ill-equipped for the battles blazing across the globe. Such was Churchill's world. Sandys and Henley show here the roots of Nazism, with its mixture of "perverted science" and Aryan mysticism. The labels are different, but the similarities between Churchill's day and ours are remarkable.

Churchill was more than a leader for his time. He was "a man for all seasons," to borrow Robert Bolt's title from his play about Sir Thomas More. "There has been no one remotely like him before or since," writes London mayor Boris Johnson.

The world is the worse for it.

Churchill, as a man for all seasons, is a model of leadership for our times. He was a full-orbed human being, and now Sandys and Henley present his spirituality as well as his humanity, showing the critical link between the two. The authors answer not only the questions of the past but also those of the present, as they show the leadership we need now for the sake of the future.

The most intriguing issue Sandys and Henley explore—one that most Churchill authors dodge—is the role of God in the making of Winston Churchill. This provokes several other questions: Does God have a plan in human history? Does God intervene in the course of human events? Does he raise up leaders at critical junctures to save civilization? If so, was Winston Churchill one of the many "deliverers" who have appeared in history's arena at just the right time and place?

In light of contemporary issues, these may be the most important concerns of all regarding the making of a leader. It's not merely the making of Winston Churchill that is in focus here, but more so the burning issues of civilization's survival and the quality of leadership needed in our times for that struggle.

INTRODUCTION

JONATHAN SANDYS

When I was a child, my sense of identity was framed in part by the knowledge that I was descended from one of history's great heroes: Sir Winston Churchill, who, as prime minister of Great Britain, had inspired the nation and her allies during the dark days of the Second World War. My grandmother, Diana, was Churchill's eldest daughter, and her son, Julian, is my father. I grew up hearing stories from family and friends who had intimate, firsthand knowledge of Sir Winston, or Great-Grandpapa as I have always known him.

One of my treasured memories as a youth was the day I met Sir Martin Gilbert, Churchill's official biographer. At a book launching I attended in London for one of Sir Martin's books, I approached the great historian for an autograph. He took one look at me and said, "You're one of Julian's boys, aren't you?" Heady stuff for a teenager, to be recognized by a man of such stature, and it made quite an impression on me.

Though during my childhood I was immersed in rich relationships with my family and at church, I suffered some setbacks along the way that shattered my innocence about the world, destroyed my cheerful self-image, and set me on a downward spiral that persisted for almost two decades.

As I approached the age of thirty, it became clear to me that something had to change to get my life back on track. That change began, surprisingly, when I "met" Winston Spencer Churchill, who was both a hero and a mystery to me. Developing an acquaintance with the spirit and soul of Great-Grandpapa, though he had died ten years before I was born, was a crucial factor in my recovering a sense of identity and purpose. Little did I realize at the time what a mighty oak Churchill had been, casting a tremendous shadow over all of us acorns.

I dreamed of embracing my great-grandfather's legacy and surprising everyone by becoming a member of Parliament. Then someday I would run for prime minister, and Churchill's DNA would once again inhabit No. 10 Downing Street.

Building on the vague notion I had of my great-grandfather as a heroic figure who had saved the world from something terribly bad, I studied everything I could about him. I probed the memories of family members, such as my great-aunt Mary Soames, Churchill's last surviving child. Along with my father and others who had known Churchill in his lifetime, she provided a vital connection through which I was able to learn so much.

Despite dyslexia and the struggles I'd had in school, I became a self-taught historian, consuming all the books I could find about Churchill and his era.

I soon discovered that, though he was arguably the greatest leader of the twentieth century, he was only a man, not a god—no better or worse than any one of us.

As it happened, bringing Great-Grandpapa down to earth was a liberating experience for me. When I realized that I could not rest my identity in someone who was just as much a frail human being as I was, I decided to step out of his shadow and embrace my own identity.

Still, I wanted to do something in life that honored the Churchill legacy, which I felt was important to share with future generations who were losing hope or had already lost it.

The primary book that helped me see Great-Grandpapa with the greatest clarity was one he himself had penned: *My Early Life.* I was struck by his accounts of hubris, heroics, and near-misses— and above all, by his honesty about himself.

As I read about his youthful struggles, I was encouraged to find that someone as great as Winston Churchill had faced personal challenges similar to my own—difficulty in school, rejection, and an early reputation as a failure. That was when I began to relate to my great-grandfather and to understand his humanity, replete with the flaws and limitations we all share. I also found within myself the kind of resolve embodied in one of his greatest lines, spoken in 1941 to the boys at his old school, Harrow. As the destiny of the nation hung by a slender thread under the onslaughts of war, he had advised the young men, "Never give in, never, never, never . . ."

As I reread his words, I was filled with renewed determination. Learning that young Winston's teachers had wanted to give up on him at times, and that he had written many unhappy letters to his parents, helped me to overcome my own self-doubts. I was captivated by a new vision: *If Winston Churchill's story and words could so inspire me with hope and confidence, they could help people everywhere.* I decided I would devote myself to keeping his legacy alive by speaking and writing about Great-Grandpapa.

As with many "great resolutions," I immediately encountered an obstacle. So much had already been written and spoken about Churchill—where would I begin? What unique facet of his life and impact could I capture and show to others? What was the essence of Churchill's character and work that others had minimized or ignored altogether?

The answer began to take shape on a 2005 trip to the United States, where a friend had arranged for me to speak about my great-grandfather at two schools in Macon, Georgia. Though I was surprised and overjoyed by the great level of interest in Churchill and the Second World War, I was disheartened to discover that a vast population of American—and even British—students had no idea who Winston Churchill was and what he had accomplished.

The nations of the world today are in desperate need of encouragement and firm, decisive leadership. Having extensively studied my great-grandfather's life and works, and catching the tone of his times and personality through my family members who had known him directly, I saw an opportunity to share something of Churchill's life that would improve the lives of others. I saw in Great-Grandpapa, in his words and deeds, in his mistakes and his greatest successes, the one thing needed by so many in the twenty-first century: *hope*.

But what had made Winston Churchill the image of hope for his day and age? I didn't know, but I wanted to find out.

Across from the Houses of Parliament in London stands one of the great statues of Churchill. It shows him resolute and firm in the face of suffering and danger. From the set of his jaw and his unwavering gaze, one gets the sense that he will press on to victory. But what gave him that strength of character? What propelled him into leadership and afforded him the strength to carry on?

By this time, I had already been trying to write books and speeches about Churchill. But the more I researched, the more I realized that his story was incomplete—despite the volumes that had already been written about him. The sense that something important was missing struck me with great force.

When I delved back into *My Early Life* not long after I had this realization, my attention was arrested by the series of near-miraculous escapes that characterized Churchill's early adult life. Even more, my eye was drawn to Churchill's apparent sense of divine destiny—even as early as his teenage years. I decided I must explore more deeply my great-grandfather's personal faith. What did he believe about God? I had assumed that his references to

Deity and Christianity were merely political platitudes. Was it possible it went deeper than that? More important, was it possible that God had played a role in making Winston Churchill the man that he became? As one who had left his faith by the wayside without abandoning belief in God, I was intrigued by these questions. Was Churchill's faith something that other historians had overlooked or neglected?

When I spoke with Sir Martin Gilbert about my thoughts, he encouraged me to press on in the pursuit of the connection between God and Churchill. In fact, he said, there was "loads of information" on the topic that others had not considered in depth. He urged me to bring it to light if I were so inclined.

Sir Martin's encouragement was greatly motivating. As I plowed into the research and developed the ideas, I became increasingly aware of God's presence and power, though I still felt distant from him. Then in 2012 I passed through a season of crisis that brought me once again to a crossroads of faith.

By then I had married Sara, a native Texan, and we were living in Houston. One night, a friend and I were talking about Moses, and our conversation became quite in-depth. At the end of the evening, my buddy suggested that we go to church the following morning—something I hadn't done in ages.

When the pastor rose to preach that Sunday, his topic was exactly the same as what my friend and I had discussed the night before—the same Bible passages and the same points of focus. Neither my friend nor I had had any idea what the pastor's topic would be, and I remember thinking that it couldn't just be a coincidence. It was all too precise. As the pastor continued, I had a strong impression that I should start reading the Bible seriously.

Not long afterward, while traveling in England, I began reading the New Testament. As I opened Matthew's Gospel, it seemed that God was speaking to me on every page. Verse by verse, I wrote copious notes, pausing frequently to pray as I felt my heart drawn back to God and as I felt him begin to heal the pain of my past experiences. I returned to America with my faith restored and with a determination to once again be open to what God wanted me to do with my life.

As I saw my own connection to God restored, I felt ready to write about the remarkable connection I had discovered between God and Churchill.

I was confident I could provide a solid history of my great-grandfather, but I felt I needed some help articulating the connection between Churchill's sense of divine destiny and the events of his life. I knew it would take a unique person who understood the complexities of national leadership and thus could appreciate Churchill the statesman, but who also grasped the importance of biblical principles in the context of historical events. Furthermore, this individual would have to understand the Second World War, its spiritual underpinnings, and the hidden challenges that Churchill faced. Finally, I needed someone who wouldn't be grasping at straws, trying to fit God into the facts, or putting words in Churchill's mouth. As my great-grandfather once said, "Words, which are on proper occasions the most powerful engines, lose their weight and power and values when they are not backed by fact or winged by truth, when they are obviously the expression of a strong feeling, and are not related in any way to the actual facts of the situation."' Those words became my standard, and when I met Wallace Henley, I quickly realized that he fit all of my qualifications.

WALLACE HENLEY

Like Jonathan, I went through a period in my life when my faith faltered and I lost track of the identity I had fervently embraced as a teenager. My crisis came in the city of Nuremberg, Germany, a town that had played a key role in the summation of the Nazi era.

I was born on December 5, 1941, two days before the Japanese attacked Pearl Harbor and brought the United States into the

Second World War. My childhood was immersed in the war and its aftermath. Almost all my Sunday-school teachers and Boy Scout leaders were returning veterans, and they were heroes in my eyes.

Another prominent memory was the countenance of Winston Churchill. His confident visage was on black-and-white newsreels at the theater, and his voice resonated on our radios. In the mind of a young boy, there was something almost mystical about the Second World War that Churchill seemed to embody. That sense of valor and courage under fire stayed with me, and even intensified, over the decades. It is part of what brought me to join with Jonathan Sandys in writing this book.

In 1964, I began preparing for a career as a preacher by enrolling in seminary and serving as a pastor at Travis Avenue Baptist Church in Fort Worth, Texas. But it wasn't long before I changed my focus from being a pastor to becoming a professor of theology. I decided I needed a degree from a European school, as had many of the great theologians under whom I had studied, and I set about figuring out a way to get to Europe with my wife, Irene, and our new baby.

One day as I walked through the seminary administration building, I noticed a bulletin board posting for an English-language Baptist church in Nuremberg, primarily serving the large American military contingent there. Nuremberg is close to Erlangen, the site of a university with a noted theology faculty. I had studied German for two years in college and was confident I could succeed there. Pastoring the Nuremberg church would provide support for my family while I was earning my European degree. I sent an application but never received a response.

Almost a year later, in the fall of 1965—long after I had put the matter out of my mind—a letter arrived from Nuremberg calling me as pastor of Antioch Baptist Church. Two weeks before Christmas 1965, Irene, our one-year-old daughter, and I flew to New York to board the Holland America Line ship *Princess Margriet*.

Even as we were headed for Nuremberg, many of the soldiers and their families in the small church we were going to serve were preparing to move out—the men to Vietnam and their wives and children back to the United States. Within four months of our arrival in Germany, the church informed me that there would soon not be enough money for my salary. Some of the soldiers were willing to get us groceries and gasoline from the PX, but with the black market still thriving in Germany twenty years after the war, I knew they risked a court-martial if they resold PX supplies. I began a futile search for work outside the church—teaching school, sacking groceries, anything I could do to support my family and continue serving the small congregation as pastor. But my dream of studying at the University of Erlangen was now up in smoke.

One day, I saw that our bank account had dwindled to five hundred dollars—a paltry amount by today's standards, but in 1966 it was still enough to either feed and house us for a few months or get us back to America. The decision was clear, and I resigned from the church the next Sunday.

We left Germany on April 1, 1966, and after a brief layover in Iceland's Arctic temperatures, we arrived in Alabama to a soft Southern spring and a room in my in-laws' house. Feeling humiliated by our sudden and premature return from Germany and disillusioned about my calling as a pastor after feeling so certain that God had directed our move to Nuremberg, I started looking for a job again—doing anything but church work.

I put in applications at three or four companies on that first day, and at my final stop, a box factory, I was told I could start the next morning. I jumped at the opportunity and was soon learning the value of good, hard work, even as I kept looking for better employment. Finally, in August I walked into the *Birmingham News*, told the interviewer that I loved to write, knocked out some sample copy, and wound up in journalism, a profession I came to love. I started as religion editor, became a general reporter, and ultimately was promoted to the editorial-page staff.

As my assignments broadened, I began to contemplate the world on a larger scale. At the time, Birmingham was still sizzling with civil-rights protests—just three years removed from the Birmingham church bombing—and I had an opportunity over the next two years to observe the growing influence of Dr. Martin Luther King Jr. This started me thinking about the nature of leadership—especially as it affects societies.

In August 1970, through circumstances too involved to describe here, I became assistant director for a White House task force working on the implementation of court-ordered school desegregation in eleven Southern states. Upon completing that mission, I moved directly into a job at the White House and spent the next two and a half years teamed with Harry S. Dent Sr., special counsel to President Richard Nixon.

From this new vantage point, I began a serious observation of leadership styles and the contrasts between raw power and true authority. But the most important thing I did while working at the White House was to participate in a prayer breakfast every Thursday morning in the West Wing. Those gatherings brought me into contact with people who believed that God works through the events of history. I had never thought much about that, but I was intrigued. When Proverbs 21:1 says, "The king's heart is a stream of water in the hand of the LORD; he turns it wherever he will,"[2] was it more than simply beautiful poetry? Does God raise up leaders and bring them down, as the prophet Daniel says?[3]

Such questions stayed on my mind in the years ahead, even as I again felt stirrings to become a preacher and took up my calling once more—a calling I pursued for the next twenty-five years before "retiring" and reentering the world of politics. After two years as district director and acting chief of staff for a United States congressman, I returned once again to church ministry. For the past thirteen years, I have served as a teaching pastor and senior associate pastor at Houston's Second Baptist Church.

In 1990, just after the collapse of the Soviet Union and of Eastern European communism, I assisted a British agency in responding to numerous urgent requests from former Soviet Bloc nations for conferences to equip leaders. Communism, I saw, had devoured the leadership infrastructure of the nations it had controlled—in families, churches, schools, governments, and businesses. The church had played a key role in the overthrowing of communism, and many people were now seeking help from the very institution that had once been all but banned in most of their nations. I even attended a conference that was held in a building that once housed the KGB.

When Jonathan Sandys invited me to work with him on this project exploring the life of his famous great-grandfather, I felt as if my entire life had been a preparation for the task. As I mentioned, I've been fascinated with Churchill all my life, and I have studied his life in some depth. During the early 1970s, Churchill became almost an obsession for me. My White House experiences had impressed on me the enormous responsibility of leading a nation and having an impact on the world. As I observed world leaders up close, I realized there was another dimension to Churchill that made him historically exceptional, a dimension I could not fully describe but wanted to explore. I collected all the books I could find that dealt with Churchill's life and leadership. For inspiration, I hung photos of the great man in my home study, which I dubbed the "Churchill Room."

When I listened to Jonathan's vision for this book, I realized that even though we come from different backgrounds and perspectives, it seemed inevitable that our paths would converge. We had both spent many years of our lives searching for God, and we both viewed Winston Churchill, in many ways, as a God-haunted man. This book represents our efforts to understand this great leader in the context of God's work in the world.

PART I

THE REMARKABLE
PREPARATION

A Vision of Destiny

This country will be subjected somehow, to a tremendous
invasion, by what means I do not know, but I tell you
I shall be in command of the defences of London, and
I shall save London and England from disaster.

WINSTON CHURCHILL, AGE 16

ON A SUMMER SUNDAY EVENING IN 1891, with the echoes of chapel evensong still resonating in their minds, sixteen-year-old Winston Churchill and his close friend and fellow Harrow student Murland de Grasse Evans sat talking in what Evans would remember years later as "one of those dreadful basement rooms in the Headmaster's House."

The conversation focused on destiny—more specifically, their own. Churchill thought that Evans might go into the diplomatic service, or perhaps follow his father's footsteps into finance.

Then Evans asked Churchill, "Will you go into the army?"

"I don't know," young Winston replied. "It is probable; but I shall have great adventures soon after I leave here."

"Are you going into politics? Following your father?"

"I don't know, but it is more than likely because, you see, I am not afraid to speak in public."

Evans was quizzical as he gazed back at his friend. "You do not seem at all clear about your intentions or desires."

"That may be," Winston shot back, "but I have a wonderful idea of where I shall be eventually. I have dreams about it."

"Where is that?"

"Well, I can see vast changes coming over a now peaceful world; great upheavals, terrible struggles; wars such as one cannot imagine; and I tell you London will be in danger—London will be attacked and I shall be very prominent in the defence of London," Winston said.

"How can you talk like that?" Evans asked. "We are forever safe from invasion, since the days of Napoleon."

"I see further ahead than you do," Winston replied. "I see into the future."

Murland Evans was so "stunned" by the conversation that he "recorded it with utmost clarity," in a letter he sent to Churchill's son, Randolph, who in the 1950s was given the responsibility of writing his father's biography.[2]

Churchill continued, undaunted, as he would many times throughout his career. "This country will be subjected somehow, to a tremendous invasion, by what means I do not know, but I tell you I shall be in command of the defences of London, and I shall save London and England from disaster."

Evans remembered Churchill as "warming to his subject" as he spoke.

"Will you be a general, then, in command of the troops?" Evans asked.

"I don't know," Britain's future leader replied. "Dreams of the future are blurred, but the main objective is clear. . . . I repeat— London will be in danger and in the high position I shall occupy, it will fall to me to save the Capital and save the Empire."[3]

NEED FOR AFFIRMATION

Were it not for events almost fifty years later, young Winston's prediction might be dismissed as the desperate effort of a lonely adolescent with a need for affirmation to assert his significance. That need would have been understandable, given the relationship between Churchill and his physically and emotionally removed parents. Of his mother, Churchill wrote later in life, "I loved her dearly—but at a distance."[4] And once, after an extended conversation with his own son, Churchill remarked, "We have this evening had a longer period of continuous conversation than the total which I ever had with my father in the whole course of his life."[5]

Today, social conventions are often determined by their political correctness. In Churchill's day, especially for people of his class, it was "Victorian correctness" that set the standard. VC demanded a certain aloofness of parents towards their children. In some households, parents met with their offspring by appointment only (determined by the parent) and in the presence of a servant. If the child became too troublesome, obnoxious, or impolite, the help could quickly take charge.

As a boy, Winston romanticized his parents at times. He saw his father as a champion of "Tory democracy." History focuses on Lord Randolph's personal morality, but Winston saw his father as a good and loyal politician who stood on principle. He noted his father's courageous stands as chancellor of the exchequer—and how, when Lord Randolph's voice was ignored, he offered his resignation. Churchill admired the fact that Lord Randolph was sometimes unpopular and that he placed the nation's needs above those of his own Conservative Party when he perceived a conflict. Winston believed his father to be a "people's politician," not a party hack. He concluded that Lord Randolph sincerely desired to serve the people he represented and was not in politics for himself, for power, or for accolades.

Churchill's mother, Jennie, was an active socialite, if not a libertine, with many (some would say scandalous) involvements; but her relationship with her young son was not especially close. Still, Churchill remembered her as "a fairy princess: a radiant being possessed of limitless riches and power."[6]

"Emotionally abandoned by both [parents], young Winston blamed himself," writes historian William Manchester. "Needing outlets for his own welling adoration, he created images of them as he wished they were, and the less he saw of them, the easier that transformation became."[7] Aristocratic families sent their boys to private boarding schools—for Winston, it was Harrow—and at a distance, Winston's fantasized image of his parents was quite easy to maintain because he did not see them often or receive communications from them.

At one point, he tried to tell his mother how lonely he was: "It is very unkind of you not to write to me before this, I have only had one letter from you this term."[8] In 1884, four years before he entered Harrow, nine-year-old Winston became sick. His doctor, who had a medical office in Brighton, on the Channel coast, felt it would be good for the boy's health if he lived for a while by the sea. Thus, Churchill started that fall as a student at a school there. But the new location made no difference in his parents' attentiveness. In fact, when he read in the Brighton newspaper that Lord Randolph had recently been in town to make a speech, Winston penned him a note: "I cannot think why you did not come to see me, while you were in Brighton. I was very disappointed, but I suppose you were too busy to come."[9]

Then there were the suffocating strictures of the upper-crust educational institutions. As William Manchester observes, "Youth was an ordeal for most boys of [Churchill's] class. Life in England's so-called public schools—private boarding schools reserved for sons of the elite—was an excruciating rite of passage."[10] Added to that misery was the continuing disregard by his parents. "It is not very kind darling Mummy to forget all about me, not answer my epistles," he wrote in one letter to his mother.[11] On another occasion, Winston asked his father to come to Harrow for Speech Day and told him, "You have never been to see me & so everything will be new to you."[12]

As difficult as his parents' seeming disinterest must have been for Churchill, it may have been a blessing in disguise. By default, his nanny, Elizabeth Everest, played a much bigger role in forming his vital foundational beliefs, and her perspective was decidedly Christian.

WOOMANY

Winston Churchill's school experience was pathetic by any measure, but right from the start, even as a seven-year-old, he demonstrated the tenacity and determination that would come to characterize his life. Subjected to institutional acts of brutality that might have destroyed another boy's morale, Churchill remained resolute. Once, after a particularly severe caning at St. George's School in Ascot, he got his revenge by defiantly stomping on the headmaster's prized straw hat.

At the bottom of his class—and also sorted towards the end of the list at roll call because of his name, Spencer-Churchill—Winston wrote pleadingly to his father to allow him to dispense with the Spencer and simply go by Churchill. Lord Randolph ignored the letter, just as he had failed to respond to the hundreds of earlier epistles in which the homesick young Winston begged them to visit for a weekend, Sports Day, Prize Giving, or any occasion.

During those dark eleven years of Churchill's primary schooling, he had only one visitor: his nanny, Mrs. Elizabeth Everest, whom he affectionately called Woomany. She was the one person to whom he "poured out [his] many troubles."[13] Churchill and Mrs. Everest remained friends and confidants until her death in

1895, five months after Lord Randolph's and three months after his grandmother's, Clarissa Jerome. "I shall never know such a friend again," Churchill wrote of Everest in a letter to his mother.[14]

During Churchill's younger years, Mrs. Everest loved him dearly and protected him as best she could. Years later, when he wrote his only novel, *Savrola*, Churchill no doubt had Mrs. Everest in mind when he described the housekeeper character:

> It is a strange thing, the love of these women. Perhaps it is the only disinterested affection in the world. The mother loves her child; that is maternal nature. The youth loves his sweetheart; that too may be explained. . . . In all there are reasons; but the love of a foster-mother for her charge appears absolutely irrational. It is one of the few proofs, not to be explained even by the association of ideas, that the nature of mankind is superior to mere utilitarianism, and that his destinies are high.[15]

Stephen Mansfield provides further insight into Elizabeth Everest's influence on Churchill. She was a "low church adherent," he notes, who wanted no part of the "popish trappings" in the Anglican Church. "But she was also a passionate woman of prayer, and she taught young Winston well. She helped him memorize his first Scriptures, knelt with him daily as he recited his prayers, and explained the world to him in simple but distinctly Christian terms."[16] Her role in the formation of Churchill's worldview was still evident later in his life when he often paraphrased or quoted Bible passages in his speeches. Even in seasons of doubt, he instinctively saw through eyes formed with a biblical outlook. This is why he could inspire hope, call for strength and faith, and most importantly, grasp the true meaning of Nazism and its threat to civilization.

Throughout his life, Winston Churchill was a man of principle, even though his understanding and application of those principles were sometimes skewed—as they are in all of us. The academics under whom Britain's future wartime leader studied would have been well acquainted with the writings of Jeremy Bentham, the prominent late-eighteenth- and early-nineteenth-century British philosopher who promoted the theory of utilitarianism and the idea that outcomes determined the ethical rightness of actions and philosophies. Churchill was a practical man, but he was not a mere utilitarian. Instead, he combined a mighty visionary perspective, strategic wisdom, and tactical knowledge in ways rarely found in one person.

Early in his political career, Churchill angered his friends and won only meager approval from his former opponents when he changed political parties over policy principles. After the seeming collapse of his leadership reputation during the First World War, Churchill only dug the ditch deeper with his attempts to warn about the intentions of Adolf Hitler during the buildup to the Second World War. To regain his credibility and stature, it would have been much easier to give way to raw pragmatism and mute his message. The more comfortable course would have been to yield to Britain's war-weariness and allow Hitler free rein in Western Europe. After all, key players in the British aristocracy didn't think all that badly of Hitler, though his style was off-putting to some of their sensibilities. But as Winston had told his school chum in 1891, he could see "further ahead." And what Churchill saw was the power of principle over sheer utility. In the absence of parental influence, some credit for this perspective must go to his "foster-mother," Elizabeth Everest, who showed him that human nature is indeed superior to mere utility.

Years later, Churchill indicated a "partiality for Low Church principles" because of the impact of Elizabeth Everest.[17] Though he respected Britain's rich historic traditions, he had no need for pomp. After the Second World War had ended, Churchill's wife, Clementine, asked her husband what memorial he would prefer. "Oh, nothing," he replied. "Perhaps just a park for the children to play in."[18]

In 1945, after Churchill had saved civilization, King George VI wanted to induct him into the Order of the Garter, Britain's oldest, most prestigious, and highest honor for chivalry. Churchill became perhaps the first commoner to decline the high honor. The political editor of the London *Daily Mail* noted that "Mr. Churchill has always insisted that he does not wish to have a title."[19] Besides, said Churchill (who had just been surprisingly defeated in the first postwar election), he could hardly accept the "garter" from the king when his people had just given him the "order of the boot."

Finally, in 1953, when Churchill was once again voted in as prime minister at the age of seventy-eight, he accepted the Order of the Garter—though still dragging his feet. Young Queen Elizabeth II, with as much fortitude as Churchill had, told him that if the prime minister would not come to her to receive the honor, then Her Royal Majesty would have to come to him, bearing the accoutrements of the Order. Churchill's regard for the monarchy wouldn't permit such a denigrating act by the queen, so he relented and became a member of the Most Noble Order. "I only accepted because I think she is so splendid," Churchill said, in describing his change of mind.

During the Second World War, Churchill gained the respect of the British people and their allies by personifying British pluck. His engagement with the public provided a link between average people and the aristocrats in high positions of power. This was crucial in forming the strong unity that was essential for the people to keep standing during the Battle of Britain and the years of bloody struggle after that.

PURSUING DESTINY

Despite the void left by his parents, Churchill's visionary outlook was awakened at Harrow. Martin Gilbert notes that Churchill's first essay there dealt with Palestine in the age of John the Baptist.

The seed of Churchill's concept of "Christian civilization" was already present when he included in the essay the notion of "the advantages of Christianity."[20]

In 1940, as British cities were languishing under the Blitz, Churchill took his son, Randolph, to Harrow. The student choirs presented songs that Churchill had sung when he was there as a pupil. "Listening to those boys singing all those well-remembered songs I could see myself fifty years before singing those tales of great deeds and of great men and wondering with intensity how I could ever do something glorious for my country."[21]

This, then, was the milieu in which sixteen-year-old Winston Churchill made his remarkable prediction of destiny to Murland Evans. It would be easy to attribute his lofty adolescent prediction to an overwrought quest for the recognition, acceptance, affirmation, and significance that his parents had not provided, except for the fact that what he predicted came curiously and remarkably true.

The path to greatness, however, was torturous and twisted. After Harrow, Churchill had high hopes of following his father into politics, even serving in Parliament at his side. Lord Randolph, however, had other ideas. When at last he visited Harrow, he told the headmaster he wanted Winston to go into the Army Class. At one point, when Winston was a young boy, Lord Randolph had surveyed his son's toy army of fifteen hundred soldiers and asked Winston if he would like to go into the military.

"I thought it would be splendid to command an army," Churchill later recalled, "so I said 'Yes' at once: and immediately I was taken at my word."[22] Churchill assumed that his father "with his experience and flair had discerned in me the qualities of military genius. But I was told later that he had only come to the conclusion that I was not clever enough to go to the Bar"—that is, to pursue a career practicing law.[23]

It was determined that Winston would be sent to Sandhurst,

the military institute where infantry and cavalry officers were trained. But he failed the entrance examination—twice—and it appeared he wouldn't qualify for Sandhurst after all. On his third try, he gained admission, but with grades insufficient for the infantry. Undaunted, he let his family know he had succeeded, with his appointment to the cavalry.

Lord Randolph was unimpressed. In fact, with his mind by then wilting under the effects of what his physicians had diagnosed as syphilis, he disparaged his son without mercy. Winston's failure to get into the infantry, his father said, "demonstrated beyond refutation your slovenly happy-go-lucky harum scarum style of work."[24] The elder Churchill told his son that he was second- or third-class at best. In fact, his father wrote to him, "if you cannot prevent yourself from leading the idle useless unprofitable life you have had during your schooldays & later months, you will become a mere social wastrel, one of the hundreds of the public school failures, and you will degenerate into a shabby unhappy & futile existence."[25]

Churchill's admiration for his father, however, was undiminished. Aspirations of serving with him in Parliament lingered in his mind until Lord Randolph died in 1895. Even then, the thought never quite left him. One evening in 1946, when Churchill was once again a member of Parliament and leader of the opposition, he sat with members of his family in the dining room at his home, Chartwell. His daughter Sarah glanced at an empty chair and then at her father. "If you had the power to put someone in that chair to join us now, whom would you choose?"

"Oh, my father, of course," Churchill replied immediately.

He then told them a story that would later become the seed of his little book titled *The Dream.*

"It was not plain whether he was recalling a dream or elaborating on some fanciful idea that had struck him earlier," Churchill's son, Randolph, would later say.[26] Churchill penned the story in

1947, when he was again feeling the disdain of the political party in power and of a sizable portion of the British public. Yet, suggests historian Richard Langworth, perhaps it was the disdain from his own father that Churchill, now at the age of seventy-three, had not overcome.[27]

In *The Dream*, Churchill said he was in his art studio at Chartwell. He had been given a portrait of his father from 1886. The canvas was badly torn, and he was attempting to make a copy. As he concentrated intensely on his father's image, his mind "freed from all other thoughts except the impressions of that loved and honoured face now on the canvas, now on the picture, now in the mirror," he felt an "odd sensation."[28] He turned to find his father sitting in the red leather armchair across the studio.

"Papa!" he exclaimed.

"What are you doing, Winston?"

After Churchill explained his project, the conversation continued.

"Tell me, what year is it?" Lord Randolph asked.

"Nineteen forty-seven."

Lord Randolph asked his son to tell him what had happened in the years since his death. Churchill gave him a broad outline and then spoke of the Second World War. "Seven million were murdered in cold blood, mainly by the Germans. They made human slaughter-pens like the Chicago stockyards. Europe is a ruin . . ."

"Winston," replied Lord Randolph, "you have told me a terrible tale. . . . As I listened to you unfolding these fearful facts you seemed to know a great deal about them. . . . When I hear you talk I really wonder you didn't go into politics. You might have done a lot to help. You might even have made a name for yourself."[29]

In the "dream," Lord Randolph did not know, and his son would not tell him, that Winston had indeed gone into politics. Military service, as we will see, was part of the path that got him there.

At age twenty-one, with that storied encounter with his father still decades into the future, Churchill was only a few months from being commissioned into the Fourth Hussars cavalry regiment. It was in this moment that his life's purpose changed, and though a tinge of youthful arrogance remained, everything he did until the day he entered Parliament was with the singular purpose he expressed in his book *My Early Life:* to pursue Lord Randolph's aims and vindicate his memory.

Despite his father's gloom at his being a mere cavalryman, Churchill looked forward with exuberance to graduating from Sandhurst and "becoming a real live cavalry officer."[30]

> At Sandhurst I had a new start. No longer handicapped by past neglect of Latin, French or Mathematics. We now had to learn fresh things and we all started equal. . . . I was deeply interested in my work, especially Tactics and Fortification.[31]

Suitably engaged, Churchill soon discovered that he "could learn quickly enough the things that mattered."[32] He graduated with honors from Sandhurst, finishing eighth in his class of 150, and thus was launched "into the world."[33]

He plunged into living and working with excitement and anticipation: "Ups and downs, risks and journeys, but always the sense of motion, and the illusion of hope," he said.[34]

Yet there was a disappointment: The world was at peace. A cavalry officer needed to stay in the saddle, so it seemed the best thing to do was play polo. Lord Randolph had died two months before Winston was commissioned as an officer in the Fourth Hussars, and Churchill's income was reduced to a relatively small allowance, which he exhausted on polo ponies.

Then he heard there was war in Cuba. Rebels there were battling the Spaniards. If he could not go as a soldier, he determined to travel to the battlefield as a correspondent. He soon found that the *Graphic* would pay him five pounds for each report. After a lengthy voyage, which he greatly disliked, Churchill peered out at Cuba from his ship as it approached the island:

> I felt as if I sailed with Captain Silver and first gazed on Treasure Island. Here was a place where real things were going on. Here was a scene of vital action. Here was a place where anything might happen. . . . Here I might leave my bones.[35]

In fact, he almost did. In Cuba came the first of those seemingly miraculous survivals that would occur several times in Churchill's life. A bullet passed a foot from his head, and another pierced the thatched hut where he slept but left him unscathed.

In the winter of 1896, when his assignment to Cuba was completed, Churchill sailed to India with the Fourth Hussars, and they were based in Bangalore. He and two of his comrades lived in what he described as "a palatial bungalow, all pink and white," set on two acres and "wreathed in purple bougainvillea."[36] There they were tended to by three butlers. There was still no war in which to exercise his military craft, so he resumed playing polo. It occurred to him that there might be other, perhaps better, pursuits—namely, that of learning.

Back in England, someone had told Churchill that "Christ's Gospel was the last word in Ethics."[37] This was a theme he often spoke about in later years, but in his young adulthood he scarcely understood the meaning. "This sounded good," he wrote, "but what were Ethics? They had never been mentioned to me at Harrow or Sandhurst. . . . Then someone told me that Ethics were concerned not merely with the things you ought to do, but with why you ought to do them."[38] With no one in Bangalore to instruct him, Churchill ordered a wide array of books.

From Darwin to Macaulay, from Gibbon to Malthus to Plato and Aristotle, Churchill read voraciously during the long, hot subcontinental afternoons as his comrades napped.[39] The religious ideas sown into him by Elizabeth Everest and others were greatly challenged by what he read. When he read *History of the Rise and Influence of the Spirit of Rationalism in Europe* and *History of European Morals* by William Lecky, an Irish historian and political theorist, Lecky's arguments induced him to briefly settle his mind on a predominantly secular view. Reflecting in later years, he said:

> If I had been at a University my difficulties might have been resolved by the eminent professors and divines who are gathered there. At any rate, they would have shown me equally convincing books putting the opposite point of view. As it was I passed through a violent and aggressive anti-religious phase which, had it lasted, might easily have made me a nuisance. My poise was restored during the next few years by frequent contact with danger. I found that whatever I might think and argue, I did not hesitate to ask for special protection when about to come under the fire of the enemy: nor to feel sincerely grateful when I got home safe to tea.[40]

That "poise" would be tested sooner perhaps than Churchill had imagined. During a trip home to England in 1897, he learned there was action on the Northwest Frontier of India, and he managed to get there as a war correspondent. Out of that experience, he penned his first book, *The Malakand Field Force*.

As the Indian conflict was winding down, Churchill heard that war had broken out in the Sudan in North Africa. He tried to get into the battle there, but his efforts were met with resistance from none other than Sir Herbert Kitchener, the commander of the Egyptian Army fighting in the Sudan. Churchill managed to get the backing of Prime Minister Salisbury, but even that was rebuffed. Kitchener had all the officers he needed, and any vacancies would be filled by "others whom he would be bound to prefer before the young officer in question."[41]

Churchill later happened to hear through a friend that Sir Evelyn Wood, the adjutant general of the British Army, had expressed resentment of Kitchener's approach to selecting officers. Sir Evelyn felt strongly that the War Office ought to be able to choose the makeup of the British Expeditionary Force. Churchill got word to Sir Evelyn that his attempts to join Kitchener's army had been refused. "This move was instantly successful," writes Violet Bonham Carter. "Sir Evelyn Wood became his *deus ex machina*."[42]

Within days, Churchill was en route to North Africa and another giant leap towards his destiny.

2

Surviving Destiny's Perilous Paths

*I raised my pistol and fired. So close were we that
the pistol itself actually struck him. Man and
sword disappeared below and behind me.*

WINSTON CHURCHILL, *MY EARLY LIFE*

THE VULTURES GATHERED that September morning in 1898 as
twenty thousand British troops marched across the battle-battered
landscape to scout a thrice-larger force of zealous Sudanese warriors (three thousand of whom were on horseback) led by Abdullah
al-Taashi. The Arab ruler was driven by his sense of destiny as the
successor to Muhammad Ahmad, the self-proclaimed Mahdi, a
messianic leader and Allah's servant in bringing koranic order to
the world in its end times.

Winston Churchill, then a twenty-four-year-old cavalryman
itching for action, estimated the number of ravenous birds that
day at about a hundred. The vultures had no appreciation for
history or religious fervor, but they grasped the significance of
carnage.

History remembers the bloody clash that followed as the Battle of Omdurman.

A BLESSED BUSTED SHOULDER

Two years before Omdurman, Churchill had landed at Bombay, India, after a long, wearying voyage from the British Isles. Eager for dry land, he scampered to get off the small tender boat that had ferried him and others from the SS *Britannia* to a rocky quay. Iron hand rings were embedded in the stone so that passengers could steady themselves as they jumped onto steps made slippery by the surf.

On the day of Churchill's arrival, the tiny tender was heaving on four- to five-foot swells. Just as the young soldier gripped one of the rings, the boat was caught in a surge and jerked away. The sudden yaw of the vessel wrenched Churchill's right shoulder— dislocating it, though he was unaware of the severity of the injury at the time. Wincing in pain, he made his way ashore, but in true Churchill style, he soon tried to put the matter from his mind.

Without proper treatment, Churchill's busted shoulder never quite healed properly, and it would forever plague him. Through the years, he never knew when the stabbing pain would again bring him up short—reaching for a book, sleeping on his side, swimming, or even laying hold of a banister. The injury kept him from participating in some sports, and most likely from dying at Omdurman.

On September 2, 1898, at a quarter to six on a hazy North African morning, Churchill and his comrades-in-arms rode into the face of an overwhelmingly strong enemy. But rather than fearing the human tsunami hurtling towards him, Churchill felt exhilarated. Later, in a letter to his mother, he described how the "Dervishes" were fearless in the face of the pounding hooves, refused to jump out of the way, and were struck down by the galloping horses of the British. The enemy slashed at the animals' hamstrings, tried to cut bridles and reins, brandished swords in frenetic swinging arcs, and fired rifles at close range. Yet Churchill pressed forward, unscathed and undaunted.[1]

As Churchill explained in his letter, the key to his success and survival that day was his ten-shot Mauser pistol.

A British cavalryman traditionally engaged the enemy with a sword, not a handgun. The blade's length enabled the rider to lean down and reach the ground with the tip, and then recoil to continue the fight. But if Churchill had been using a sword and not a pistol on this occasion, it's unlikely he would have left the battlefield alive.

As Churchill rode into the fray, an enemy warrior hurled himself to the ground in front of him. A glint of light flashed from the blade of a scimitar as the warrior got ready to hamstring Churchill's horse. Firm in his saddle, Churchill quickly spun his mount away from the sweeping sword and shot the enemy infantryman from a distance of three yards.

He barely had time to straighten up and regain his bearings before another warrior lunged at him with a sword.

"I raised my pistol and fired," he wrote years later. "So close were we that the pistol itself actually struck him. Man and sword disappeared below and behind me."[2]

With his bum shoulder, it is doubtful whether Churchill, using his sword, would have been able to reach down and strike the first Dervish attacker. But even if he had managed that feat, it is improbable that he would have recovered his balance in time to defend against the second foe at much closer range.

That the injury to his shoulder at Bombay led to his survival at Omdurman might reinforce the idea that someone was watching over him.

After the battle, the valiant cavalryman wrote to his mother: "Bullets—to a philosopher my dear Mamma—are not worth considering. Besides I am so conceited I do not believe the gods would create so potent a being as myself for so prosaic an ending."[3] If he faced the possibility of death on the battlefield, at least he'd had a "pleasant" life. It would be regrettable to give up his life so soon, but at least if he were dead, it would be a regret he wouldn't have to experience.[4]

It was all, of course, sheer hubris. There is no record of a reply from Lady Randolph, but any parent can imagine the thoughts that must have filled her mind.

SURVIVAL IN SOUTH AFRICA

In October 1899, war broke out between Great Britain and the South African Republic. Churchill had by now left the army, but he was still yearning to see action. After obtaining a contract to serve as a war correspondent for the *Morning Post* newspaper, he set sail from Southampton on October 14 aboard the RMS *Dunottar Castle*.

Arriving in Cape Town on October 31, Churchill and two of his fellow correspondents took a train to East London, and from there they caught a steamer to Durban. In Durban, Churchill heard that his old friend Ian Hamilton, now a general in the army, had traveled by rail to Ladysmith. Churchill immediately followed. Though he was now a civilian, he felt certain that Hamilton would afford him the same respect as if he were still in uniform.

Churchill and J. B. Atkins, a correspondent for the *Manchester Guardian*, began their journey, only to find that Hamilton's train was the last to get through before the Boers cut the line near Chieveley. Disappointed, and now stranded at Estcourt, Churchill and Atkins pitched their tents in the railway yard, where they proceeded to take their meals, drink wine, and entertain friends around a campfire each night.

By November 9, Churchill had become frustrated with his situation, and he let it be known around town that he was looking for a guide to take him to Ladysmith—even though he knew that a sizable army of Boers was situated between Estcourt and Ladysmith. His determination to insinuate himself into the thick of the action was clearly leading him down a very unwise path of unnecessary danger. And once again, destiny—or Providence—interceded.

Churchill discovered that an armored train was scheduled to leave that afternoon for Colenso, a small town in no-man's-land that was about twenty miles from Ladysmith. The thought of seeing action, his first since Omdurman, was too irresistible to pass up, and when the train pulled out of the station, Churchill was aboard. When Captain Helmsley, the officer in charge of the train, stopped short of Colenso and proceeded on foot with his sergeant, Churchill disembarked as well and followed.

After reconnoitering Colenso, Churchill reported in his dispatch for the day that "[we] had learned all there was to learn—where the line was broken, that the village was deserted, that the bridge was safe, and we made haste to rejoin the train. . . . So we rattled back to Estcourt through the twilight."[5]

From Estcourt, Churchill continued his correspondence. While sitting around the campfire with the commanding officer of the garrison, Colonel Long, he suddenly heard shouting and metallic clanging. The colonel explained that soldiers were loading the field guns to move to a safer location in anticipation that Estcourt would be taken by the Boers. Churchill boldly suggested that the move might be seen as a sign of evacuation and could lead the cautious enemy to become daring in their advance.

Colonel Long left the campfire, and soon the noise stopped. However, a few minutes later, the scraping and banging began again, and Churchill saw the weapons being removed from the train, apparently to remain at Estcourt.

I did that, Churchill mused. Then he caught himself, and assumed a more modest attitude. "*We* did that," he said.[6]

It would not be the last time that Churchill voiced his opinion nor the last time he advised resistance rather than surrender. And though at times he may have seemed arrogant or rash, his intentions were good and his judgment usually sound. He respected the officers making the decisions, and his previous military service afforded him a credible voice.

Around that same time, in a letter to Sir Evelyn Wood, Churchill raised the question of punishment for officers who surrendered troops under their command. He hated surrender. He believed that wars should be fought until the last man is standing.[7]

Years later, when he was pressed by high-ranking government officials in the early days of his first term as prime minister to seek a truce with Hitler, even if it meant surrender, he famously replied, "If this long island story of ours is to end at last, let it end only when each of us lies choking in his own blood upon the ground."[8] And he meant it.

What he had seen in Africa many years earlier had no doubt taught him the importance of all-out victory. The mere thought of surrender at Omdurman had made the word sour to his palate, and occurrences such as the events at Estcourt only intensified his distaste. Once again, events in his early life prepared him for the grand assignment that still lay ahead.

ABOARD "WILSON'S DEATH TRAP"

Though Churchill was unsuccessful in securing a guide to take him to Ladysmith, he soon found another way to get himself into the action. Through a seemingly coincidental—but perhaps, in hindsight, providential—circumstance, he bumped into the temporary commander of the Dublin Fusiliers, Captain Aylmer Haldane, while wandering along the single street in town.

Churchill and Haldane had been friends from their frontier days in India, and Haldane had helped Churchill secure an appointment to Sir William Lockhart's staff during the Tirah Expedition, a war fought between the British and the Afridi tribe in 1897–1898 for control of the Khyber Pass in mountainous northern India (now Pakistan). Now in South Africa, Haldane was preparing to take an armored train on a reconnaissance mission. Believing that Churchill would be a good companion and knowing that he had previous experience, Haldane happily invited him to join the mission.

Churchill soon stood beside the beast of a train, which had been nicknamed Wilson's Death Trap, watching as the soldiers clambered aboard six armored railcars—three on each end, with the locomotive and the tender set in the middle. Mounted at the head of the train was a six-pound naval gun to be operated by sailors from the HMS *Terrible*.

As the train set off from Estcourt, neither Haldane nor Churchill knew that a Boer artillery unit with three field guns and a quick-firing Maxim gun held a position overlooking the railway about fourteen miles down the track.

The train departed on schedule and arrived at Frere Station around 6:20 in the morning. No enemy had been seen. At Frere, Churchill spoke to a party of eight Natal Mounted Police, who informed him that they comprised an advance patrol reconnoitering towards Chieveley.

The train traveled on and reached Chieveley around 7:10, at which time they received a message instructing them to remain at Frere because Chieveley was now occupied by the enemy. The message came with a specific and alarming warning: "Do not place reliance on any reports from local residents, as they may be untrustworthy."[9]

Upon acknowledging receipt, they were further informed that a party of about fifty Boers and three wagons had been spotted "moving south on the west side of the railway."

About that time, Haldane spied "a number of small figures moving about and hurrying forward" about six hundred yards behind the train, back in the direction of Estcourt.[10] With no time to lose, Haldane ordered the troops to reboard, and they began their return journey.

As Wilson's Death Trap approached a hill along the way, Churchill, who was standing on a box in one of the troop cars with his head and shoulders rising above the steel plating, saw a cluster of Boers along the crest. "A huge white ball of smoke sprang into being," he said, "and tore out into a cone, only as it seemed a few feet above my head. It was shrapnel—the first I had ever seen in war, and very nearly the last!"[11]

Suddenly, an almighty crash was heard, "a tremendous shock." Churchill, Haldane, and "all the soldiers in the truck were pitched head over heels onto its floor."[12] Scrambling to his feet, Churchill peered over the top of the carriage. The front three cars of the train had derailed, but it was unclear at the time what the cause had been.

Churchill and Haldane jumped from the railcar and quickly agreed that Haldane would go to the rear to man the small naval gun, attempt to draw the enemy's fire, and keep them at bay while Churchill made his way to the front of the train to investigate the cause of the crash and see what could be done. Bullets ricocheted off the sides of the carriages as the Boers opened fire on the unfortunate British troops, who scrambled to take cover behind the armored railcars.

Upon reaching the front of the train, Churchill surveyed the scene with alarm. The Boers had apparently rolled several large stones onto the track, and because the locomotive was situated in the middle of the train, the driver hadn't seen them. Even if he had, the sheer weight of the train and its speed would have made it impossible to stop in time to avoid the boulders.

Although two of the derailed cars were partially blocking the track, Churchill surmised that, with some help from the soldiers, they might be pushed out of the way by the locomotive. Under steady fire from the enemy—their lives in imminent danger and the outcome uncertain for more than an hour—Churchill, the engineer, and several soldiers worked to free the train and clear a path towards home.

Eventually, the locomotive and tender car were able to travel again, and a gradual retreat began towards the Blaauwkrantz River. In the process of clearing the track, they had detached all the railcars from the locomotive, and these now had to be left behind. The wounded from the battle were loaded onto the locomotive, and the rest of the soldiers ran alongside, using the engine for cover as they made their way towards safety.

As the train moved away, the Boers increased their fire. Fearing that the locomotive would be crippled by the artillery fire, the engineer increased his speed, and Churchill watched helplessly as the troops on foot, unable to keep up with the train, scrambled furiously to avoid being exposed to enemy fire.

"At last I forced the engine-driver to stop altogether," Churchill later wrote, "but before I could get the engine stopped, we were already three hundred yards away from our infantry."[13] Churchill jumped from the cab and ordered the engineer to continue on, across the Blaauwkrantz River, and to wait on the other side of the bridge. Churchill then turned and ran back up the line to aid the stranded soldiers and inform Haldane of the revised plan.

Just then, he noticed two figures in plainclothes hurriedly approaching him at a distance of about one hundred yards. His first thought was that they were plate layers from the railroad, but he soon realized they were Boer soldiers.

Once again under fire, Churchill ran back towards the engine as two bullets narrowly missed him on either side. After unsuccessfully attempting to take cover in a narrow ditch, he quickly concluded that continuing to move was his only chance of escape. Two more bullets whistled past his ears as he looked for an opportunity to get to higher ground.

Scrambling up the left side of the ditch, Churchill scaled the embankment and slipped through a hole in a wire fence. On the other side, he crouched down in a tiny depression and tried to catch his breath. From his new position, he could see a small cabin fifty yards away—the perfect cover. Two hundred yards further along was the rocky gorge of the Blaauwkrantz River.

ACCEPTING THE REPUGNANT

Determined to make a dash for the river, Churchill stood and took a quick glance back towards his enemy. To his dismay, the two Boers on foot had been joined by a third man on horseback, who was now galloping towards him at full speed.

Although officially a noncombatant, Churchill had decided that morning to carry his Mauser pistol with him on patrol. From a distance of forty yards, Churchill was confident he could shoot the mounted soldier.

When he put his hand to his belt, his heart sank as he discovered the gun was missing. While working on clearing the track, he had removed the pistol and left it in the cab of the train. He was now standing forty yards from a man mounted on a horse and pointing a rifle directly at him with every intention of killing him. Churchill looked towards the river and then back at the plate-layer's cabin, quickly realizing there was no chance for escape and that the horseman thundering down upon him had a perfect shot.

"I held up my hands and surrendered myself a prisoner of war," he later said.

Though Churchill found surrender most repugnant, "in the poignant minutes that followed" he thought of Napoleon's axiom: "When one is alone and unarmed, a surrender may be pardoned."[14]

The Boer lowered his weapon and beckoned Churchill towards him. Vanquished, he obeyed, and the two made their way back to where Churchill had left Haldane and his company. But there was no one there: They had already been taken prisoner.

The weather, like Churchill's mood, turned grim as he was compelled to join the other captives. From the start, he contended that he was not a combatant but merely a war correspondent. However, he knew too well that by accompanying a military company and taking part in the fight, he had undermined his claim to civilian status—especially given that he was half dressed in uniform. The Boers would have been within their rights to shoot him on the spot as a possible spy. No doubt Churchill saw the irony of his situation, as years later he would define a prisoner of war as "a man who has tried to kill you and, having failed to kill you, asks you not to kill him."[15]

While deciding the fate of their prisoners, the Boers separated Churchill from the others. As he stood in the rain, alone, he half expected a "drumhead court martial" and summary judgment.[16] Finally, a field cornet approached him with the verdict.

"We are not going to let you go, old chappie, although you are a correspondent. We don't catch the son of a lord every day."[17]

With mixed feelings, Churchill rejoined the others, now officially a prisoner of war. Naturally relieved that he would not be shot, he was nevertheless discouraged by his circumstances. His outlook did not improve when the men were ordered to begin a sixty-mile march to the railhead at Elandslaagte, where they would board a train to Pretoria.

With every step during the three-day journey, Churchill regretted his decision to surrender, replaying the moment over in his head while looking for a chance to escape. Sadly, no opportunity presented itself, and along with the officers at whose side he had fought, he entered confinement at the State Model Schools in Pretoria, which had been converted to an officers' prison.

Unbeknownst to him, Churchill was already a hero. The *Natal Witness* ran a most enthusiastic report from Captain Wylie, an officer wounded in the battle, who said that Churchill's actions had enabled a safe escape. Wylie described Churchill's conduct as "that of as brave a man as could be found."[18] Inspector Campbell of the Natal government railways, on behalf of the civilian trainmen accompanying Churchill, wrote to the General Messenger of the Railways Department:

> The railway men who accompanied the armored train this morning ask me to convey to you their admiration of the coolness and pluck displayed by Mr. Winston Churchill, the war correspondent who accompanied the train, and to whose efforts, backed up by those of Driver Wagner, is due the fact that the armored engine and tender were brought successfully out after being hampered by the derailed trucks in front. . . . The whole of our men are loud in their praises of Mr. Churchill, who, I regret to say, is a prisoner. I respectfully ask you to convey this admiration to a brave man.[19]

The letter was duly published in newspapers as far away as New Zealand. Many of the reports suggested that Churchill should be awarded the Victoria Cross, "the highest award for gallantry that a British and Commonwealth serviceman can achieve."[20] Though perhaps deserved, the award was never given.

In the first volume of his biography of his father, Winston's son, Randolph, includes a most moving report, sent to Churchill's mother by his manservant, Thomas Walden, and later published in the *Morning Post*:

> My Lady,
>
> I am sorry to say Mr Churchill is a prisoner, but I am almost certain he is not wounded. I came down to Maritzburg yesterday to bring all his kit until Mr Winston gets free. . . . I have joined the Imperial Light Horse on Colonel Long's advice, although I asked him first if I could join as I wanted to be near Mr Winston as soon as he is free. So Colonel Long said he would arrange for me to leave the regiment as soon as Mr C. wanted me. I came down in the armoured train

with the driver, who is wounded in the head with a shell. He told me all about Mr Winston. He says there is not a braver gentleman in the Army.[21]

Numerous other reports, all similar in their compliments, were sent, each one drawing particular attention to Churchill's bravery and the sadness the writers felt at his subsequent capture. However, the adventure for Winston Churchill, special war correspondent to the *Morning Post*, was just beginning.

Though he referred to his capture as "a melancholy state," Churchill recognized that being held as a prisoner of war was "the least unfortunate kind of prisoner to be," especially when compared to being "confined for years in a modern convict prison . . . each day exactly like the one before, with the barren ashes of wasted life behind, and all the long years of bondage stretching out ahead."[22]

"Hours crawl like paralytic centipedes. Nothing amuses you. Reading is difficult; writing, impossible." In assessing the boredom of prison life, Churchill allowed that "dark moods come easily across the mind of a prisoner. . . . But when you are young, well fed, high spirited, loosely guarded, able to conspire with others, those moods carry thought nearer to resolve, and resolve nearer to action."[23]

Thus, from within the converted-schoolhouse jail, Churchill began to protest his captivity. He first wrote directly to Transvaal Secretary of State for War Louis de Souza, hoping to gain his release. Perhaps the South African officials would recognize him as a noncombatant and let him go.

On the other hand, if they ignored his requests—as they likely would—his correspondence would at the very least occupy their minds and divert them from considering him a flight risk. It was an ingenious strategy, but it sadly had the reverse effect. General Piet Joubert, the senior Boer commander, wrote to F. W. Reitz, the Transvaal State Secretary, advising against Churchill's release—and, in fact, suggesting that he be more closely guarded. "Otherwise he can still do us a lot of harm."[24]

HIGH-RANKING VISITORS

Though Churchill was something of a prize possession to the Boers, they allowed him to receive many high-ranking visitors at the prison. He entertained them with conversations about the progress of the war, and they provided him with their own views.

By now, he was determined to lull the enemy into a false hope that he had given up on the possibility of release and had resigned himself to incarceration for the duration of the war. However, quite the contrary was true. Along with Haldane and a South African colonist named Brockie, who had passed himself off as a sergeant-major in order to be sent to the officers' prison rather than the camp for regular soldiers, Churchill was hatching a plan to escape.

On December 7, days before the planned escape, two other prisoners jumped the fence of the State Model Schools and were captured on the outskirts of Pretoria. Though this incident raised Haldane's confidence in their escape plan, it also added urgency, as the threat of tighter prison security or restrictions on movement would surely scupper any future attempts. It was quickly decided that they would proceed as soon as possible.

On the evening of December 11, Churchill and Haldane strolled separately to the latrine building, which was to be their "leg up" for climbing over the fence to escape. Brockie had agreed to meet them once they were in place, and he would bring the maps and a compass.

The plan failed to get off the ground that night because the sentry refused to budge from his assigned position. Disappointed, the three men decided to postpone for twenty-four hours and returned to their dormitories. Churchill was very fortunate not to have been discovered. Unwisely, he had left on his pillow a note for Louis de Souza, which he now urgently retrieved. The note read, in part:

> I do not consider that your government was justified in holding me
> . . . and I have consequently resolved to escape. The arrangements I
> have succeeded in making in conjunction with my friends outside are
> such as give me every confidence. . . . Regretting that circumstances
> have not permitted me to bid you a personal farewell . . .
>
> Yours vy sincerely,
> Winston S. Churchill [25]

Though laced with foolhardy arrogance, the note's purpose was not only to be humorous but also to lead de Souza to believe that Churchill had received help from the outside, which he hoped would keep the Boers busy looking for phantom accomplices and investigating anyone who had come remotely near the school. Strategically, it was a masterstroke.

Irony has its moments. Unbeknownst to Churchill, on December 12, the day planned for the second escape attempt, General Joubert telegraphed Reitz, withdrawing his objections to Churchill's release. The telegraph had yet to be delivered to the authorities in Pretoria when Churchill and Haldane once again made their way towards the latrine.

With the sentry once again standing firm, the prospects once again looked bleak. If they made a run for it and were seen, they knew that a shot at such close range would most definitely hit them.

Churchill and Haldane returned to the verandah and informed Brockie. Not satisfied with their review, Brockie went over to observe for himself. Churchill and Haldane waited for some time, and then Churchill made his way back to see what Brockie was doing. Moments later, Brockie returned to Haldane, while

Churchill remained in position, waiting for the guard to move, determined that yet another night not be wasted.

When the sentry at last turned from his position, Churchill took the opportunity to scale the fence. On the way over, his waistcoat snagged on the wire, and the ripping noise almost gave him away. But when he looked back towards the sentry, he saw the man cup his hands and light a cigarette. Relieved, Churchill lowered himself into the garden below, where he hid among the shrubs and waited for Haldane and Brockie to follow him over the fence so they could escape together.

After an hour had passed with no sign of his companions, Churchill finally saw the two men through the fence. He risked signaling with a cough, and they noticed him; but it soon became apparent that they would not be able to escape that night. Because Churchill was already over the fence and unable to return easily, he decided to proceed alone.

Churchill describes what happened next:

> The gate which led into the road was only a few yards from another sentry. I said to myself, "*Toujours de l'audace*," put my hat on my head, strode into the middle of the garden, walked past the windows of the house without any attempt at concealment, and so went through the gate and turned to the left. I passed the sentry at less than five yards. Most of them knew me by sight. Whether he looked at me or not I do not know, for I never turned my head. I restrained with the utmost difficulty an impulse to run. But after walking a hundred yards and hearing no challenge, I knew that the second obstacle had been surmounted. I was at large in Pretoria.[26]

LONG JOURNEY TO FREEDOM

Churchill now faced a three-hundred-mile trek to Delagoa Bay and freedom. Unable to speak Dutch or Kaffir, not knowing anyone to whom he could turn for help, and without either a map or a compass, he had little money, no water, and only four slabs of chocolate—nothing that would sustain him for very long.

Sentries were stationed throughout the towns, and the countryside was routinely patrolled. Knowing that all trains were searched and the lines guarded, Churchill could proceed only on foot. Urgently aware that by morning his absence would be noticed, he proceeded with determination, avoiding the beams of streetlights by walking in the middle of the road.

He began to form a plan for his uncharted journey. His challenge in getting to Delagoa Bay Railway with no map or compass would be solved by following the rail line from a safe distance. Knowing he would be unable to walk the full three hundred miles, he determined to board a moving train and hide himself somewhere out of the way.

After two hours of walking, he saw the signal lights of a station and hid in a ditch about two hundred yards beyond it. He reasoned that any train stopping at the station would still be moving slowly enough for him to board when it passed his position.

After another hour, a train pulled into the depot and stopped. Churchill readied himself. When the train resumed its journey, he waited for the engine to pass his hiding place and then began running alongside the rails, looking for a way to clamber aboard. He quickly realized that he had underestimated the acceleration of the locomotive, and it took him several tries to successfully board the train. When he climbed into one of the cars, he discovered it was filled with sacks of empty coal bags, which proved a warm and comfortable bed. Uncertain of the train's destination or whether he was even going in the right direction, he decided that anything was better than being trapped in the enemy's capital. At peace with his decision, he soon fell asleep.

"I woke suddenly with all feelings of exhilaration gone, and only the consciousness of oppressive difficulties heavy on me."[27] He knew he had to leave the train before dawn or risk detection.

Quickly scrambling over the top of the railcar, he took hold of the iron handle at the back and jumped clear at the first opportunity.

"The train was running at a fair speed," he later said, "but I felt it was time to leave it. . . . My feet struck the ground in two gigantic strides, and the next instant I was sprawling in the ditch, considerably shaken but unhurt. The train, my faithful ally of the night, hurried on its journey."[28]

By now he was desperately thirsty, and he immediately began to search for water. Finding a clear pool in the waning moonlight, he gulped down as much as he could hold and then made his way up into the surrounding hills to hide in a grove of trees. As he watched the sun rise over the railroad, he was relieved to see that he had chosen the right rail line to follow.

The day was soon sweltering, and Churchill was hungry. He ate one of his chocolate bars, which took the edge off his hunger but greatly increased his thirst. He waited for an opportunity to run back to the pool for another drink but watched with dismay as several Boers happened by throughout the day. He finally resigned himself to wait until dark before hazarding his next move. As he later recalled, "My sole companion was a gigantic vulture, who manifested an extravagant interest in my condition, and made hideous and ominous gurglings from time to time."[29]

But as at Omdurman, the voracious bird would not make a meal of Winston Churchill that day.

CHURCHILL'S PRAYER

When night fell on Churchill's second day at large, he quickly made his way to the pool and drank. Knowing he would be unable to board a train moving at the speed it had been traveling when he jumped off the night before, he made his way to where the line sloped upward, and he waited. Six hours passed, and no train appeared. As another hour lapsed, Churchill began to lose hope. He decided to proceed on foot, determined to walk at least ten miles before dawn. Because of the heavily guarded bridges and huts placed in frequent intervals along the rail line, he made little progress. Still, "there was nothing for it but to plod on—but in an increasingly purposeless and hopeless manner. I felt very miserable."[30]

Meanwhile, the Boers were determined to recapture Churchill as quickly as possible. A notice was copied, delivered, and posted, offering a £25 reward for his recapture, *dead or alive*. Though he didn't know it at the time, Churchill now had not only a price on his head but a death sentence as well.

Churchill now saw a row of lights on the horizon, which he assumed came from another station along the railway. Off to the left, he saw the gleam of fires, and he was encouraged by the possibility that they came from a *kraal*, a cluster of huts inhabited by tribal Africans. Though he didn't speak a word of the local language, he hoped that, by offering the British bank notes he had in his pocket, he might be given food, water, and shelter for the night and would not be turned over to his enemies.

As Churchill walked towards the lights in the distance, he began to lose confidence. He stopped, looked back, and began to retrace his steps. He made it halfway back to the rail line before he again halted, this time slumping to the ground in desperate depression. He was, he said, "completely baffled, destitute of any idea what to do or where to turn."[31]

Churchill's thoughts and actions at that moment provide a clear view of his personal spirituality:

> I found no comfort in any of the philosophical ideas which some men parade in their hours of ease and strength and safety. They seemed only fair-weather friends. I realised with awful force that no exercise of my own feeble wit and strength could save me from my enemies, and that without the assistance of that High Power which interferes in the eternal sequence of causes and effects more

often than we are always prone to admit, I could never succeed. I prayed long and earnestly for help and guidance. My prayer, as it seems to me, was swiftly and wonderfully answered.[32]

"Suddenly," Churchill recalled, "without the slightest reason all my doubts disappeared. It was certainly by no process of logic that they were dispelled. I just felt quite clear that I would go to the Kaffir *kraal*."[33]

TOWARDS THE FLAMES

The fires he had thought were only a few miles away were in fact much farther. Still, with determination and his never-surrender attitude, Churchill continued towards the flames that had become a beacon of hope.

After walking for more than an hour, he drew close enough to realize that the fires were not from a *kraal*. "I saw that I was approaching a group of houses around the mouth of a coal-mine . . . and I could see that the fires which had led me so far were from the furnaces of the engines."[34]

Churchill now had to make a decision: If he turned back, he would wander in the wilderness until "hunger, fever, discovery, or surrender" ended his journey. Before his escape, he had heard that "in the mining district of Witbank and Middleburg there were a certain number of English residents who had been suffered to remain in the country in order to keep the mines working. Had I been led to one of these?"[35]

With some hesitation, Churchill knocked on one of the doors. When there was no answer, he tapped again. This time, a light went on and a man's voice came from a window.

"*Wer ist da?*"

Churchill replied in English, telling the man he needed help. Within moments, the door opened and a tall man peered out, pale-faced and sporting a black mustache.

"What do you want?" the man said, this time in English.[36]

Knowing that he needed to be invited inside in order to negotiate, Churchill made up a tale, claiming to have fallen off a train in an accident. He claimed he had been unconscious for hours and had dislocated his shoulder. The story, he said, "leapt out as if I had learnt it by heart. Yet I had not the slightest idea what I was going to say or what the next sentence would be."[37]

The stranger invited him into a dark room. When the lamps were lit, Churchill noticed a revolver lying on the table. He wondered if this room would now become his prison.

"I think I'd like to know a little more about this railway accident of yours," the man said.

"I think I had better tell you the truth," Churchill replied.

"I think you had."[38]

When Churchill identified himself as a British war correspondent and told of his escape from Pretoria, the man stepped forward and offered his hand.

"Thank God you have come here!" he said. "It is the only house for twenty miles where you would not have been handed over. But we are all British here, and we will see you through."

As it turned out, John Howard, Churchill's "good Samaritan," was a British subject who had been forced to remain in South Africa during the conflict. He ran the coal mine and was happy to hide Churchill in the mine until he could be safely loaded onto a freight train and taken across the border to safety.

After three "anxious and uncomfortable" days on the train, Churchill crossed into Portuguese territory (present-day Mozambique) and made his way to the British Consulate in Louranço Marques (today called Maputo). From there, he caught a steamboat down the coast to Durban.

Churchill arrived in Durban to much acclaim, finding himself "a popular hero . . . as if I had won a great victory."[39] Flags festooned the harbor, bands played, crowds cheered. Churchill said he was "nearly torn to pieces by enthusiastic kindness" as he was swept up onto the shoulders of the crowd and carried to the town hall steps, "where nothing would content them but a speech, which after a becoming reluctance I was induced to deliver."[40]

A "SOLITARY TREE" IN PARLIAMENT

For the first time in his life, Churchill was an international hero. Upon his return to England in 1900 after a second stint in South Africa with a cavalry regiment, he stood for election to the House of Commons from Oldham, where he had lost a bid prior to his experience in the Boer War. This time, however, he "received the warmest of welcomes" as Oldham "almost without distinction of party accorded me a triumph."[41]

The catalytic voice that would one day move a nation—and much of the world—was heard for the first time in Parliament on February 18, 1901. Churchill quickly found his own voice and purpose, securing his father's legacy in his maiden speech to a packed House.

Like his father before him, the youthful politician fearlessly rose to challenge his own political party and government on policies that he believed were not in Britain's best interests. "I was brought up in my father's house to believe in democracy. 'Trust the people'—that was his message."[42]

Winston Churchill was a moderate who firmly disagreed with Joseph Chamberlain, secretary of state for the colonies and father of the same Neville Chamberlain whom Churchill would one day succeed as prime minister.

Joseph Chamberlain's "Party before Country" belief was evident in 1902, when he asked Churchill: "What is the use of supporting your own Government only when it is right? It is just when it is in this sort of pickle that you ought to come to our aid."[43]

Churchill paid the price for his moral stands several times: losing Parliamentary seats; being overlooked for appointments;

and finding himself cooling his heels on the glum backbenches of the House of Commons, staring at the heads of younger, less experienced members who advanced because they made no waves in the party.

Within a few years of entering Parliament, Churchill, in conflict with the Conservative government over free trade, crossed the floor of the House of Commons, leaving the Conservatives and taking a seat on the Liberal benches. He would return to the Tory side twenty years later, but his decision to switch sides branded him for many as traitorous and untrustworthy. This characterization was further exacerbated by his stance against Indian independence and, later, by his alarm over Germany's rearmament program and Adolf Hitler's rise.

On the latter issues, Churchill correctly predicted bloodshed. Tragedy might well have been avoided had the government listened to his early warnings.

During these barren years, Churchill studied the life of Moses and reflected on what went into building such a strong leader.

> Every prophet has to come from civilization, but every prophet has to go into the wilderness. He must have a strong impression of a complex society and all that it has to give, and then he must serve periods of isolation and meditation. This is the process by which psychic dynamite is made.[44]

Churchill would not have believed he was describing his own route to "psychic dynamite," and he may not have been a prophet in the Old Testament sense; but he had remarkable intuition. Many of his contemporaries recognized it, including Violet Bonham Carter, daughter of Prime Minister H. H. Asquith and a close Churchill friend. She wrote that her father was "deeply impressed" by Churchill's forecast of the beginning of the First World War. Churchill, then in his thirties, provided a prediction "uncanny in its exactitude." Three years later, the sequences and timing he listed in his analysis "were almost literally verified," Carter writes. "Once again Winston's daemon was 'telling him things.'"[45]

That "daemon" also gave Churchill a strong intuitive understanding of military strategy.[46] As he moved through the ranks of government in the years ahead, his tactical understanding would be sharpened on the biting edge of failure as well as success.

3

From the Admiralty to the Trenches

What vile & wicked folly & barbarism it all is.

WINSTON CHURCHILL, IN A LETTER TO HIS WIFE,
CLEMENTINE, SEPTEMBER 15, 1909

"AFTER HIS ADVENTURES in the Boer War, Winston Churchill was the most petted young man in England," writes René Kraus.[1] But Churchill had little time to rest in the caress of glory. He was moving inexorably towards headlines that would blare his humiliation and downfall. He would soon be reminded that public acclaim is fickle and that no one should trust his heart to the fleeting siren of fame.

Churchill learned this truth with wrenching painfulness slightly more than a decade after his return from South Africa as a conquering hero. Through the ensuing years, he rose through the governmental ranks to his initial major wartime leadership role as first lord of the Admiralty during the First World War.

The run-up to that conflict included rising tensions in the

Balkans, saber rattling among the European powers in North Africa, and a naval armaments race between Britain and Germany. In August 1911, at the ebb of one of the many crises that had brought the world to the brink of war, Churchill—now thirty-seven and bearing the stresses of his role as home secretary—went to Somersetshire, the site of Prime Minister Asquith's manor house, for a much-needed rest. It was "a place of magical beauty, stillness and peace," writes Violet Bonham Carter. But during those tense days, three years before the outbreak of war, Churchill was restless even looking out on the soft countryside with the lines of a poem by A. E. Housman:

> On the idle hill of summer,
> Sleepy with the sound of streams,
> Far I hear the steady drummer
> Drumming like a noise in dreams.
>
> Far and near and low and louder
> On the roads of earth go by,
> Dear to friends and food for powder,
> Soldiers marching, all to die.[2]

Housman's verse was so evocative to Churchill's soul because, as he wrote later, "I could not think of anything else but the peril of war."[3] Churchill went about his duties, but the looming conflict was the "only . . . field of interest fiercely illuminated in my mind."[4]

Seated on a hilltop, Churchill surveyed "the smiling country which stretches around Mells"[5] as Housman's words roamed through his mind. Viewed against the backdrop of Churchill's concerns about war, Housman's lines become specters.

In 1920, two years after the end of the First World War, Churchill would return to Mells and would paint a portrait there of an archway leading to a pergola washed in subtle violets. But in 1911 there was no settling tone—only "anxieties," as Churchill himself put it.[6]

Meanwhile, Asquith was wrestling with conflicts within the Committee of Imperial Defence, where some believed that the Admiralty was failing to work cooperatively with the Imperial General Staff. Lord Haldane, leader of the War Office and one of Asquith's dearest friends, told the prime minister he would no longer bear responsibility if the clash between his staff and the Admiralty could not be quieted. In September, Asquith went to Scotland, hoping to find a measure of calm on the golf course. However, "his mind was preoccupied with the change at the Admiralty."[7]

Churchill joined Asquith in Scotland on September 27, and they golfed in "golden autumn sunshine with sea gulls circling overhead."[8] Asquith's mood began to lift, and laughter rang over the links. However, tension returned with a visit from Haldane.

Churchill was called away for an evening on Home Office business, but he returned by the next afternoon and again went golfing with Prime Minister Asquith.

When the men came in from the links, Violet Bonham Carter writes, "I saw in Winston's face a radiance like the sun."

"Will you come out for a walk with me—at once?" he asked.

"You don't want tea?"

"No, I don't want tea. I don't want anything—anything in the world. Your father has just offered me the Admiralty."

Never had Carter seen such happiness and fulfillment in her friend.

"This is the big thing," Churchill said. "The biggest thing that has ever come my way—the chance I should have chosen before all others. I shall pour into it everything I've got."[9]

As Churchill walked back to his guest quarters, he looked out at the Firth of Forth, the vast waterway opening Scotland to the

North Sea. In the distance, he saw two British battleships, moving under plumes of steam. "They seemed invested with a new significance to me," he later recalled.[10]

BIBLICAL GUIDANCE

As Churchill entered his room, his head still spinning from his appointment as first lord of the Admiralty, his first thought was of the danger facing his nation. "Peace-loving, unthinking, little-prepared" Britain, he had always felt, was characterized by "power and virtue" and a mission among the nations "of good sense and fair-play."[11] Then his mind shifted to Germany and how he had been enthralled in 1907 when he had watched fifty thousand soldiers march in a thundering military display. Churchill contemplated Germany's "cold, patient, ruthless calculations." He recalled "the army corps I had watched tramp past, wave after wave of valiant manhood." He remembered another time when he had observed maneuvers at Würzburg consisting "of the thousands of strong horses dragging cannon and great howitzers up the ridges and along the roads."[12]

With these thoughts racing through his mind, Churchill's eye landed on a large Bible on his bed table. Opening at random to Deuteronomy 9, he read these words:

> Hear, O Israel: Thou art to pass over Jordan this day, to go in to possess nations greater and mightier than thyself, cities great and fenced up to heaven, a people great and tall, the children of the Anakims, whom thou knowest, and of whom thou hast heard say, Who can stand before the children of Anak! Understand therefore this day, that the LORD thy God is he which goeth over before thee; as a consuming fire he shall destroy them, and he shall bring them down before thy face: so shalt thou drive them out, and destroy them quickly, as the LORD hath said unto thee. Speak not thou in thine heart, after that the LORD thy God hath cast them out from before

thee, saying, For my righteousness the LORD hath brought me in to possess this land: but for the wickedness of these nations the LORD doth drive them out from before thee. Not for thy righteousness, or for the uprightness of thine heart, dost thou go to possess their land: but for the wickedness of these nations the LORD thy God doth drive them out from before thee, and that he may perform the word which the LORD sware unto thy fathers, Abraham, Isaac, and Jacob.[13]

Churchill later said that "it seemed a message full of reassurance."

Having observed the German military maneuvers firsthand in the company of Kaiser Wilhelm, Churchill may well have focused on the description of the Anakim as "a people great and tall." He had been impressed by the Teutonic soldiers and had noted their prowess with their powerful weapons. Now as he contemplated the possibility of having to stand against such a formidable power, he may have been tempted to adapt the words of Moses—"Who can stand before the children of Anak?"—and ask himself, "Who can stand before the children of Germany?" Whereas Moses had anchored his hope in the "consuming fire" of an almighty God, Prime Minister Asquith apparently laid his hopes on the Royal Navy and had now set the Royal Navy squarely on the shoulders of Winston Churchill.

Reading in Deuteronomy, Churchill may have found his reassurance in the overwhelming power of God, who had promised Moses that God himself would be the Great Displacer, going before the armies of his covenant people, Israel, and dislodging the enemy from the ground it occupied.

What Churchill could not have foreseen in that moment was the German leader who would arise in years to come and who would turn his back on God, try to eradicate the Jews, and impose his own kingdom (Reich) in the place of God's. He would try to use the church to advance his goals, and when the faithful church refused, he would try to destroy it.

As Churchill read this portion of Deuteronomy 9, he would

have noted God's warning about taking pride in victory. As human conquerors, men were not to take credit for victory or to declare that it was because of their "righteousness" that God had favored them over their enemy. Indeed, the divinely wrought victory would come not because of the superior worthiness of the victorious nation but because of the God-defying wickedness of the conquered.

Churchill was a prideful man, but not in the style of Lucifer, who sought to ascend to the very throne of God to displace the rightful Ruler. Beneath Churchill's hubris was a heart of humility, sown perhaps through rejection by his father and further wrought by seasons of setbacks that were soon to follow.

Hitler, on the other hand, would one day try to present himself as a new messiah, and that same impulse was already in the heart of his spiritual predecessor, Kaiser Wilhelm, in 1911. Of course, as René Kraus aptly notes, "What mortal man would not become a megalomaniac if he were deified day in and day out as 'the world's most glorious prince,'" as Wilhelm had been?[14] Ultimately, the Kaiser's armies would not prevail, but only after the European continent had been drenched with the blood of its rising generations.

There was much puffery associated with being first lord of the Admiralty—plumed hats, cannon salutes, and acclamation as the leader of the world's greatest navy. But as Churchill would soon learn, the higher the position, the greater the potential for humiliation.

THE DARDANELLES DISASTER

The winter of 1914 would inscribe the most painful of memories on Churchill's mind, as an icy grip throttled the combatants in the First World War. "Russia, mighty steam-roller, hope of suffering France and prostrate Belgium—Russia is falling," he wrote.[15] The wintery blast had frozen Russia, cutting her off from her allies, including Britain, and rendering her unable to receive their aid.

Ice covered the seas, and where there was open water, there lay the Germans. Turkey, as one of Germany's allies, had slammed shut the other access route to Russia: the Straits of the Dardanelles. Something had to be done.

Three months into the First World War, Britain and her allies had already lost about a million men, and Churchill was gravely concerned about the terrible human toll in the trenches along the western front. Meanwhile, in the east, the Turks were pressuring the Russians in the Caucasus. Churchill believed that freeing the Russian military to open a new front in the east by attacking Berlin would prevent more soldiers in the west from being sent to "chew barbed wire."

Lord Hankey, who held the dual position of secretary to the Committee of Imperial Defence and secretary to the War Council, shared Churchill's concern. Independently, they wrote to Prime Minister Asquith about the necessity of breaking the trench-warfare stalemate.

Meanwhile, the Russian Grand Duke Nicolas wrote an urgent appeal to Lord Kitchener, the British secretary of state for war, asking for immediate action to pull away the Turkish armies that were closing in on Russian forces in the Caucasus. Kitchener wrote to Churchill, suggesting that "the only place that a demonstration might have some effect in stopping reinforcements going east would be the Dardanelles,"[16] the narrow strait connecting the Aegean Sea to the Sea of Marmara in northwestern Turkey. Such a maneuver also would open the way to the Turkish capital of Constantinople (Istanbul) and the Black Sea.

Kitchener committed Britain to action by telegraphing the grand duke that "steps will be taken to make a demonstration against the Turks."[17] Though Kitchener had no troops available to support an operation in the Dardanelles, he embraced a plan proposed by Hankey for a naval expedition "to bombard and take the Gallipoli Peninsula, with Constantinople as its objective."[18] The optimistic hope was that "the mere threat of naval bombardment would force the Ottoman Empire out of the war."[19] The British battleship HMS *Queen Elizabeth* had recently been equipped with fifteen-inch guns, and it was proposed that they be tested by using Turkish military installations for target practice. However, as Lord Hankey noted in his War Council minutes, Kitchener stipulated that "we could leave off the bombardment if it did not prove effective."[20] Thus, the War Council voted unanimously in favor of the operation.

The conclusion seemed logical and clear: Remove Turkey from the war, and the Dardanelles would be open all the way to the Marmara Sea, through the Bosporus, into the Black Sea, and onward to the doorstep of Russia.

Churchill conceived a bold plan that found great support from the War Cabinet. He proposed using a combined navy and army attack to break through the Straits and march on Constantinople. If it worked, Churchill was confident it could force Turkey to surrender, tipping the balance of power in favor of the Allies and bringing the First World War to an early end. On paper, the strategy seemed inventive and the best shortcut to victory.

In the auspicious Admiralty buildings, the "possibilities seemed limitless."[21] In the Dardanelles, the initial bombardment seemed successful. Constantinople braced for an almost certain assault. The Turkish sultan readied to move himself and his entourage away from the city.

On March 18, 1915, fourteen British and four French battleships sailed into the Narrows and furiously pounded the Turkish positions. Following a line of minesweepers, the fleet eased its way up the Straits. Not all the mines were destroyed, however, and three battleships went down. Two others were disabled.

The sudden turn in the battle stunned the British fleet commander, Admiral John de Robeck, who suspended the attack until ground troops could be deployed and given an opportunity to capture the high ground along the Gallipoli peninsula. This unexpected pause ultimately led to the defeat of the British in the Dardanelles.

Commander Roger Keyes, chief of staff for the Dardanelles expedition, believed that the Turks were already beaten and that a "sweeping force" to "reap the fruits of our efforts" was what was needed. In his 1934 memoirs, Keyes says he believed that "from the 4th April, 1915, onwards, the Fleet could have forced the Straits, and, with losses trifling in comparison with those the Army suffered, could have entered the [Marmara Sea] with sufficient force to destroy the Turko-German Fleet."[22]

Enver Pasha, the Turkish minister of war at the time of the Dardanelles operation, agreed:

> If the English had only had the courage to rush more ships through the Dardanelles they could have got to Constantinople; but their delay enabled us thoroughly to fortify the Peninsula, and in six weeks' time we had taken down there over two hundred Austrian Skoda guns.[23]

Despite the failed naval attack, the Allies went ahead with troop landings on April 25, 1915. The British and French, along with troops from Australia and New Zealand, established two beach-heads, but were unable to advance inland. Indecision on the part of the Allied command gave the Turks time to bring reinforcements and deepen the stalemate. Finally, on December 7, 1915, the British began evacuating their positions.

Before it was over, more than half a million casualties had been suffered on the battlefield—about 250,000 on each side. Of the 480,000 Allied soldiers sent to Gallipoli, 46,000 died there. With the failure of the British and French warships to advance through the Dardanelles Strait, and the resulting evacuation of the ground troops, Gallipoli was regarded as a massive defeat for the British. Churchill, as first lord of the Admiralty, was made the principal scapegoat, largely because of the loss of the battleships at the beginning of the campaign.

Unable to call upon exculpatory evidence from Cabinet meetings and correspondence that would have shown his true role in the operation, Churchill honorably resigned the Admiralty, though he later said, "The archives of the Admiralty will show in utmost detail the part I have played in all the great transactions that have taken place. It is to them that I look for my defence."[24]

With one hundred years of hindsight, the evidence today shows that the failure of the Gallipoli campaign was due to mismanagement and division within the War Cabinet. Churchill had asked for ground troops to be deployed along with the naval bombardment, but his request was initially refused. Then, just days before the planned attack, the troop support was granted, but with only half the number Churchill said he needed. Even after the ships were sunk, he wanted to advance the naval attack, but he was instructed to delay until the army arrived. By the time the ground forces were in position, too much time had passed, and the Turks had prepared their defenses for the attack.

"Time will vindicate my administration of the Admiralty," Churchill said at the time, "and assign me my due share in the vast series of preparations and operations which have secured us the command of the seas."[25]

In a 2013 Discovery Channel documentary on the Gallipoli campaign, Peter Doyle—a military historian, geologist, and battlefield specialist—suggested that the campaign never would have succeeded even with the best leadership because the Turkish forces held advantages of terrain over the beachheads on which the Allies landed. Still, the debate about Gallipoli continues.

Whatever history decides, the 1915 campaign and its heavy British casualties will always be considered among the greatest failures in military history. And rightly or wrongly, Winston Churchill's legacy will always be colored to some degree by those events.

"I have a clear conscience which enables me to bear any responsibility for past events with composure," Churchill said in his letter of resignation to Prime Minister Asquith. Asquith subsequently appointed Churchill to an inconsequential post, the chancellery of the Duchy of Lancaster. Perhaps he meant well by allowing Churchill to continue as a member of the War Cabinet, but it was pure torture for Churchill. Though in his new role he could attend the meetings and hear reports from the battlefield and discussion of plans, he could neither enter the talks nor vote. "He was condemned to passivity while the storm raged over England, and all hands were feverishly occupied on deck,"[26] writes René Kraus. As Churchill himself described it:

> The change from the intense executive activities of each day's work at the Admiralty to the narrowly measured duties of a councillor left me gasping. . . . I had great anxiety, and no means of relieving it. I had vehement convictions and small powers to give effect to them. I had to watch the unhappy casting-away of great opportunities, and the feeble execution of plans which I had launched and in which I heartily believed. I had long hours of utterly unwanted leisure in which to contemplate the frightful unfolding of the war.[27]

Once the dynamo of the world's greatest navy, Churchill now took up, among other things, oil painting. Though it would prove a delight for the rest of his life, it was not enough to assuage the frustration of being pushed aside while his nation was at war. When Prime Minister Asquith reduced his War Cabinet to a committee of five, excluding Churchill from the inner circle, Churchill wrote to him, "I am an officer, and I place myself unreservedly at the disposal of the military authorities, observing that my regiment is in France."[28]

Within days, he requested a posting to the western front in France, and he served there until March 1916 alongside troops who no doubt blamed him for the disaster at Gallipoli that had cost so many Allied lives.

FACING PARLIAMENT

Before Churchill left for the front, he went to the House of Commons to explain his resignation. The members were cordial but skeptical as he rose. What followed was one of the signature speeches of his political career, as he rallied Parliament in the face of the recent military reversals.

> There is no reason to be disheartened about the progress of the war. We are passing through a bad time now and it will probably be worse before it is better, but that it will be better, if we only endure and persevere, I have no doubt whatever. . . . Some of these small States are hypnotised by German military pomp and precision. They see the glitter, they see the episode; but what they do not see or realise is the capacity of the ancient and mighty nations against whom Germany is warring to endure adversity, to put up with disappointment and mismanagement, to recreate and renew their strength, to toil on with boundless obstinacy through boundless suffering to the achievement of the greatest cause for which men have fought.[29]

When Churchill finished his remarks, thunderous applause erupted from members who only moments earlier had been reluctant to even welcome him to the House.

On November 18, 1915, Churchill crossed over to France to take up a posting in the Oxfordshire Hussars. En route, he was intercepted by Sir John French, the commander-in-chief at St. Omer, who offered him a brigade to command. Churchill jumped at the chance.

Upon hearing that Churchill was to serve on the French front, his friend Violet Bonham Carter wrote to him: "For one who knows as you do what he has to offer the world, it is a very great thing to risk it all as you are doing. So fine a risk to take that I can't help rejoicing proudly that you should have done it."[30]

Field Marshal French kept his promise to arrange Churchill's command, and it was agreed that he would train with the Grenadier Guards. Churchill met with the senior divisional officers, who encouraged him greatly. "They highly approved of my course of action & thought it vy right & proper," he wrote to Clementine from St. Omer, adding that "the Army is willing to receive me back as 'the prodigal son.'"[31]

On November 20, Churchill was attached to the second battalion of the Grenadier Guards, commanded by Lieutenant Colonel George Jeffreys. The battalion was destined for Neuve Chapelle, and Churchill later recalled that first day:

> It was a dull November afternoon, and an icy drizzle fell over the darkening plain. As we approached the line, the red flashes of the guns stabbed the sombre landscape on either side of the road, to the sound of an intermittent cannonade. We paced onwards for about half an hour without a word being spoken on either side.[32]

Jeffreys was not pleased to have had Churchill foisted upon him.

"I think I ought to tell you that we were not at all consulted in the matter of your coming to join us," he said.[33]

Churchill replied respectfully, saying that he'd also had no idea which battalion he would be assigned, "but that I dared say it would be all right. Anyhow we must make the best of it."[34]

Upon his arrival at battalion headquarters, a ruin called Ebenezer Farm, Churchill received an icy reception from the troops. Undaunted, he pressed ahead with making the proper introductions, and soon his personality and wit won the day. Before long, he commanded the respect and good wishes of everyone under his leadership—a remarkable feat considering the untenable nature of his situation: an international disgrace, stepping down from the Admiralty under a cloud, and now serving among troops who neither liked nor trusted him. However, on reflection, the years Churchill had spent in Parliament, and the times he had been cast aside by those he once considered friends had prepared him for this great challenge.

> It will always be a source of pride to me that I succeeded in making myself perfectly at home with these men and formed friendships which I enjoy to-day. It took about forty-eight hours to wear through their natural prejudice against "politicians" of all kinds, but particularly of the non-Conservative brands.[35]

On November 26, 1915, Churchill's career and life once again nearly came to an abrupt end. While serving three miles behind the front lines, he received an unusual but urgent summons from Lieutenant General Richard Haking to meet at Merville. Churchill set off on a dangerous walk "across sopping fields on which stray bullets are always falling, along tracks periodically shelled."[36]

A driver was supposed to meet him at the Rouge Croix crossroads, but when Churchill arrived, he found no car and no driver. Finally, hours later, the escort arrived, but without a motor car. Heavy shelling had forced the vehicle off the road, making it late to fetch Churchill. As it turned out, the meeting with the corps commander had been canceled.

Annoyed that his time had been wasted, Churchill returned to his previous location behind the lines. He was frustrated that the officer's order and subsequent cancellation had resulted in "dragging me about in rain & wind for nothing."[37] He "reached the trenches without mishap," only to discover that, a mere fifteen minutes after he had left, a German shell had exploded just a few feet from where he had been sitting. The shack-like structure built into the trench was demolished, and one of the three men inside had been killed. "When I saw the ruin I was not so angry with the general after all," he wrote.[38]

THE UNSEEN HAND

In contemplating his brush with death in the trenches of the First World War, Churchill wrote to Clementine:

> Now see from this how vain it is to worry about things. It is all chance or destiny and our wayward footsteps are best planted without too much calculation. One must yield oneself simply and naturally to the mood of the game and trust in God which is another way of saying the same thing.[39]

Churchill could not have known at the time how all of these events, high adventures, miraculous unscathings, and even the most dire setbacks and failures were preparing him for the day when his number would be called to step up and lead the free world against the incursions of tyranny. Yet without his even realizing it, it seems he had adopted a very biblical perspective: "Don't worry about anything" (Philippians 4:6).

PART II

DESTINY

4
Hitler's Vision

*More than a million German soldiers . . . are drawn up ready
to attack . . . ; and the decision rests in the hands of a haunted,
morbid being, who, to their eternal shame, the German
peoples in their bewilderment have worshipped as a god.*

WINSTON CHURCHILL, MARCH 30, 1940

WHILE LIEUTENANT COLONEL WINSTON CHURCHILL was bonding with his countrymen in the trenches of the western front, Corporal Adolf Hitler, on the other side of the conflict, began to pulsate with his own life vision in the muddy, vermin-infested ditches of that same war.

Though surrounded by death and destruction, the twenty-five-year-old Hitler narrowly escaped harm on several occasions. When his regiment sustained an 83 percent casualty rate (2,500 men killed, wounded, or missing) in its first engagement of the war at Ypres, Hitler walked away "without a scratch."[1] As he watched his comrades being blown to bits or dying horribly by breathing poison gas, he noted that none of it touched him. Though eventually

61

he sustained a leg wound from a shell fragment in the Battle of the Somme,[2] he began to believe he was "predestined for greatness . . . [and] his sense of invincibility was later reinforced by his survival of several assassination attempts."[3]

Like Churchill before him, Hitler was sixteen years old when he predicted a grandiose role for himself in the future.

"IN THAT HOUR IT BEGAN"

Hitler's friend August Kubizek was with him on the night in 1905 when he claimed that his destiny was set and the spirit that would drive it entered into him. "It was the most impressive hour I ever lived through with my friend," Kubizek noted. "It was not a voluntary act but rather a visionary recognition of the road that had to be followed and which lay beyond his own will."[4]

August and Adolf had just come from a performance of *Rienzi*, Richard Wagner's five-act opera based on the rise and fall of a fourteenth-century Italian populist politician. Unable to secure seats, they had stood near the pillars in the opera house promenade, "burning with enthusiasm, and living breathlessly through Rienzi's rise to be tribune of the people of Rome, and his subsequent downfall."[5]

It was past midnight before August and the future Nazi leader left the theater. "My friend, his hands thrust into his coat pockets, silent and withdrawn, strode through the streets and towards the outskirts," writes Kubizek in his memoir, *The Young Hitler I Knew*. "He looked almost sinister, and paler than ever."

Suddenly, Hitler turned and gripped his friend's hands tightly. "His eyes were feverish with excitement," Kubizek recalled. "The words did not come smoothly from his mouth as they usually did, but rather erupted, hoarse and raucous. From his voice I could tell even more how much this experience had shaken him."

When Hitler began to speak, Kubizek was "struck by something strange. . . . It was as if a second ego spoke from within him."

Even Hitler showed "astonishment" at "what burst forth from him with elementary force." With "complete ecstasy and rapture," he seemed to transfer Rienzi's character "with visionary power, to the plane of his own ambitions."[6]

> He conjured up, in grandiose, inspiring pictures, his own future and that of his people. . . . He was talking of a mandate which, one day, he would receive from the people, to lead them out of servitude to the heights of freedom.
>
> It was a young man whose name then meant nothing who spoke to me in that strange hour. He spoke of a special mission which one day would be entrusted to him and I, his only listener, could hardly understand what he meant. Many years had to pass before I realised the significance of this enraptured hour for my friend.[7]

Decades later, after Hitler had come to power in Germany, Kubizek visited him and they talked about the night they had attended the opera. "In that hour it began," said Hitler. In fact, Hitler asked for Wagner's original manuscript of the *Rienzi* opera, and it was given to him on his fiftieth birthday.

"It is not difficult to see how Hitler might have been mesmerized by Rienzi's theatrical embodiment of a charismatic *Führerprinzip* [leadership principle]," writes Wagner scholar Thomas Grey. "In every step of Rienzi's career—from [his] acclamation as leader and savior of the *Volk* [the German people], through military struggle, violent suppression of mutinous factions, betrayal, and the final immolation at the hands of a world that has failed to follow his vision—Hitler would doubtless have found sustenance for his fantasies."[8]

Hitler and his compatriots, in their hubris, thought they were the heralds of a new order that would cleanse the world of its impurity. With stunning brutality, they pursued their fantastical vision right up until the moment when they were defeated by "the world," led by Winston Churchill. Still, before the full truth of Hitler's vision came to light, there were sympathizers in the United States, Great Britain, and elsewhere who watched with interest how the Nazis would implement this new order.

THE ROOTS OF HITLER'S NAZISM

During and after the Second World War, specialists tried to construct psychological profiles and histories of Adolf Hitler, hoping to predict, while the war raged, where and how he might strike; or hoping to understand, in the war's aftermath, how to recognize and prevent the rise of another of his type. But few have delved deeply into Hitler's spiritual roots. Spirituality gives rise to personal psychology and is the bulb from which the psychological roots spread.

"Hitler's actions have been given a variety of psychological explanations," writes Tufts University professor George Scarlett. But "they do not add up to explaining how it was possible for this odd man first to seduce a highly educated nation and then to nearly destroy it along with millions of non-Germans."[9]

Both Churchill and Hitler suffered from dysfunctional fathers. Churchill felt the pain of rejection from Lord Randolph's emotional abandonment, whereas Hitler experienced physical and emotional pain from his father's violent temperament.

Anyone who has experienced parental rejection knows that mental and emotional distress can be as severe as physical abuse. Nevertheless, Churchill developed admiration for his father's public career at least, and aspired to follow in his footsteps. Hitler's infliction of violence on entire nations may indicate that he never rose above the hatred he felt for his father.

Childhood development expert George Scarlett cautions against taking too narrow a view of Hitler's formative character. Quoting psychiatrist Fritz Redlich, Scarlett writes, "'To study the psychosocial transactions between Hitler and his followers is a crucial task, perhaps also more feasible than solving the riddle of the inner man.'"[10] Scarlett then adds: "Hitler does not fit neatly into a psychiatric category, and his problems cannot be derived simply from his childhood early experience. . . . [His] problems are combinations of psychological and spiritual problems."[11]

Whatever else might be said about Hitler, he was not a crazed religious nut. Labeling Hitler as *crazy* is tantamount to acquitting him and his legacy by reason of insanity. Hitler was not insane; he was evil. There was a cold calculation behind his actions. Though there is no question that he burned with demonic hatred for the Jews and was driven to exterminate them, there was also the practical matter of needing huge sums of money for the war he was planning, which he would either have to borrow or steal. Persecuting the Jews enabled him to also confiscate their wealth. Hitler's paintings—which, like any piece of art, is an expression of the artist's personality—have been criticized for their tedious rigidity. Hitler's art shows that he was starkly logical, and that is what made him so evil.

History's definitive events—both good and bad—are often noted in the Bible and other literature as occurring "on that day," "on a certain day," or at a momentous time that is weightier than others in a given period.[12] And so there was "a certain day" when Adolf Hitler became obsessed with the glories of war and unification of the German people. He describes the experience in his autobiographical *Mein Kampf*:

Rummaging through my father's library, I stumbled upon various books on military subjects, and among them I found a popular edition dealing with the Franco-Prussian war of 1870–71. These were two volumes of an illustrated journal of the period which now became my favorite reading matter. Before long that great heroic campaign had become *my greatest spiritual experience*. From then on I raved more and more about everything connected with war or with militarism.[13]

Though Hitler grew up at a time when Western culture was becoming fascinated with industrialization and the emerging concepts of Darwin's evolutionary theories, there was still a strong mythic influence, primarily from the romanticists and their tales of knights, wizards, and grand crusades. This strange syncretism between mechanical and mystical elements is similar to what we find in our own postmodern age, except now the mix is between spirituality and cybernetics.

For Hitler, the mystical aspect was found in his engagement with occultism. Whereas Churchill's spiritual foundation was established in large part by his nanny, Elizabeth Everest, Hitler was influenced by occultists such as the founders of the Thule Society, whose major goal was to "create a new race of Nordic Aryan Atlanteans";[14] mystics like Guido von List (who linked racial ideology with occultism), Lanz von Liebenfels (who fostered the pro-Aryan views known as Ariosophy), and Rudolf von Sebottendorf (who had studied spiritualist and occult systems in Turkey); and other believers in the occult, including Karl Haushofer, Dietrich Eckart, and Helena Blavatsky.

Hitler's views were also shaped by the writings of the philosophers Friedrich Nietzsche and Martin Heidegger. Nietzsche had filled the German mind with the idea of the Superman, the concept that God was dead, and the principle that the primal force in human society was "the will to power."

With all these formative influences, it's easy to see how Hitler could allow himself to be revered as a messianic deliverer and how he gained power over the German people, Europe, and the world itself.

HITLER'S SPIRITUAL GUIDE

French philosopher Emmanuel Faye believes that Martin Heidegger was Hitler's direct spiritual guide later in life, and that Heidegger viewed himself as "the 'spiritual' Führer of Nazism."[15]

Furthermore, according to Faye, "his writings continue to spread the radically racist and human life-destroying conceptions that make up the foundation of Hitlerism and Nazism."[16]

Heidegger, briefly rector of the University of Freiburg in the early Nazi era, gave philosophical credentials to the anti-Semitism that led to the Holocaust. This can be seen in his *Black Notebooks*, a personal philosophical diary written between 1931 and 1941 and released in 2014.[17] According to Heidegger, questions of God and eternity are not relevant. What matters at the end of our lives is the cumulative impact of our existence in time. There is no real accountability or glory beyond death, so we must live fully and gloriously in the *Zeitgeist* to which fate has affixed us as individuals.

According to this way of thinking, the Jews happened to be consigned by fate to live in a period of grandeur (for the German people) in which they were the tragic counterpoint (the race of ignominy) simply because they were *there* at that point in time. Heidegger inferred, however, that the German people had both the right and the responsibility to pursue their destiny.

As it was for Churchill, civilization was a major theme for Hitler. However, their visions differed dramatically. From Hitler's perspective, civilization meant the systemic order of the Reich, with its fascist control over the destiny of the *Volk* (the mass of the population). That destiny could be determined only by the Führer and his regime. In fact, in keeping with the views of Heidegger, the Führer was a spiritual leader, and each institution had to have its own Führer, carrying out the vision of the supreme leader.

One cannot explore Hitler's spiritual roots without finding a Frenchman, Arthur de Gobineau, buried deep in the soil. Gobineau, who authored *An Essay on the Inequality of the Human Races*, believed that purity of race is the determining factor in the rise and fall of civilizations.

In line with Gobineau's theories, Hitler and the Nazis believed that the Jews had polluted the pure Aryan stock and that it was up to the Germans to restore racial purity.

At the time, many Europeans and Americans were intellectually and spiritually prepared to accept Nazi theories. John Lukacs writes that, in the years before the war, "Hitler . . . appeared as the greatest leader and statesman that the German people had had in one thousand years—as well as the most powerful national leader in Europe, perhaps even in the world."[18] In fact, "he represented an enormous tide in the affairs of the world in the twentieth century."[19]

American industrialist Henry Ford was among Hitler's early admirers, as was Joseph Kennedy, father of President John F. Kennedy and ambassador to Great Britain from 1938 to 1940. Even former Prime Minister David Lloyd George initially "admired Hitler," calling him "the greatest living German."[20] Lloyd George also "thought that Britain had no chance of winning [the] war against Hitler's Third Reich."[21]

THE DAY GERMAN DEMOCRACY DIED

On January 30, 1933, the stage was set for Hitler's ascendance when German president Paul von Hindenburg was forced to recognize the National Socialists as the leading party in the Reichstag, the German parliament. Reluctantly, Hindenburg called for Hitler, who was sworn in as Germany's chancellor in a brief meeting. President Hindenburg was very popular among the German people, and Hitler therefore had to act with restraint, biding his time until he could control the president's popularity and power.

On the evening of February 27, 1933, as Hitler dined with Joseph Goebbels and family, Ernst Hanfstaengl, an aide to Hitler, telephoned to report that the Reichstag building was on fire. Goebbels and Hitler immediately went to the site. Hermann Goering was already there, claiming that the blaze was arson, started by the Communists. The accusation gained credibility when Dutch Communist Marinus van der Lubbe, a known arsonist who had boasted that he would burn down the Reichstag, was arrested at the scene.

Van der Lubbe's short trial was a farce. Evidence was presented by experts, proving that the fire "had been set with considerable quantities of chemicals and gasoline."[22] William Shirer notes that the large quantity of chemicals and gasoline required to generate the conflagration would have been far too much for one man to carry. In an attempt to legitimize the allegation, Goering arrested the Communist parliamentary leader Ernst Torgler and Bulgarian Communist Georgi Dimitroff. At trial, both Torgler and Dimitroff were acquitted, but van der Lubbe was found guilty and executed.

Those who were truly responsible for the fire may never be known, but its occurrence created the advantage that Hitler needed to establish the Nazis as the only legitimate political party in Germany. The day after the Reichstag fire, Hitler pressured Hindenburg to sign a decree that Hitler claimed was "for the Protection of the People and the State."[23] The decree established draconian measures, including "restrictions on personal liberty, on the right of free expression of opinion, including freedom of the press; on the rights of assembly and association; and violations of the privacy of postal, telegraphic, and telephonic communications; and warrants for house searches, orders for confiscation as well as restrictions on property."[24]

Thus, on February 28, 1933, democracy died in Germany and was not to be revived for twelve long years, during which time millions would lose their lives as a result of Hitler and his Nazis. After the war, Winston Churchill hoped the world had learned a lesson from the way Hitler insinuated himself into power with the promise of bringing glory to Germany. During a speech given in Amsterdam on May 9, 1948, Churchill offered this warning:

Tyranny presents itself in various forms, but it is always the same, whatever slogans it utters, whatever name it calls itself by, whatever liveries it wears. It is always the same and makes a demand on all free men to risk and do all in their power to withstand it.[25]

Having legitimized both his party and its right to arrest, detain, and execute without trial those who were considered to be enemies of the state, Hitler looked to remove the remaining obstacles: President Hindenburg and those who stood in opposition to Hitler's rule as dictator of Germany. Hindenburg was by this time very ill and dying, and Hitler knew that within a matter of weeks the president would be gone. He therefore focused his attention on others who might become thorns in his side and much more difficult to neutralize once Hindenburg was dead. On June 30, 1934, Hitler launched what came to be known as the Night of Long Knives, in which his primary opponents were removed, either through arrest or death.

When President Hindenburg died on August 2, 1934, Hitler combined the offices of president and chancellor and thus ruled Germany absolutely. Now free to do as he wished without fear of consequences, Hitler began to put his ultimate plans into effect— namely, to raise a perfect Aryan Germanic empire that the world would admire and fear; to declare war on the rest of Europe; and to rid the world of Jews.

Though Hitler had successfully secured the political position of the Nazi Party, he knew it was only a matter of time before those he trusted would attempt to oust him and seize control. Needing the unwavering support of the army and the adoration of the German people, Hitler endorsed the creation of a new oath of allegiance that recognized him as the ultimate power:

> I swear by God this sacred oath, that I will render unconditional obedience to Adolf Hitler, the Führer of the German Reich and people, Supreme Commander of the Armed Forces, and will be ready as a brave soldier to risk my life at any time for this oath.[26]

The oath is similar to that of the British oath of allegiance to the monarch:

> I do swear that I will be faithful and bear true allegiance to Her Majesty Queen Elizabeth, her heirs and successors, according to law. So help me God.

However, there is a clear provision in the British oath not found in Hitler's oath: the morality of *law*.

A soldier in the British armed forces is called upon to bear true allegiance, unless an order contradicts the law of the land as laid out by Parliament. Therefore, if commanded to march into a shopping mall and randomly shoot unarmed people, it is a British soldier's moral duty to question that order. In Germany under the Hitler Oath, questioning any order was a punishable crime; Hitler *was* the law.

The Führer moved quickly to consolidate his power and expand the German economy by any means possible, including threats and acts of violence. Despite Churchill's warnings between 1933 and 1939 of the rising evil in Germany, most observers were impressed by how quickly Hitler began to transform the ailing country he had inherited.

Among other accomplishments, his full-employment policy led to the creation of the Autobahn, an infrastructural feat that was envied (and later would be adopted) around the world. As with other Nazi innovations, however, Hitler's Autobahn was designed for more sinister reasons than the mere creation of a high-speed automobile expressway. His plan was to enable the quick and efficient movement of troops and munitions from one end of the country to the other, in preparation for war.

Despite claims that Hitler was merely trying to restrain the communist Bolsheviks, the evidence indicates otherwise. The creation of a vast army, navy, and air force, which began in 1933 and gained momentum in 1935 when Hitler reinstated conscription and announced that he would create an army of a half-million men, proves beyond a doubt that Hitler's intentions were not limited solely to the elimination of the Bolshevik movement. He was preparing for war.

With his economic and employment policies in full swing, Hitler was now free to focus his attention on what he believed to be the cause of Germany's past troubles and the primary obstacle to the ascendance of the new German empire: the Jews. The anti-Jewish Nuremberg Laws of 1935 were an essential component of that dark scheme. Crucial to the plan was the emerging idea that the German people were a demographic mass, the *Volk*. If one was not part of the *Volk*, one was not a German and therefore was not entitled to the rights and protections of citizenship. According to the laws, Jews and other minorities were excluded from inclusion in the *Volk*.

The Nuremberg Laws thus divided the German people into two major classifications: Aryan (pure-blooded Germans with four German grandparents) and non-Aryan (people of mixed ancestry). Aryans were afforded every privilege: citizenship, the right to marry and procreate with other Aryans, and the privilege to work for or on behalf of the government. The Nuremberg Laws deprived Jews and other non-Aryans—gypsies and blacks, for example—of citizenship and prohibited racially mixed sexual relations and marriages.

Hitler's direct action against the Jews—called God's chosen people in the Bible—marked another turning point in his transformation into a false messiah. Just a year earlier, the Nazis had created and imposed a new "Lord's Prayer" and table grace, addressed directly to their Führer.

The New Lord's Prayer: Adolf Hitler, you are our great Leader. Thy name makes the enemy tremble. Thy Third Reich comes, thy will alone is law upon earth. Let us hear daily thy voice and order us by thy leadership, for we will obey to the end even with our lives. We praise thee! Heil Hitler!

The New Table Grace: Führer, my Führer, sent to me from God, protect and maintain me throughout my life. Thou who hast saved Germany from deepest need, I thank thee today for my daily bread. Remain at my side and never leave me, Führer, my Führer, my faith, my light. Heil my Führer![27]

Hitler claimed he was sent by God and that Providence was guiding him on his path. His Ministry of Enlightenment and Propaganda had the audacity to parallel him with Jesus in a dictation that schoolchildren were ordered to write and learn:

As Jesus freed men from sin and Hell, so Hitler freed the German people from destruction. Jesus and Hitler were persecuted, but while Jesus was crucified, Hitler was raised to the chancellorship. . . . Jesus strove for heaven, Hitler for the German earth.[28]

Meanwhile, in Britain, as Churchill watched the military buildup in Germany and the growing spiritual adulation of Hitler, he knew it would take people of remarkable courage to defeat a force in which mysticism and might joined to destroy what he would increasingly refer to as "Christian civilization."

Later in life, Churchill would describe how learning to paint gave him a "heightened sense of observation of Nature."[29] Preparing colors for the canvas taught him how to see "the tint and character of a leaf, the dreamy purple shades of mountains, the exquisite lacery of winter branches, the dim pale silhouettes of far horizons."[30] However, by the 1930s he was already able to discern the vagaries of human nature.

With growing alarm, Churchill sensed that the British government wasn't seeing the true picture of Hitler's character. Prime

Minister Neville Chamberlain clearly did not perceive the Nazi leader as a potential enemy but rather as a fair-minded man who would happily negotiate an agreement and keep it. The nation itself dozed in the blissful assurances given by Chamberlain and others of his stature and position.

Churchill, however, was not similarly deceived. When Hitler launched his blitzkrieg against Poland, violating the handshake-sealed "gentleman's agreement" with Chamberlain, the war was on. As the House of Commons sat somberly reflecting and recriminating, Churchill rose to address the prime minister. In despair over Chamberlain's naiveté, he quoted from the Bible, as he often did: "Thou art weighed in the balances and found wanting."[31]

Churchill knew that the British could not afford to come up short. They would have to stand and fight or be captured as a prime prize and enfolded into Hitler's Third Reich, which was now on the march. Britain would need "weighty" leadership for the fight ahead.

5

Prime Minister at Last

When great causes are on the move in the world . . . we learn that
we are spirits, not animals, and that something is going on in
space and time, which, whether we like it or not, spells "duty."
WINSTON S. CHURCHILL, *THE UNRELENTING STRUGGLE*

Before 1940, it was not easy for [Churchill] to be taken
seriously as the man of destiny he believed himself to be.
DAVID CANNADINE, *ASPECTS OF ARISTOCRACY*

ON APRIL 7, 1935, Ralph Wigram, head of the Central Department
at the Foreign Office, visited Chartwell, Churchill's home in Kent.
He stayed overnight, talking to Churchill about the fears he had of
the coming danger and offering secret documented evidence that
revealed the true figures of German air strength in comparison to
Britain's.

A week later, Wigram sent Churchill the government's assessment, ranking German first-line air strength at 800 aircraft against
Britain's 453.

"These are grave and terrible facts for those who are charged
with the defence of this country," Wigram noted in an internal
minute entry.[1] Churchill now knew more clearly than ever that he

had been right in 1933 when he told Parliament that the renewal of war in Europe was "within a measurable distance" as Germany attained "full military equality with her neighbours."[2]

As far back as 1931, Churchill's first publicly spoken warnings had only been predictions. But now, thanks to the factual foundation that Wigram had supplied, Churchill felt the urgency of certainty. He immediately began to increase the pressure for a quick and thorough rearmament program for Britain. He laid out the dire truth that German air strength would reach parity with the United Kingdom by the end of 1935, and unless the British government took action, the Nazis' air force would be double the size of Britain's by 1937.[3] On May 2, 1935, when Churchill again spoke to the House of Commons, he grimly reported that "German ascendancy in the air is already a fact. The military part is far advanced, and the naval part is now coming into view."[4]

Only five months earlier, on November 28, 1934, Stanley Baldwin—then lord president of the Privy Council—had assured the House that the British government would see to it that "in air strength and air power this country shall no longer be in a position inferior to any country within striking distance of our shores."[5] But during the May 1935 debate, the government continued to deny the truth Churchill had revealed.

The cabinet had met the previous day to discuss the matter, and they decided that the next day's debate would not be "the occasion for further details" but that they would reaffirm Baldwin's earlier assurances.[6] "The Government takes the earliest opportunity, at the opening of the present debate, to state publicly that the President's declaration stands."[7]

Nevertheless, the May debate caused the government great discomfort. For the first time since his warnings began, and because of the documents Wigram had supplied him, Churchill had them on the run. Over the years leading up to the outbreak of war on September 1, 1939, Churchill's credibility continued to grow. No matter how hard the government tried, they were unable to silence his voice.

By the sixth month of the war, Britain's neck was in Hitler's noose, which was tightening moment by moment. Escape appeared impossible—not only because of the Nazi armies squeezing continental Europe and threatening British shores, but also because of the impossible political crisis within Britain itself.

Prime Minister Neville Chamberlain's naiveté had been exposed by his dealings with Hitler, and his idealized, false hope for "peace for our time" was now scorned by both Parliament and the people. He tried to lead on, but as the Germans continued their advance towards the English Channel, gobbling up the Low Countries and closing in on Paris, Chamberlain began to realize the impossibility of his leading Britain through the war alone.

Forming a coalition government seemed like a wise choice, but both opposition parties, Labour and the Liberals, refused to be part of a governing coalition in which Chamberlain was prime minister.

Finally, forced by circumstance, Chamberlain agreed to resign. As majority leader, however, he had the right to recommend his own successor to King George VI.

Lord Halifax was an obvious possibility, with his experience in foreign affairs and his favor with the king, who had even given him a key to Buckingham Palace's royal garden. But if Halifax refused or was rejected by his fellow Conservatives, then who would succeed Chamberlain? Winston Churchill? Impossible!

Decades after the fact, it is difficult to grasp just how unlikely it was for Churchill to become Britain's wartime prime minister and thus to fulfill the vision he'd had as a sixteen-year-old schoolboy. To fully appreciate what a stunning miracle it was for Churchill to be named the leader of Great Britain at the very moment when the nation was about to come under direct attack, we must consider how many in the British establishment and public disdained him.

Consider Lord Hankey, chancellor of the Duchy of Lancaster, who provides a ripping example of how the aristocratic class viewed Churchill. On May 10, 1940, when word came of Churchill's appointment as prime minister, Lord Hankey wrote the following to his son:

> The net result of it all is that today, when the greatest battle of the war and probably the greatest battle of our history has begun, when the fate of the whole Empire is at stake, we are to have a Government of politicians, . . . quite a number of whom are perfectly futile people.[8]

There was no question that Lord Hankey placed Churchill at the head of the pack of "futile people." In another letter, two days later, Hankey opined to pro-appeasement politician Samuel Hoare, "God help the country . . . which commits its existence to the hands of a dictator [Churchill] whose past achievements . . . have never achieved success!"[9] Hankey saw Britain's "only hope" in a coalition of Churchill, Chamberlain, and Halifax, but he doubted "whether the wise old elephants [Chamberlain and Halifax] will ever be able to hold the Rogue Elephant [Churchill]."[10]

Lord Hankey was not the only highborn person who did not like Churchill. "Although he was an aristocrat by birth, Churchill was widely believed to be not really a gentleman at all," writes David Cannadine.[11]

> It was not just that Churchill was widely distrusted as a man of unstable temperament, unsound judgement, and rhetorical (and also alcoholic) excess. . . . It was also that for most of his career, there hung around him an unsavoury air of disreputability and unseemliness, as a particularly wayward, rootless and anachronistic product of a decaying and increasingly discredited aristocratic order. . . . During the inter-war years, he remained a shameless cadger and incorrigible scrounger.[12]

Proper people didn't think much of Churchill's friends, either. He associated with people from "raffish worlds," writes Cannadine.[13] By the mid-1930s, as the world crisis deepened, Churchill had become, in the view of many Britons, "almost a parody of the paranoid aristocrat: intransigent, embittered, apocalyptic."[14]

Churchill's parentage was often scorned in establishment opinion. He was a "half-breed" and a "mongrel" because he had an American mother, "a woman of more than one past."[15] Lord Randolph Churchill, despite holding high office, had been noted as a womanizer and gambler. And if denigrating his family wasn't enough, when Churchill became prime minister in 1940 his newly formed government was characterized as a band of "crooks," "gangsters," and "wild men" by important British opinion makers.[16]

APPEASEMENT AND ASCENDANCE

Churchill's reputation hit the skids at the very time when acclaim for Adolf Hitler was soaring to its zenith. As Churchill continued his warnings about Hitler and the Nazis and spoke out against appeasement, his reputation in the public eye sank even lower.

> In that year [1938] Hitler's Third Reich became the greatest power in Europe and perhaps in the world. . . . All over Europe, governments recognized that their existence depended on being on good terms with Germany. . . . At Munich everyone gave in to Hitler; and many people welcomed what they saw as [Neville] Chamberlain's act of wise statesmanship. Churchill did not.[17]

But by 1938, Churchill was battling to hold on to his seat in Parliament. His opposition to the Chamberlain-Hitler pact was viewed as another break with the Conservative Party. The voters of Epping believed that Churchill, as a duly elected Conservative member of the House of Commons, should have supported the

Conservative prime minister, Neville Chamberlain. Following Churchill's speech in Parliament criticizing the Munich accord, Sir Harry Goschen, a highly respected constituent, wrote to the local Conservative Party chairman:

> I cannot help thinking it was rather a pity that he broke up the harmony of the House by the speech he made. Of course he was not like a small ranting member, and his words were telegraphed all over the Continent and to America, and I think it would have been a great deal better if he had kept quiet and not made a speech at all.[18]

On November 4, Churchill survived a no-confidence vote in his constituency, but as Martin Gilbert puts it, he "sensed a mood of restraint among many [members of Parliament] who might have been his allies."[19]

Thus, when we consider the whole of Churchill's glum situation leading up to May 10, 1940, his appointment as prime minister must be ranked as one of the most unlikely political outcomes of modern times. To sum it up:

- Churchill was "widely distrusted."
- He was regarded by most as an irrelevant old man, the leftover of a past generation.
- He was disdained by many in the public as a privileged aristocrat with whom they could not identify. At the same time, he was viewed by many in the aristocracy as not worthy of their class.
- He was called an "aristocratic adventurer" who lacked good judgment and political skills.
- He was "unlucky."
- Churchill, according to a popular view at that time, was the son of a dysfunctional father and a wayward mother.
- His friends were "raffish," vulgar, and crude.

- Churchill was considered to be "rootless . . . unstable . . . unsound . . . an undeniable cad."
- He was an embarrassment to important people in his constituency and in the Conservative Party.
- He was thought to be a "real danger" who was impetuous and tended not to count the cost of his endeavors.

When Chamberlain decided to resign as prime minister, he called Churchill and Lord Halifax, then Secretary of State for Foreign Affairs, to No. 10 Downing Street. Seated opposite the two men in the Cabinet Room, Chamberlain informed them of his decision to step down and said that one of them would become the next prime minister.

Chamberlain favored Lord Halifax and made it clear that the viscount would be his choice if he wanted the job. Halifax was most certainly a very ambitious man, but, like Chamberlain, he looked at the situation they were facing and saw eventual surrender as inevitable. Not relishing the thought of being remembered as the man who handed Hitler the keys to Britain, Halifax declined.

When Churchill returned to his office at the Admiralty, he immediately entered a meeting with the Dutch minister, whose country had been attacked without provocation and was battling for its life. Churchill focused on the issue at hand, forcing the conversation at Downing Street to the back of his mind. He was interrupted by a message saying that Prime Minister Chamberlain had gone to see King George and resign as prime minister, in accordance with the requirements of the constitutional monarchy.

Shortly before 6 p.m., Churchill received an invitation from Buckingham Palace to visit King George VI. Later he recalled:

I was taken immediately to the King. His Majesty received me most graciously and bade me sit down. He looked at me searchingly and quizzically for some moments, and then said: "I suppose you don't know why I have sent for you?" Adopting his mood, I replied: "Sir, I simply couldn't imagine why." He laughed and said, "I want to ask you to form a Government." I said I would certainly do so.[20]

As Churchill left Buckingham Palace after his meeting with the king, his bodyguard, Walter Thompson, stated the truth that was on both of their minds: "You have an enormous task." With tears welling in his eyes, Churchill replied, "God alone knows how great it is. . . . I hope that it is not too late. I am very much afraid that it is. We can only do our best."[21]

Churchill returned to the Admiralty and immediately began the task of forming a coalition government. He asked Neville Chamberlain to serve as Lord President of the Council and Leader of the House of Commons, and Chamberlain accepted; but it was to be a very short appointment. When Chamberlain died of cancer later that year, Churchill paid a beautiful, heartfelt tribute to him in the eulogy at his funeral.

In his first book on the Second World War, *The Gathering Storm*, Churchill recalls his thoughts and feelings from the day when he was named prime minister.

At last I had the authority to give directions over the whole scene. I felt as if I were walking with destiny, and that all my past life had been but a preparation for this hour and for this trial. Ten years in the political wilderness had freed me from ordinary party antagonisms. My warnings over the last six years had been so numerous, so detailed, and were now so terribly vindicated, that no one could gainsay me. I could not be reproached either for making the war or with want of preparation for it. I thought I knew a good deal about it all, and I was sure I should not fail. Therefore, although impatient for the morning, I slept soundly and had no need for cheering dreams. Facts are better than dreams.[22]

Throughout the Second World War, Churchill employed everything he had learned throughout his life to mastermind the victory the Allies would achieve on May 8, 1945. In humility he proceeded, and with humanity he led.

The day after his appointment as prime minister, Churchill met with Labour Party leader Clement Attlee, inviting him to join the coalition government. Despite being from opposite sides of the political divide, the two men worked harmoniously throughout the crisis.

Churchill asked Lord Halifax to remain as Foreign Secretary, against the wishes of those who sought retribution for the men responsible for leaving Britain unprepared for war, among whom they included Halifax. Churchill came to the defense of those who had formerly been his greatest opponents. "If we open a quarrel between the past and the present, we shall find that we have lost the future," he told Parliament.[23] Churchill had every right to cast aside those who had caused him such pain in the decade leading up to the war. Instead, he chose to put the country's best interests before his own.

Churchill's magnanimous spirit towards his fellow leaders gave him the authority and credibility needed after the war to speak of forgiveness for the German people. Had those in authority after the First World War practiced the forgiveness that Jesus taught and Churchill displayed, the Second World War might never have happened. Unforgiveness breeds resentment, and the Second World War was resentment in action. As Churchill assumed power, he united the parties politically, and his appointment united the people in the great and terrible cause that lay before them.

BLOOD, TOIL, TEARS, AND SWEAT

On May 13, 1940, Churchill made his first speech to the House of Commons as prime minister. He was honest and realistic about the situation, but clear in the policy and aim of his government:

We are in the preliminary stage of one of the greatest battles in history. . . . I would say to the House, as I said to those who have joined this government: "I have nothing to offer but blood, toil, tears and sweat." We have before us an ordeal of the most grievous kind. We have before us many, many long months of struggle and of suffering. You ask, what is our policy? I can say: It is to wage war, by sea, land and air, with all our might and with all the strength that God can give us; to wage war against a monstrous tyranny, never surpassed in the dark, lamentable catalogue of human crime. That is our policy. You ask, what is our aim? I can answer in one word: It is victory, victory at all costs, victory in spite of all terror, victory, however long and hard the road may be; for without victory, there is no survival. . . . I take up my task with buoyancy and hope. I feel sure that our cause will not be suffered to fail among men.[24]

Parliament gave a cautious endorsement, but the public at large were fired up in great support of Churchill and his determination. A crowd of well-wishers had gathered outside the Admiralty building to which Churchill had gone by foot from Downing Street. Lord Hastings Ismay recalled this walk in his memoirs:

A number of people waiting outside the private entrance greeted him with cries of "Good luck, Winnie. God bless you." He was visibly moved, and as soon as we were inside the building, he dissolved into tears. "Poor people," he said, "poor people. They trust me, and I can give them nothing but disaster for quite a long time."[25]

Churchill's humility and humanity—seeing himself as one of the people, no better or worse—was what electrified his supporters and made them love him. Those characteristics even turned the opinion of many of his severest critics. Among them was John Colville, who had served as Chamberlain's secretary and would continue with Churchill. Colville's snarky attitude appeared in his diary entry of

May 13: "Went down to the House to hear the new P. M. . . . He made a brilliant little speech. . . . I spent the day in a bright blue new suit from the Fifty-Shilling Tailors, cheap and sensational looking, which I felt was appropriate to the new Government."[26]

Within three days of working with Churchill, however, Colville's tone had changed. By May 18, respect seeped in as he comments on the great care and seriousness with which Churchill worked: "Such is the change that high office can work in a man's inherent love of rash and spectacular action."[27]

Colville's conversion earned him the rancor of his old friends. "I am really very sorry that you are no longer one of the [Chamberlain] team," wrote R. A. Butler, who was Halifax's undersecretary at the Foreign Office, "and that you have been sacrificed for the Coalition."[28] Perhaps Colville's former colleagues believed that leadership requires aloofness. Churchill, however, believed that his presence among his embattled countrymen was needed so that he could give them hope.

It is ironic to think that if Churchill's predecessors as prime minister, Stanley Baldwin and Neville Chamberlain, had listened to him, they might have been the ones hailed as heroes instead of Churchill. If Britain had rearmed in the early 1930s, the Second World War might well have been avoided. Hitler may have been compelled to negotiate with a militarily strong Britain. And if that had happened, God may never have had to use Winston Churchill.

Without the war, Churchill's unpopularity throughout the 1930s would most certainly have led to his slipping away into insignificance. History would have forgotten Winston Churchill, but Stanley Baldwin and Neville Chamberlain would be remembered as great leaders. If Hitler hadn't introduced the Nuremberg Laws and hadn't provoked the war, history might remember him as a great restorer of his nation.

By openly acknowledging that only God could see Britain

and Europe through the crisis of the war, Churchill honored God through the words he spoke to the people of Britain:

> We shall not flag or fail. We shall go on to the end, we shall fight in France, we shall fight on the seas and oceans, we shall fight with growing confidence and growing strength in the air, we shall defend our Island, whatever the cost may be, we shall fight on the beaches, we shall fight on the landing grounds, we shall fight in the fields and in the streets, we shall fight in the hills; we shall never surrender, and even if, which I do not for a moment believe, this Island or a large part of it were subjugated and starving, then our Empire beyond the seas, armed and guarded by the British Fleet, would carry on the struggle, until, in God's good time, the New World, with all its power and might, steps forth to the rescue and the liberation of the old.[29]

"BE YE MEN OF VALOUR"

In his first nationwide broadcast as prime minister, on May 19, 1940, Churchill reached for words "written [centuries ago] to be a call and a spur to the faithful servants of Truth and Justice."[30] Then he paraphrased 1 Maccabees 3:58-60 from the Apocrypha, a section of the Bible held sacred by many Christians:

> Arm yourselves, and be ye men of valour, and be in readiness for the conflict; for it is better for us to perish in battle than to look upon the outrage of our nation and our altar. As the Will of God is in Heaven, even so let it be.

Knowing the historical context for these words, Churchill did not choose them lightly. In 166 BC, the Maccabees were struggling against powerful Hellenistic rulers who wanted to impose their control and culture on the Jews. Mattathias, a rural Jewish priest, ignited a revolt and took his five sons into the rugged Judean wilderness rather than submit. Upon the death of Mattathias,

Judas, one of his sons, picked up the banner to lead an army against the Greeks. Compared to the power of the Hellenistic forces, the Jewish warriors seemed no more than a tattered group of amateurs. But the Greeks did not fully comprehend what drove Judas and his fellow warriors: *Their very identity and freedom were at stake. They had to fight or else become slaves.*

No wonder this passage fired up Churchill's resolve. It mirrored the situation that Britain now faced. Hitler underestimated the determination of the British people, and the world assumed that the British military, in the wake of the First World War, was nothing but a ragtag group of amateurs. And certainly the evacuation at Dunkirk at the end of May would do nothing to bolster the image of the British Expeditionary Force. Still, "it is better for us to perish in battle than to look upon the outrage of our nation."

The passage in 1 Maccabees that Churchill drew upon bears a resemblance to another passage from the Old Testament book of Judges. In Judges 6, when God calls Gideon to lead the people of Israel against the Midianite invaders, he sends an angel to say to Gideon, "The Lord is with thee, thou mighty man of valour. . . . Go in this thy might, and thou shalt save Israel from the hands of the Midianites: have I not sent thee?"[31]

In the 1 Maccabees text, the phrase is, "Be ye men of valor," but Churchill's wording evokes the passage in Judges, in which *valor* refers to bravery and courage in war.

Churchill recognized that Britain, like Mattathias and Judas in 1 Maccabees, faced an enemy crowded on the borders of their nation, wanting to enslave them and destroy their culture. In May 1940, Churchill knew that Adolf Hitler had the whole of Europe—and more—in his sights. Britain represented the "men of valor" on whom the outcome of the battle rested. Thus, with great care, Churchill chose his words.

Though the Blitz would soon set London and other English cities ablaze, Churchill believed that "under Providence, all will be well," as he said in a February 9, 1941, message to President Franklin Roosevelt.[32]

Churchill's call for valor and courage had its intended effect. "You have never done anything as good or great," wrote War Secretary Anthony Eden, adding, "Thank you, and thank God for you."[33] Former prime minister Stanley Baldwin, at whose feet lay much of the blame for Britain's lack of preparedness, wrote:

> My dear PM, I listened to your well known voice last night and I should have liked to have shaken your hand for a brief moment and to tell you that from the bottom of my heart I wish you all that is good—health and strength of mind and body—for the intolerable burden that now lies on you. Yours always sincerely, SB [34]

The great weight that Churchill carried was, to his mind, nothing less than the survival of "Christian civilization" against the greatest threat it had ever faced. Churchill knew it was not just Britain's survival that had been laid upon him, but also all the values of justice, freedom, respect for humanity, and peace inherent in Western culture. He sensed that, if he failed, the world would become hellish.

It was indeed an "intolerable burden," but one that Winston Churchill was willing not only to tolerate but to carry all the way to victory—or, if need be, to death.

PART III

SAVING "CHRISTIAN CIVILIZATION"

6

Churchill and the Sermon
on the Mount

*I expect that the battle of Britain is about to begin. Upon
this battle depends the survival of Christian Civilisation.*

WINSTON CHURCHILL, "THEIR FINEST HOUR"
SPEECH, JUNE 18, 1940

WHAT WAS IT THAT WINSTON CHURCHILL—who was neither
an engaged churchman nor a pious religious devotee—saw in
"Christian civilization" that, to his mind, made its survival worth
the immense sacrifices required to stop Hitler and the Nazis?

In a 1943 speech at Harvard University, he said that it was nothing less than the choice between "world anarchy or world order."[1]

The degree of Winston Churchill's passion for Christian civilization is evident in the number of times he spoke or wrote about it.
Here is a brief list of his statements, enough to establish the point:

- In a 1931 article in *The Strand Magazine*, Churchill wrote
  about "our duty to preserve the structure of humane,
  enlightened, Christian society."[2]
- In a speech to the House of Commons about the Munich
  Agreement in 1938, Churchill said, "There can never be

friendship between the British democracy and the Nazi power, that power which spurns Christian ethics, which cheers its onward course by a barbarous paganism."[3]

- In an appeal to Benito Mussolini in 1940 to keep Italy from joining the war on Germany's side, Churchill said, "Down the ages above all other calls comes the cry that the joint heirs of Latin and Christian civilisation must not be ranged against one another in mortal strife."[4]

- As he contemplated the defense of London during the Battle of Britain, he referred to the metropolis as "this strong City of Refuge which enshrines the title-deeds of human progress and is of deep consequence to Christian civilisation."[5]

- "It is no exaggeration to say that the future of the whole world and the hopes of a broadening civilisation founded upon Christian ethics depends upon the relations between the British Empire or Commonwealth of Nations and the USA," Churchill said in 1941.[6]

- In his famous "Iron Curtain" speech on March 5, 1946, Churchill was still sounding the warning. The Communist parties that had infiltrated postwar nations "constitute a growing challenge and peril to Christian civilisation," he said.[7]

- In October 1946, Churchill revealed to the Conservative Party leadership what he felt its "main objectives" should be. The list begins: "To uphold the Christian religion and resist all attacks upon it."[8]

- In a 1949 speech to scientists at the Massachusetts Institute of Technology, Churchill said, "The flame of Christian ethics is still our highest guide. To guard and cherish it is our first interest, both spiritually and materially. The fulfilment of spiritual duty in our daily life is vital to our survival. Only by bringing it into perfect application can we hope to solve for ourselves the problems of this world and not of this world alone."[9]

• Churchill also believed that "the more closely we follow the Sermon on the Mount, the more likely we are to succeed in our endeavours."[10]

Stephen Mansfield believes this urgent focus came through the influence of Elizabeth Everest, Churchill's childhood nanny. "In an age of mounting skepticism, Churchill proclaimed the cause of 'Christian civilization,'" notes Mansfield.[11] Churchill saw external threats in the "barbarous paganism" of the Nazis, who embodied principles that were the polar opposites of "Christian ethics." Furthermore, Churchill was concerned about the internal threats from some of his own countrymen who had lost their Christian vision. Every Christian, thought Churchill, had a "duty to preserve the structure of humane, enlightened Christian society." To neglect this would send society spinning into chaos because, said Churchill, "once the downward steps are taken, once one's moral intellectual feet slipped upon the slope of plausible indulgence, there would be found no halting-place short of general Paganism and Hedonism."[12]

ALL THAT MAKES EXISTENCE PRECIOUS

Churchill tells us generally what he meant by the term "Christian civilization" in a 1938 radio broadcast to America:

> Since the dawn of the Christian era a certain way of life has slowly been shaping itself among the Western peoples, and certain standards of conduct and government have come to be esteemed. After many miseries and prolonged confusion, there arose into the broad light of day the conception of the right of the individual; his right to be consulted in the government of his country; his right to invoke the law even against the State itself. . . . Now in this resides all that makes existence precious to man, and all that confers honour and health upon the State.[13]

For Churchill, what was at stake was the well-being not merely of a privileged few but of all who could benefit from the fruits of a beneficent, coherent society. Richard Langworth reminds us that Churchill believed that Christianity's "principles applied broadly to all of mankind regardless of religion." Thus, "when Churchill in speeches referred to 'Christian civilization' . . . he did not mean to exclude Jews or Buddhists or Muslims. He meant those words with a much broader sense. Just as, to Churchill, the word 'man' meant humankind, his allusions to Christianity embodied principles he considered universal."[14]

Under the tutelage of Elizabeth Everest, Churchill no doubt would have read—and probably memorized—Jesus' teachings in the Sermon on the Mount.

> And seeing the multitudes, he went up into a mountain: and when he was set, his disciples came unto him: And he opened his mouth, and taught them, saying, Blessed are the poor in spirit: for theirs is the kingdom of heaven. Blessed are they that mourn: for they shall be comforted. Blessed are the meek: for they shall inherit the earth. Blessed are they which do hunger and thirst after righteousness: for they shall be filled. Blessed are the merciful: for they shall obtain mercy. Blessed are the pure in heart: for they shall see God. Blessed are the peacemakers: for they shall be called the children of God. Blessed are they which are persecuted for righteousness' sake: for theirs is the kingdom of heaven.[15]

Let's look briefly at how these teachings, commonly known as the Beatitudes, intersected with the life of Winston Churchill.

Blessed are the poor in spirit: for theirs is the kingdom of heaven

The poverty of spirit to which Jesus refers is the humble recognition of one's own need. Churchill recognized it while hiding in a trench in South Africa in his youth; and again, decades later, when he stepped into No. 10 Downing Street as prime minister. Churchill knew that humility of spirit must also apply to his nation and its allies, and he said as much amid the deepening gloom of 1940.

> We shall never surrender, and even if, which I do not for a moment believe, this Island or a large part of it were subjugated and starving, then our Empire beyond the seas, armed and guarded by the British Fleet, would carry on the struggle, until, *in God's good time*, the New World with all its power and might, steps forth to the rescue and the liberation of the old.[16]

Churchill knew where the ultimate outcome of the struggle rested—in the hands of God. This, as much as anything, distinguished Churchill's confidence from Hitler's arrogance.

Blessed are they that mourn: for they shall be comforted

Elizabeth Nel, one of Churchill's personal secretaries during the war, writes, "When a city had received a bad bombing, he would try whenever possible to pay it a visit, to cheer up the inhabitants, but his grief at the sight of the devastation was moving to see."[17]

Yet Churchill understood the importance of controlling his grief, and "he was always on top of his feelings, and the people, revitalized, would show their delight at the sight of him."[18]

Blessed are the meek: for they shall inherit the earth

Meekness is an unlikely characteristic for a man characterized as a *bulldog* and a *lion*. However, when we look at the original Greek, the language in which Jesus' words were recorded in the Bible, we see that meekness is an apt description.

The Greek word *prautes* actually refers to *strength under proper restraint*. A common example is that of a mighty stallion under control of a bridle. But true meekness is not based on *external* restraint, for that would imply an inner weakness that required the control and enforcement of law. Rather, the idea is that of *self-control*. Churchill would have known Edmund Burke's words:

> Men are qualified for civil liberty in exact proportion to their disposition to put moral chains upon their own appetites. . . . Society cannot exist unless a controlling power upon the appetite be placed somewhere, and the less of it there be within, the more there must be without. It is ordained in the eternal constitution of things that men of intemperate minds cannot be free. Their passions forge their fetters.[19]

Blessed are they which do hunger and thirst after righteousness: for they shall be filled

Churchill was not known for his piety, nor did he pretend to it. Once when he was told he could not imbibe in the presence of the king of Saudi Arabia because of the ruler's Muslim beliefs, he replied, "If it was his religion that made him say such things, my religion prescribed as an absolute sacred ritual smoking cigars and drinking alcohol before, after, and if need be during, all meals and the intervals between them."[20]

However, as with *meekness*, we understand what *righteousness* may have meant to Churchill when we see it in the original language of the New Testament. There, *righteousness* refers to that which is *upright* and *straight*. Another word for it might be *alignment*. Proverbs speaks of those "whose paths are crooked and who are devious in their ways."[21] A "crooked path" veers away from the true course.

The standard for such alignment is nothing less than the perfect character of God. Thus, God must be the reference point for personal behavior and for the character of a civilization. Though Churchill at times leaned away from God's perfect standard—as we all do—he certainly understood its importance in society. Such ethical alignment is what he likely had in mind when he offered this perhaps idealized assessment of Britain and a Christian consensus:

There are a few things I will venture to mention about England. They are spoken in no invidious sense. Here it would hardly occur to anyone that the banks would close their doors against their depositors. Here no one questions the fairness of the courts of law and justice. Here no one thinks of persecuting a man on account of his religion or his race. Here everyone, except the criminals, looks on the policeman as a friend and servant of the public. Here we provide for poverty and misfortune with more compassion, in spite of all our burdens, than any other country. Here we can assert the rights of the citizen against the State, or criticize the Government of the day, without failing in our duty to the Crown or in our loyalty to the King.[22]

Blessed are the merciful: for they shall obtain mercy

"The finest combination in the world is power and mercy," Churchill wrote to his mother, Jennie, in 1919. "The worst combination in the world is weakness and strife."[23] These values, expressed early in his career, were what guided Churchill throughout the most crucial periods of his life. Both power and mercy were evident in Churchill's speech to the House of Commons on July 14, 1940, when he said, "We may show mercy—we shall ask for none."[24]

Churchill felt that Neville Chamberlain's weakness had placed Britain in peril as Hitler's power grew. Nevertheless, he revealed an understanding of the importance of mercy in his eulogy of Chamberlain:

It fell to Neville Chamberlain in one of the supreme crises of the world to be contradicted by events, to be disappointed in his hopes, and to be deceived and cheated by a wicked man. But what were these hopes in which he was disappointed? . . . What was that faith that was abused? They were surely among the most noble and benevolent instincts of the human heart—the love of peace, the toil for peace, the strife for peace, the pursuit of peace, even at great peril, and certainly to the utter disdain of popularity or clamour. . . . We can be sure that Neville Chamberlain acted with perfect sincerity according to his lights and strove to the utmost of his capacity and authority . . . to save the world from the awful, devastating struggle in which we are now engaged.[25]

Blessed are the pure in heart: for they shall see God

To be "pure in heart" is to be free from corruption. Winston Churchill was not pure in the sense of functional perfection; but the term also refers to a purity of motive that others can trust, and there Churchill is amply acquitted. In Churchill's example, we find the idea of sincerity, of "something that has been cleansed by shaking to and fro as in a sieve or in winnowing."[26]

This understanding becomes clearer in the Bible's admonition to "purify your hearts, you double-minded."[27] Ambivalence about belief in God, or about right and wrong, constitutes double-mindedness. It is the position of the agnostic and thus is among the reasons we disagree with those who believe that Churchill retained the agnosticism of his youth. Throughout his life, he spoke of God and his providence with confident certitude.

The British people recognized Churchill as a man with a single-ness of heart and mind. This quality, perhaps more than anything else, gave Churchill the capacity to lead and to guide through the Second World War. The British citizenry sensed that they could trust him, that he spoke with no hidden agenda. This purity of trust and its attendant credibility had not come easily but was hard-earned through all the "winnowing" trials through which Churchill had passed.

Blessed are the peacemakers: for they shall be called the children of God

Churchill is sometimes accused of being a warmonger. "Some critics characterized Churchill as a bold, but impetuous buccaneer, long on character but short on judgment," writes Kenneth W. Thompson. "However, the picture of the prime minister as a soldier of fortune, an adventurer and a troublemaker was misleading."[28]

Churchill's first and continual hope was peace. On December 3, 1936, he said:

> If we wish to stop the coming war—if coming it is—we must in the year that lies before us—nay, in the next six months—gather together the great nations, all as well armed as possible and united under the Covenant of the League [of Nations] in accordance with the principles of the League, and in this way we may reach a position where we can invite the German people to join this organisation of world security; where we can invite them to take their place in the circle of nations to preserve peace, and where we shall be able to assure them that we seek no security for ourselves which we do not extend most freely to them.[29]

In his appeal, Churchill added "peace and strength" to his equipoise of "power and mercy." Rather than desiring war, this old soldier yearned for peace. But he did not delude himself about human nature or the character of the enemy—Hitler. Churchill's insistence on rearmament was crucial to the establishment and maintenance of his real objective—peace. Indeed, Churchill's foreign policy was based on strength with diplomacy, power, and negotiation, as Kenneth Thompson points out.

Even after the Second World War, there were still some who tried to stick the "warmonger" and "adventurer" label on Churchill. Finally, in 1951, the *Times* of London had had enough.

> It will be seen by historians as an extraordinary perversion that Mr. Churchill should have come to be regarded by so many critics and opponents in politics as a man eager for war. . . . Perhaps because so much of his fame and character has been

made—with uncommon zeal and gusto—in the midst of world carnage, his thought has always been, between the wars, upon the means of making peace among the peoples.[30]

Thompson concludes, "Someone who possessed only a passion for war would hardly have been as tireless in exploring the narrow paths to peace. No one who was incurably a warmonger would have been willing to pay so high a price for peace."[31]

Blessed are they which are persecuted for righteousness' sake: for theirs is the kingdom of heaven

Winston Churchill didn't suffer for the Christian cause in the same sense as the early followers of Christ. However, if we view righteousness as a desire for rightness, fairness, and justice aligned with God's revelation of himself in Jesus Christ and the Bible, then Churchill endured much scorn for such a cause. Jesus' teachings would have prompted Churchill to expect derision and would have steeled him to keep standing. At the same time, Churchill was not a passive target; he could fire back with the best of them at those who took shots at him.

"It is perhaps worth noting," writes British historian Andrew Roberts, "that it was surely from the Beatitudes that Churchill took the inspiration for his famous moral for his memoirs of the Second World War: 'In War; Resolution. In Defeat; Defiance. In Victory; Magnanimity. In Peace; Goodwill.'"[32]

BEYOND THE BEATITUDES

While the Beatitudes describe some of the undergirding principles of Christian civilization, Jesus says much more in the Sermon on the Mount that may have instructed Winston Churchill and informed his perspective. In fact, Churchill referred to the Sermon on the Mount as "the last word in ethics."[33]

The following are some of the principles Churchill may have

learned from the Sermon on the Mount and allowed to shape his thoughts and actions.

The importance of being "salt" and "light" in the world

> You are the salt of the earth. But what good is salt if it has lost its flavor? Can you make it salty again? It will be thrown out and trampled underfoot as worthless.
>
> You are the light of the world—like a city on a hilltop that cannot be hidden.[34]

To those listening to Jesus teaching on the hillside that day, "salt" would have signified flavor, healing, and preservation. Without salt, food was flat, wounds might go unhealed, and decay would set in. Jesus was referring to spiritual and moral "salt," the truths that give zest to civilization, health to a society, and longevity to its principles.

Winston Churchill embodied these ideas as he led Britain and the Allies during the Second World War. He was thoroughly *salty*. Elizabeth Nel writes, "From first to last we were utterly devoted to him, not because he was prime minister but because he was himself."[35] Nel also said that she had been careful to teach her children about Churchill "and the things he has stood for in his long lifetime. Courage. Strength. Resolution. Steadfast loyalty. Love of country. If I can only teach them these things, I shall have done something."[36]

Churchill was a conservative in the sense of *preservation*—conserving what is of value. He believed that Christian civilization and the institutions that propagated it were worth keeping—even dying for. He was not a bourgeois conservative, whose sole focus is on preserving the commercial order. Rather, he was a historic conservative in the style of Edmund Burke, whose concern was not merely the preservation of the economic order but also the conservation of those deeper values and principles on which all civilization rests.

"Do not let spacious plans for a new world order divert your energies from saving what is left of the old," he told his Minister for Works and Buildings in 1941.[37] No doubt, to his own mind at least, Churchill was referring not only to the reconstruction of bombed sections of London but also to the civilization they had once symbolized.

Jesus said that his followers are "the light of the world." One of Churchill's gravest concerns in the face of the Nazi incursion was that "the lights are going out" all over Europe.[38] He recognized the darkness of Nazism as a vast abyss, the pit of evil.

Churchill sought to warn others "of what may easily come to pass if Civilization cannot take itself in hand and turn its back" on the alternatives, the "City of Destruction" and the "City of Enslavement."[39] Centuries earlier, Augustine had set before humanity the concept of the City of God, the embodiment of light. Churchill's words echoed the stark choice between the City of God and the City of Darkness.

God's revealed morality and ethics are absolute, not relative

> Don't misunderstand why I have come. I did not come to abolish the law of Moses or the writings of the prophets. No, I came to accomplish their purpose. I tell you the truth, until heaven and earth disappear, not even the smallest detail of God's law will disappear until its purpose is achieved. So if you ignore the least commandment and teach others to do the same, you will be called the least in the Kingdom of Heaven. But anyone who obeys God's laws and teaches them will be called great in the Kingdom of Heaven.[40]

Winston Churchill has been accused of being impious. Actually, he valued *morality*, but disdained *moralism*. "The life and strength of our authority springs from moral and not from physical forces," he said in a 1903 speech.[41] In fact, such morality was crucial to national endurance and survival. Morality was the broad attitude of heart and behavior that followed the values of the highest principles for individuals and society. Moralism, on the other hand, is "a double standard of conduct" in a person's "private and public" life.[42] True morality should guide a nation's foreign relations.

On July 6, 1944—exactly one month after D-Day—Churchill left the House of Commons, where he had just reported to the members that a Nazi V-1 rocket attack had killed 2,752 of their countrymen. Those missiles forced Churchill to conduct his staff conference in the underground war rooms. Churchill left the session and headed wearily to his office, where he dictated his thoughts to Marian Holmes, one of his secretaries, in a memorandum to his chiefs of staff.

With the carnage from the rocket attack weighing heavily on his mind, he raised the possibility of using nonlethal mustard gas, "from which nearly everyone recovers," against the Germans. This strategy would be employed only if "it was life or death for us" or "to shorten the war by a year," saving multitudes of lives.

Churchill's hope was to use a form of gas that would have only a temporary effect on an enemy soldier, allowing him to be taken prisoner and out of the war.

Then he reflected on the issue of morality regarding the use of mustard gas:

> It is absurd to consider morality on this topic when everybody used it in the last war without a word of complaint from the moralists or the Church. On the other hand, in the last war bombing of open cities was regarded as forbidden. Now everybody does it as a matter of course. It is simply a question of fashion changing as she does between long and short skirts for women.[43]

To Churchill's mind, the moral imperative was to defeat the Nazis. On this depended the survival of the civilization that could extend blessings of freedom and prosperity to the entire world. He found the moralists who objected to certain tactics to be reminiscent of the Pharisees of Jesus' day: preoccupied with small legalisms that obscured the "weightier matters."[44]

Still, Churchill's dilemma reveals the complexity and contradictions facing those in high leadership who must sort through the ethics of war and survival. It also reveals both his own struggles with moral questions and the limitations of his humanity in coming to grips with the highest ethical values and their application on the battlefield. Churchill's position is not morally satisfying, but in the mood of the moment it addressed the contradictions between the ideal and the necessary—to his own mind at least. Here, however, Churchill's pragmatism almost pushed him over the edge into an argument that the ends may justify the means— an attitude that does not align with Christian ethics.

But no one could accuse Churchill of being a mere moralist. Neither could anyone reproach him for not believing in absolute morality, as revealed in the Bible. Churchill saw Moses as a historical figure who "received from God that remarkable code upon which the religious, moral, and social life of the nation was so securely founded."[45]

The importance of restraining anger, and its proper expressions

> You have heard that our ancestors were told, "You must not murder. If you commit murder, you are subject to judgment." But I say, if you are even angry with someone, you are subject to judgment! If you call someone an idiot, you are in danger of being brought before the court. And if you curse someone, you are in danger of the fires of hell. . . . When you are on the way to court with your adversary, settle your differences quickly.[46]

Once, during an outbreak of tensions regarding Ireland, Churchill and Lord Birkenhead, chancellor of the exchequer and a close friend of Churchill's, were in a private and tense meeting with the

Irish leader Michael Collins. The chancellor was intense in his opposition to Irish home rule, and Collins, according to Churchill, was in his most difficult mood, "full of reproaches and defiances."[47] The atmosphere was like a tinderbox awaiting a match, and an outbreak of temper might have sparked a conflagration. Here is Churchill's account of the exchange:

> "You hunted me night and day," [Collins] exclaimed. "You put a price on my head."
>
> "Wait a minute," I said. "You are not the only one."
>
> And I took from my wall the framed copy of the reward offered for my recapture by the Boers. "At any rate it was a good price— £5,000. Look at me—£25 dead or alive. How would you like that?"[48]

After a moment, Churchill writes, Collins "broke into a hearty laugh [and] all his irritation vanished."[49]

Humor and restrained temper were part of Churchill's political and diplomatic toolbox throughout his career. He counseled candidates who faced angry constituents to always "smile, be natural, detach yourself from the fray, never lose your temper, and the worse it gets, the more you must treat it as a puppet show."[50]

The importance of being reconciled to one's brothers

> If you are presenting a sacrifice at the altar in the Temple and you suddenly remember that someone has something against you, leave your sacrifice there at the altar. Go and be reconciled to that person. Then come and offer your sacrifice to God.[51]

Churchill's battle to hold his seat in Dundee in 1922 was one of the most painful in his many years of electioneering. His opponent was Edwin Scrymgeour, a perennial adversary dating all the way back to 1908. Scrymgeour's prime issue was Prohibition— for which Churchill had no enthusiasm. Churchill was colonial secretary in Prime Minister Lloyd George's Cabinet, and he was dogged constantly by indignant suffragettes, who didn't appreciate what they perceived to be his opposition to allowing women to vote. On top of it all, around this time he was forced into the hospital for an appendectomy.

This time, Scrymgeour crushed Churchill by 10,000 votes. Nevertheless, Churchill was understanding towards Scrymgeour when recalling the events many years later:

> I felt no bitterness towards him. I knew that his movement represented after a fashion a strong current of moral and social revival. . . . He lived a life of extreme self-denial; he represented the poverty and misery of the city and its revolt against the bestial drunkenness for which it bore an evil reputation, and which I must admit I have never seen paralleled in any part of the United Kingdom.[52]

Perhaps that attitude towards his "British brothers" helped Churchill in the great challenge of forming and working with a coalition government as wartime prime minister. He had managed to offend all the parties and their members with whom he sat at the cabinet table, and they him. Nevertheless, the unity that Churchill forged with his opponents was an example to the nation that helped its outspoken, philosophically diverse people pull together to defeat Hitler.

The foundation of wholesome families that compose a healthy nation

> You have heard the law that says, "A man can divorce his wife by merely giving her a written notice of divorce." But I say that a man who divorces his wife, unless she has been unfaithful, causes her to commit adultery. And anyone who marries a divorced woman also commits adultery.[53]

Churchill resonated with Jesus' high view of marriage, for he cherished Clementine. One of his letters to her, written in 1935, was named as one of *Time* magazine's Top Ten Famous Love Letters:

> My darling Clemmie, in your letter from Madras you wrote some words very dear to me, about having enriched your life. I cannot tell you what pleasure this gave me, because I always feel so overwhelmingly in your debt, if there can be accounts in love. . . . What it has been to me to live all these years in your heart and companionship no phrases can convey.[54]

That love brought the whole family into its embrace and gave them all strength when the Churchills lost one of their children, Marigold, who died of septicemia as a toddler in 1921. The following year, when Clementine was pregnant with Mary, Winston wrote her notes of encouragement. Decades later, Mary wrote of her childhood, "From the early days of his marriage to my mother, Winston had always been most attentive to their nursery world, regularly reporting its news to Clementine when she was away; now, many years on [at the news of the pregnancy], he seemed delighted to find nursery life revived."[55]

"My father and I evidently enjoyed each other's company," Mary continues, quoting from a February 1926 note from Winston to Clementine:

> Mary is very gracious to me & spends 1/2 an hour each morning in my bed while I breakfast. Some of her comments are made in the tone & style of a woman of thirty. She is a sweet.[56]

There would be hard times as Churchill's responsibilities increased and the children grew older, but his marriage of fifty-six years endured until his death at the age of ninety.

Churchill's concern for his children never flagged. There would be "broken marriages and other tribulations" for the family, as one newspaper report put it.[57] But the Churchills were not deprived of the many happy events of family life, couched in love and lived with exuberance.

The nature of oaths and vows

> You have also heard that our ancestors were told, "You must not break your vows; you must carry out the vows you make to the LORD." But I say, do not make any vows! Do not say, "By heaven!" because heaven is God's throne. And do not say, "By the earth!" because the earth is his footstool. And do not say, "By Jerusalem!" for Jerusalem is the city of the great King. Do not even say, "By my head!" for you can't turn one hair white or black. Just say a simple, "Yes, I will," or "No, I won't." Anything beyond this is from the evil one.[58]

As a statesman, Churchill understood the importance of trust with respect to treaties and agreements. He had a high view of the Bible, reading and meditating on it often. He tried to connect its broad principles to his own times and personal challenges. For example, in considering Pharaoh's behavior when Moses challenged him to free the Hebrews, Churchill was struck by the Egyptian ruler's vacillations. "Great interest attaches to Pharaoh," he writes. "Across the centuries we feel the modernity of his actions."[59]

Churchill saw the leader of Egypt as a cautionary example for all who would lead nations, and Pharaoh's fluctuations were among the characteristics that attracted Churchill's attention. "At first he was curious, and open to conviction" as the plagues came in sequence and Moses kept coming at Pharaoh like a plague. Finally, Pharaoh acquiesced and declared the Hebrew slaves free to leave Egypt. But then he realized how losing this base of laborers would, in Churchill's words, frustrate his "building plans" and "cause considerable derangement in the economic life of his country." Therefore, Pharaoh "hardened his heart and took back in the evening what he had promised in the dawn, and in the morning what he had promised the night before."[60]

Churchill thought sanctity of covenant was crucial to world peace. In a speech to the House of Commons in 1936, he said, "I desire to see the collective forces of the world invested with overwhelming power . . . all bound rigorously by the Covenant and the conventions which they own. . . . [Then] you have an opportunity of making a settlement which will heal the wounds of the world."[61]

The proper principles of retaliation

> You have heard the law that says the punishment must match the injury: "An eye for an eye, and a tooth for a tooth." But I say, do not resist an evil person! If someone slaps you on the right cheek, offer the other cheek also. If you are sued in court and your shirt is taken from you, give your coat, too.[62]

Churchill has been pilloried for ordering bombing attacks on German cities and especially for what some call the wanton destruction of Dresden. Yet in June 1943, as Churchill watched film footage of an intense British attack on targets in Germany's industrial Ruhr region, he cried out to a member of the War Cabinet sitting nearby: "Are we beasts? Are we taking this too far?"[63]

Three years earlier, Churchill had fallen into an argument with a member of Parliament in the smoking room of the House of Commons. The man was pressing for saturation bombing against German cities to break the nation's morale. Parliamentary Secretary Harold Nicolson, standing nearby, jotted down the exchange. "My dear sir," Churchill replied, "this is a military and not a civilian war. You and others may desire to kill women and children. We desire . . . to destroy German military objectives."[64]

Churchill's objective was to wage war to the point of complete victory. However, it was to be a moral war, a *just* war, not one that included the "terrorism" of unrestricted bombardment.[65]

So what sparked the change in Churchill's policy from 1940 to 1943?

During a raid on August 24, 1940, German planes that were bombing military objectives on London's outskirts strayed and released bombs on the city itself, resulting in civilian casualties. Hitler had originally ordered that London not be touched, fearing retaliation against his own cities. However, when London's center was bombed, Churchill assumed it marked a change in Hitler's strategy, and he ordered the bombing of Berlin—though, initially, only forty British bombers could get through.

Churchill knew he had to strike back in kind, for two reasons. First, nonretaliation would have caused Hitler to believe he had license to target civilians. Second, Parliament would have questioned Churchill's fitness to continue as wartime leader of the nation.

When Britain struck back against Berlin, the Nazis launched an aerial blitz against British cities, and the battle was on. Churchill was encouraged by Franklin Roosevelt, who contended that the Axis powers had "asked for it" and now should be bombed "heavily and relentlessly."[66]

The biblical worldview seems to set the bar impossibly high, creating tension in our flawed, limited human understanding. Churchill may well have experienced this tension as he wrestled with decisions about the proper and necessary response to the enemy.

The challenge of reaching towards Jesus' ethical ideals produces three effects in those who want to follow him. First, it makes us aware of our own flaws and failures, producing self-awareness and humility. Second, Jesus' exhortations motivate us to keep reaching to a higher—even transcendent—quality of living. Finally, what seems an impossibly high standard makes us aware of our need for grace. Churchill, in his admiration for the Sermon on the Mount, would have known what Jesus taught about retaliation, and he may have recognized his own failure to measure up in his practical management of the war. This awareness may have helped to produce the humility that Churchill sometimes exhibited. More important, it could have made him realize how much he needed grace.

Whatever the case, Churchill's heart ached for many years. During his 1949 trip to the United States, someone told him about a monument to the Hiroshima victims at Alamogordo, New Mexico, where the atomic bomb had been tested. Churchill wondered aloud if this meant the Americans "had a bad conscience because the atom bomb was dropped."[67] Randolph, Churchill's son, remarked that saturation bombing during the Second World War was "an equal horror." Churchill's eyes filled with tears as he talked about the bombing of Germany's cities. "Tens of thousands of lives were extinguished in one night," he said. "Old men, old women, little children—yes, yes, little children about to be born."[68]

Thus, Churchill's "impression of a future catastrophe," which he had written about in the aftermath of the First World War, proved to be prophetic.[69]

It was not until the dawn of the twentieth century of the Christian era that war began to enter into its kingdom as the potential destroyer of the human race. . . .

It is established that henceforward whole populations will take part in war, all doing their utmost, all subjected to the fury of the enemy. It is established that nations who believe their life is at stake will not be restrained from using any means to secure their existence. . . .

Mankind has never been in this position before. Without having improved appreciably in virtue or enjoying wiser guidance, it has got into its hands for the first time the tools by which it can unfailingly accomplish its own extermination.[70]

The ethical treatment of enemies

> You have heard the law that says, "Love your neighbor" and hate
> your enemy. But I say, love your enemies! Pray for those who
> persecute you! In that way, you will be acting as true children
> of your Father in heaven. For he gives his sunlight to both the
> evil and the good, and he sends rain on the just and the unjust
> alike.[71]

Churchill believed in "two opposite sides of human nature." There
was a place for righteous indignation or anger to defend a nation
and a place for a gentle side, ready to make peace when the fighting was done. The two sides could not be "simultaneously en
gaged."[72]

Confidence in prayer

In Matthew 6:6, Jesus teaches his disciples about prayer: "When
you pray, go away by yourself, shut the door behind you, and pray
to your Father in private."

Though Churchill understood the importance of public prayer—such as when he "join[ed] fervently together" with
President Roosevelt "in the prayers and hymns familiar to both"
aboard the HMS *Prince of Wales* in 1941[73]—he reflected the attitude of Jesus about the privacy of personal prayer.

But what part did personal prayer continue to play in his
life? A clue is found in a letter he wrote to Clementine, on
August 10, 1922, when she was pregnant with Mary. Both parents still mourned the loss of Marigold. Clementine wrote of
her continuing sadness to Churchill in a previous letter. Then
he answered her:

> I think a gt deal of the coming kitten & about you my sweet pet. I
> feel it will enrich yr life and brighten our home to have the nursery
> started again. I pray to God to watch over us all.[74]

The treasure of true value

> Don't store up treasures here on earth, where moths eat them and
> rust destroys them, and where thieves break in and steal. Store
> your treasures in heaven, where moths and rust cannot destroy, and
> thieves do not break in and steal. Wherever your treasure is, there
> the desires of your heart will also be.[75]

Among the reasons Churchill was so focused on the survival
of Judeo-Christian civilization were its intrinsic universal values. Of the biblical events at Mount Sinai, he observed, "Here
Moses received from Jehovah the tables of those fundamental laws
which were henceforth to be followed, with occasional lapses, by
the highest forms of human society."[76] Churchill readily agreed
with designating the highest civilization as *Judeo*-Christian. The
Hebrew tribes wandering in the wilderness, though "indistinguishable from numberless nomadic communities, grasped and
proclaimed an idea of which all the genius of Greece and all the
power of Rome were incapable."[77]

The Lord over this splendid society, said Churchill, is "the only
God, a universal God, a God of nations." All the values that mattered are embodied in him and arise from his holy character. He
is "a God not only of justice, but of mercy; a God not only of
self-preservation and survival, but of pity, self-sacrifice, and ineffable love."[78]

Churchill embraced these values, "with occasional lapses," and
believed they were worth fighting for. There is much more from
the teaching of Jesus that Churchill would have incorporated into
his thinking and worldview. "I try to pursue, as it seems to me, a
steady theme, and my thought as far as I can grasp it, measure it,
is all of one piece."[79]

Among other things, it is clear that Churchill did not separate
the principles revealed in the Bible from other areas of thought.

"One piece" meant there were no separate compartments in his thinking—not one for the "sacred" and another for the "secular."

Churchill may have been an external "flying buttress" in his relationship with the church, but he was a serious Bible student, as his reflections and other writings and statements show. He liked to think systematically, and the teachings of Jesus were an integral part of that vast "one piece" that comprised his worldview.

Judeo-Christian presuppositions shaped not only many of his responses but also his views of the conduct of civil society. In a 1949 speech at the Massachusetts Institute of Technology, Churchill repeated his conviction that "the flame of Christian ethics is still our highest guide," which should be guarded, cherished, and brought into "perfect application."[80]

The perspective and values arising from the Sermon on the Mount, and from the Judeo-Christian worldview in general, framed a quality of society that, to Churchill's mind, no enemy should be allowed to destroy. He was ready and willing to lead the battle for the survival of that cherished civilization and its "certain way of life."[81]

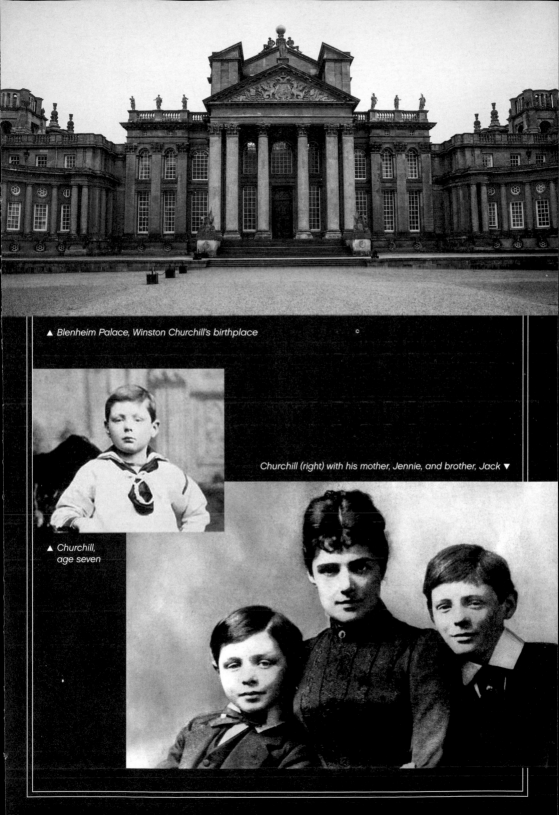

▲ Blenheim Palace, Winston Churchill's birthplace

Churchill (right) with his mother, Jennie, and brother, Jack ▼

▲ *Churchill, age seven*

Elizabeth Ann Everest, Churchill's nanny ▼

▲ As a schoolboy, in his full Harrow uniform

◀ Serving in India with the British Army, 1897

▲ Churchill (right) with other prisoners of war during the Second Boer War, 1899

As a war correspondent in South Africa, 1900 ▼

Future prime ministers David Lloyd George (left) and Winston Churchill in London, 1907, when both were in the new Liberal Cabinet ▶

Churchill's acclaim as a bricklayer at Chartwell became public in 1928 when he was chancellor of the exchequer. For years he laid brick as a form of relaxation. ▼

Christening of Julian George Winston Sandys, the author's father, in the House of Commons crypt, November 3, 1936. From left: Churchill, Duncan Sandys, Rosamund Lister (front), Diana (Churchill) Sandys (holding Julian), unknown guest (background), Mary Churchill ▼

December 29, 1940:
St. Paul's Cathedral
in London survives
amidst incendiary
bombs during the
second great fire
raid of the Blitz.

Prime Minister
Churchill (left) and
Brendan Bracken
in the bombed-out
ruins of the House of
Commons following
a German air raid
in 1941 ▶

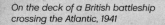
On the deck of a British battleship crossing the Atlantic, 1941

◄ The British War Cabinet, October 25, 1941. Seated left to right: Sir John Anderson, Churchill, Clement Attlee, Anthony Eden. Standing left to right: Arthur Greenwood, Ernest Bevin, Lord Beaverbrook, Sir Kingsley Wood.

Churchill returning from the 1943 Tehran Conference. Foreground, from left: Clementine Churchill, Julian Sandys (front), Winston Churchill, Diana (Churchill) Sandys ▶

▲ Churchill delivering his "Iron Curtain" speech in 1946, with President Harry Truman on his right

▲ Making the "victory" gesture outside 10 Downing Street in 1943

▲ VE Day 1945: Churchill and the British royals greeting the crowd from the balcony of Buckingham Palace. From left: Princess Elizabeth II, Queen Mother Elizabeth, Churchill, King George VI, Princess Margaret

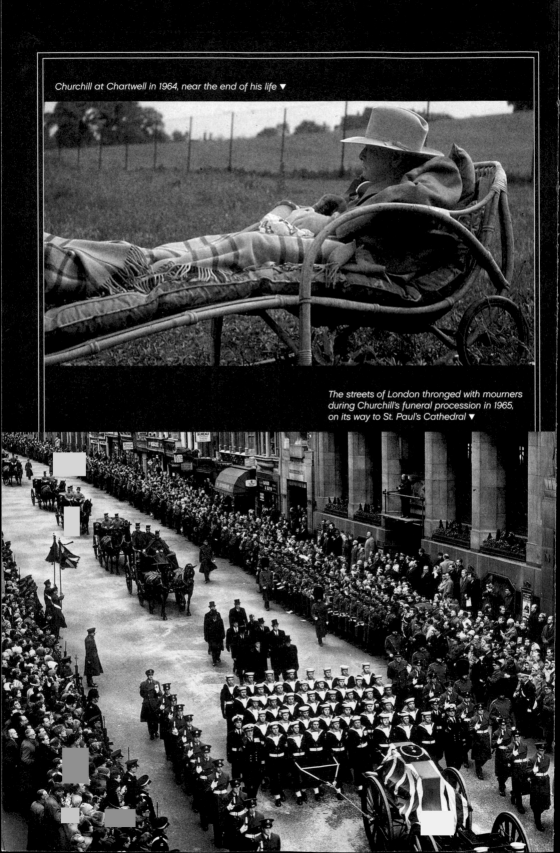

Churchill at Chartwell in 1964, near the end of his life ▼

The streets of London thronged with mourners during Churchill's funeral procession in 1965, on its way to St. Paul's Cathedral ▼

7

Preserving a "Certain Way of Life"

WINSTON CHURCHILL TREASURED "a certain way of life" to the extent that he thought it was worth the sacrifice of one's own life. Churchill knew the source of that cherished manner of living. It had arisen at "the dawn of the Christian era."

Thus, for Churchill the Bible was not only a book of mystical revelation; it was also an "operator's manual." Its principles spoke not just of heavenly, unseen things but also of earth and its rawest realities.

Churchill the historian had great admiration for King Alfred, the ninth-century monarch who Churchill believed had laid the foundation in the British realm for what would emerge as "Christian civilization." It was Alfred who linked biblical principles with existential practices and who connected the dots so skillfully between revelation and reason, faith and function.

In the first volume of *A History of the English-Speaking Peoples*, Churchill writes that King Alfred's Book of Laws "attempted to blend the Mosaic code with Christian principles and old Germanic customs." These prototypical laws, "continually amplified by his successors," led to the common law that has since guided Western civilization. The results in Alfred's day were clear, especially in contrast with other societal forces. "The Christian culture of his Court sharply contrasted with the feckless barbarism of Viking life."[1] No doubt these contrasts were in the back of Churchill's mind as he contemplated the viciousness of the Nazi regime.

In studying King Alfred, Churchill wrote, "We are watching the birth of a nation. The result of Alfred's work was the future mingling of Saxon and Dane in a common Christian England."[2] Alfred himself gave a clue to his vision for a biblically structured society in a missive he sent to the Bishop of Worcester:

> I would have you informed that it has come into my remembrance what wise men there formerly were among the English race, both of the sacred orders and the secular; and what happy times those were throughout the English race, and how the kings who had the government of the folk in those days obeyed God and His Ministers; and they on the one hand maintained their peace and morality and their authority within their borders, while at the same time they enlarged their territory abroad; and how they prospered both in war and wisdom, . . . how foreigners came to this land for wisdom and instruction.[3]

Alfred's letter to the bishop was prompted by the king's great concern that such an understanding of Christian civilization had "so clean . . . fallen away in the English race that there were very few

. . . who could understand their Mass-books in English, or translate a letter from Latin into English."[4]

Thus, when Churchill spoke of "Christian civilization," he was not using a facile platitude for political purposes nor describing an ominous theocracy; rather, he was drawing from the example established by King Alfred's application of biblical principles. It was this high civilization, so meticulously, tragically, and sacrificially formed, that Churchill feared would be destroyed by the Nazis. The Third Reich would be to Christian civilization what matter is to antimatter: The collision might obliterate the anti-civilization Nazis, but it might also wipe out Christian civilization in the process.

A theocracy is a society ruled by God through his chosen leaders. Old Testament Israel was unique in that regard, and only for a portion of its history. At its best, Israel was to be an example of the blessings inherent in a God-honoring culture. Israel's high mission as a theocracy was to display the fruits that come to a healthy society when God truly rules, and to provide a partial foreshadowing of the great day when God's Kingdom is established on earth.

Though Churchill had high regard for Moses and for the universal authority of the law given through him, he did not see Christian civilization as a theocratic domain. He had studied the Old Testament and apprehended the significance of Israel in that context.

Kingdoms and other forms of human government exist because humanity has fallen away from God. In human society, the default is always towards anarchy and chaos—as the history of the twentieth century in particular amply illustrates. Something must resist and restrain the downward spiral into disorder. Therefore, God institutes and permits governments.

Even in the theocracy of ancient Israel, God mediated his rulership through humans: Moses, Aaron and the priests, the judges, and a succession of prophets. But God's desire is that everyone be their own "governor," embracing God's principles at the core of their being. According to God's ideal, love and grace are the natural restraints against the influx of evil and discord.

God's model of government is not from the external to the internal but from the inner core of the human soul to our relationships in the external world. As Jesus says, "A good person produces good things from the treasury of a good heart, and an evil person produces evil things from the treasury of an evil heart."[5]

Edmund Burke referred to this ideal when he said that people "are qualified for civil liberty in exact proportion to their disposition to put moral chains upon their own appetites."[6] Thus, when humanity rejects love and grace as natural restraints against anarchy and chaos, law becomes necessary and essential. Governments are instituted to secure the rights threatened by tyrants—whether kings, priests, or mobs.

THE CORE PRINCIPLES OF CHRISTIAN CIVILIZATION

As we survey Churchill's speeches and writings, the specifics of what he meant by "Christian civilization" become quite clear. In the previous chapter, we surveyed what the principles meant to Churchill personally, as evidenced by his writings and actions. Here, we examine what Churchill believed about the ways those principles shape civilization.

Christian civilization rests upon the foundation of the Bible

Churchill agreed with "the words of a forgotten work of Mr. Gladstone [that] we rest with assurance upon 'The Impregnable Rock of Holy Scripture.'"[7]

The Bible was vital not only to civilization, but also to Churchill personally. The King James Bible, notes Darrell Holley, was Churchill's "primary source of interesting illustrations, descriptive images, and stirring phrases."[8]

His knowledge of the Bible manifests itself in direct quotations, in paraphrased retellings of Biblical stories, and in his frequent, perhaps even unconscious, use of Biblical terms and phrases. . . . For him it is the *magnum opus* of Western civilization.[9]

When Churchill and Franklin Roosevelt were planning for a rendezvous in Egypt, Roosevelt sent a cable warning that if they met in Cairo they might be exposed to air attacks by the German Luftwaffe. Churchill's reply to Roosevelt's concern was simple: "John 14:1-4." If Roosevelt opened the King James Bible to John 14, he would have read these words of Jesus:

Let not your heart be troubled: ye believe in God, believe also in me. In my Father's house are many mansions: if it were not so, I would have told you. I go to prepare a place for you. And if I go and prepare a place for you, I will come again, and receive you unto myself; that where I am, there ye may be also. And whither I go ye know, and the way ye know.

Churchill understood Jesus' words in personal terms. "The old man is very good to me," he once remarked to Sir David Maxwell-Fyfe.

"What old man?" Fyfe asked.

"God," Churchill replied.[10]

Churchill believed the Bible to be true history, not fantasy or myth. His view of the historically literal nature of Scripture was displayed unambiguously in his essay "Moses: The Leader of a People":

We believe that the most scientific view, the most up-to-date and rationalistic conception, will find its fullest satisfaction in taking the Bible story literally, and in identifying one of the greatest of human beings [Moses] with the most decisive leap forward ever discernible in the human story. . . . We may be sure that all these things happened just as they are set out according to Holy Writ."

However, Churchill did not want squabbles over literal interpretation to block people from the Bible's important principles. He also pondered biblical themes that very likely affected his own self-perception. Recall his idea that "every prophet has to go into the wilderness . . . [and] must serve periods of isolation and meditation."[12] Perhaps such insight from his reflections on the Bible encouraged Churchill during the periods he was exiled from public life.

In another section of his essay, Churchill paraphrases God's command to Moses from the burning bush.

> You cannot leave your fellow-countrymen in bondage. Death or freedom! Better the wilderness than slavery. You must go back and bring them out. Let them live among this thorn-scrub, or die if they cannot live. But no more let them be chained in the house of bondage.[13]

Such words from the Scripture resonated with Churchill, and perhaps buttressed his own resolution.

> God went a good deal further. He said from the Burning Bush, now surely inside the frame of Moses, "I will endow you with superhuman power. There is nothing that man cannot do, if he wills it with enough resolution. Man is the epitome of the universe. All moves and exists as a result of his invincible will, which is My Will." [14]

Was Churchill perhaps unknowingly foreshadowing his ironclad determination to meet and beat the Nazis on the field of battle?

Churchill may have been a humanist, but he was one in the sense of classical Christian humanism—which, unlike secular humanism, starts with God at the center. Whatever is good in human beings is because of the indwelling presence of God.

There is little doubt that Churchill understood that the well-springs of Judeo-Christian civilization were both the historical experience of Israel recorded in the Old Testament and the fulfillment of its "types and shadows" in the New Testament. Furthermore, Churchill believed that the history of the Jews recorded in the Old Testament pointed to a great event coming in the future.

> Many centuries were to pass before the God that spake in the Burning Bush was to manifest Himself in a new revelation, which nevertheless was the oldest of all the inspirations of the Hebrew people—as the God not only of Israel, but of all mankind who wished to serve Him; a God not only of justice, but of mercy; a God not only of self-preservation and survival, but of pity, self-sacrifice, and ineffable love.[15]

Thus, Churchill concluded,

> Let the men of science and learning expand their knowledge and probe with their researches every detail of the records which have been preserved to us from these dim ages. All they will do is to fortify the grand simplicity and essential accuracy of the recorded truths which have lighted so far the pilgrimage of man.[16]

Christian civilization recognizes healthy pride but rejects destructive arrogance

In war, Resolution.
In defeat, Defiance.
In victory, Magnanimity.
In peace, Goodwill.

Churchill first proposed that this maxim be carved into a war memorial in France after the First World War—an offer that was rejected. The phrase became a centerpiece of his memoirs of the Second World War, capturing his personal attitude. For Churchill, and the civilization for which he fought, "the life and strength of our authority springs from moral and not physical forces."[17]

Christian civilization uses wealth and strength to serve, not to master

In a radio broadcast on March 21, 1943, Churchill included his own homily from the Old Testament as he made the point that the government should be the servant, not the master, of society. "In the Bible," he said, "the Shunammite acted out of kindness and not for personal gain."[18] Churchill was referring to a story in 2 Kings 4 in which a woman provides food and lodging for the prophet Elisha. The woman of Shunem was a prominent person, probably more affluent than her neighbors. Churchill observed that the world's wealthier nations, some of which constituted Christian civilization, had a responsibility to be a servant to other societies.

He also considered that servanthood should guide the formation of foreign policy. "Churchill believed firmly," writes Richard Langworth, "that the Empire had been a boon to the native peoples within it."[19] However, as Kenneth Thompson notes, "Churchill was too clear-eyed and self-critical for the moral ambiguities of imperialism to escape him."[20] Thus, as early as 1901, Churchill recognized that British colonial policy was good only as long as it was based on "a higher reason . . . a moral force—the Divine foundation of earthly power—which, as the human race advances, will more and more strengthen and protect those who enjoy it."[21]

> In spite of every calumny and lie uttered or printed, the truth comes to the top, and it is known alike by peoples and by rulers that on the whole British influence is healthy and kindly, and makes for the general happiness and welfare of mankind.

And we shall make a fatal bargain if we allow the moral force which this country has so long exerted, to become diminished, or perhaps even destroyed.[22]

Call him idealistic or just plain wrong about colonial perceptions of the British presence in their societies, but Churchill spoke an important caution to all the colonial powers in that age of empire. A Christian nation should have a different approach to colonial policy: one of service, not mastery. Though much of what Churchill said might be considered politically incorrect today, he emphasized a principle that nonetheless ought to guide foreign policy and international relations—namely, that wealthier, more powerful nations should see themselves as serving the global community.

In his mind, Churchill's vision of the servant role that is ideally characteristic of a Christian society applied to the bloody struggles of lonely Britain against the Nazis before the Atlantic Alliance took shape. "Bearing ourselves humbly before God," he said, "but conscious that we serve an unfolding purpose . . . [we] are fighting by ourselves alone; but we are not fighting for ourselves alone."[23]

Christian civilization values and promotes the discipline of self-restraint, making true liberty possible

"It is evident that Christianity, however degraded and distorted by cruelty and intolerance, must always exert a modifying influence on men's passions, and protect them from the more violent forms of fanatical fever, as we are protected from smallpox by vaccination," Churchill wrote in 1897.[24] He contrasted the restraining element in Christianity with Islam, which "increases, instead of lessening, the fury of intolerance."[25]

Churchill would have been familiar with a passage from Edmund Burke, who (though he did not use the term) describes qualities of Christian civilization in which Churchill believed so passionately:

What is liberty without wisdom and without virtue? It is the greatest of all possible evils; for it is folly, vice, and madness, without tuition or restraint. Those who know what virtuous liberty is, cannot bear to see it disgraced by incapable heads, on account of their having high-sounding words in their mouths.[26]

Christian civilization understands the importance of the Golden Rule in the formation of government policy

After France capitulated to Germany in 1940, leaving Britain alone to withstand Hitler and the Nazis, Churchill saw the importance of the principles laid down in the Golden Rule. In a Bastille Day broadcast on July 14, 1940, he said, "When you have a friend and comrade at whose side you have faced tremendous struggles, and your friend is smitten down by a stunning blow, . . . you need not bear malice because of your friend's cries of delirium and gestures of agony. You must not add to his pain; you must work for his recovery."[27]

In an ultimate test of that principle, Churchill extended the same attitude towards the German people during the reconstruction of their devastated land after Hitler's defeat. There is always an element of pragmatism in the Golden Rule because it focuses on reciprocal behaviors. Jesus was as much a realist as he was a visionary. The theme of sowing and reaping is both implied and overtly stated in the Scriptures. Thus, in his desire to help postwar Germany, Churchill practiced principled pragmatism, an important component of Christian civilization.

Christian civilization recognizes the Ten Commandments as the basis of all morality and law

Again we recall Churchill's statement from 1903: "The life and strength of our authority springs from moral and not physical forces."[28] That conviction only deepened through his later life experiences.

Churchill clearly knew the source of all ethical laws and universal values. In writing about Moses' leadership, Churchill calls him "the supreme law-giver, who received from God that remarkable code upon which the religious, moral, and social life of the nation was so securely founded."[29]

Christian civilization fosters true liberty of belief and practice

Churchill had the opportunity to engage with non-Christian belief systems throughout his life. During the time he served in North Africa, he observed the Muslim faith firsthand. In his younger days, perhaps influenced by the romanticism of Lawrence of Arabia, Churchill seemed enthusiastic about Islamic culture. In 1907, Lady Gwendoline Bertie, who later married Churchill's brother, Jack, wrote to Churchill, expressing her concern. "Please don't become converted to Islam," she pleaded. "Your conversion might be effected with greater ease than you might have supposed."[30]

In *Churchill and the Islamic World*, Warren Dockter concludes:

> Churchill's fascination with Islam proved only to be aesthetic and passing. His knowledge of Islam was largely predicated on Victorian notions, which heavily romanticized the nomadic lifestyle and honour culture of the Bedouin desert tribes. As a result, Churchill never really acquired a deeper understanding of Islam.[31]

In his 1899 account of the Sudan War, titled *The River War*, Churchill expressed his views of Islam in terms that some have seized upon in our day:

> Besides the fanatical frenzy, which is as dangerous in a man as hydrophobia in a dog, there is this fearful fatalistic apathy. The effects are apparent in many countries. . . . A degraded sensualism deprives this life of its grace and refinement; the next of its dignity

and sanctity. . . . Far from being moribund, Mohammedanism is
a militant and proselytising faith. It has already spread throughout
Central Africa, raising fearless warriors at every step; and were it
not that Christianity is sheltered in the strong arms of science, the
science against which it had vainly struggled, the civilisation of
modern Europe might fall, as fell the civilisation of ancient Rome.[32]

Churchill emphasized that, without the union of reason and spirituality, destructive fanaticism could result from any religious system—even Christianity.

Since the events of September 11, 2001, Churchill's views of
Islam, especially those expressed in *The River War*, are often taken
out of context and used by those who see all Muslims, without
regard, as evil. The brutality of emerging Islamic terror movements has reinforced this simplistic conclusion. However, reflecting the worldview of Christian civilization, Churchill sought
to see the human beings within the movement, not merely the
movement itself. He drew a careful distinction between fanatical
Muslims and peaceful Muslims, albeit in terms that today may
appear rather patrician and condescending: "Individual Moslems
may show splendid qualities. Thousands become the brave and
loyal soldiers of the Queen."[33]

For Churchill, the charity of Christian civilization meant justice and fairness, freedom and equality. There was no official policy by which the British sought to force people into Christianity.
Hinduism continued to flourish in India, and mosques continued
to dot the landscapes of the Middle East and Africa. Christian
missionaries were free to propagate their faith, but the people in
the far-flung reaches of the British Empire were also free to reject
Christianity. There was no subjugation based on religious affili-
ation, no special tax imposed on nonbelievers, and certainly no
executions for those who followed other faiths. Such would be the
antithesis of Christian civilization.

Christian civilization promotes the importance of forgiveness

Upon becoming prime minister, Churchill could have sought revenge against those who had mistreated him. Like Hitler, he could have sought to arrest those who were opposed to his leadership of the nation. He could no doubt have used the army or British Secret Service to murder those people, just as Hitler had done at the end of June 1934. As prime minister, Churchill could have labeled all Germans as evil. However, throughout the Second World War, he was determined to distinguish between the German people in general and the Nazis.

In his *Commentary* review of Martin Gilbert's *Winston S. Churchill: Finest Hour, 1939–1941*, Spencer Warren writes:

> Churchill's generosity was displayed in his attitude toward Germany. Even when the German threat to Britain was at its greatest, he spoke of the need for a magnanimous peace after what he was sure would be Britain's final victory. Only the Nazis, he once commented, "would be made to suffer for their misdeeds." His hatred of the "Huns," as he called the Germans in his (usual) fighting mood, was only "professional."[34]

Christian civilization celebrates and encourages
true courage, not mere bravado

In the Judeo-Christian worldview, courage results from faith in God and in oneself as a servant of God and humanity. As God said to Joshua just before the nation of Israel crossed the Jordan River to take possession of the Promised Land: "This is my command— be strong and courageous! Do not be afraid or discouraged. For the LORD your God is with you wherever you go."[35]

Bravado is different from genuine courage. Courage comes from humility—the recognition that we draw our strength from a power beyond ourselves. Bravado is merely the bluster and arrogance of pride. Goliath blazed with bravado. The youngster

David, aware of his limitations, trusted God and went forward in courage.

As a young man, Churchill saw much of the bravado of his age. Barbara Tuchman describes the worldview that flourished in Europe prior to the First World War.

> Since [the end of] the Napoleonic wars, the industrial and scientific revolutions had transformed the world. . . . Industrial society gave man new powers and new scope while at the same time building up new pressures. . . . Science gave man new welfare and new horizons while it took away belief in God and certainty in a scheme of things he knew. . . . Society at the turn of the century was not so much decaying as bursting with new tensions and accumulated energies.[36]

The Britain of Churchill's early years "had an air of careless supremacy" and a mind-set of "splendid isolation," writes Tuchman. The British "felt no need of allies and had no friends."[37] It was this attitude of pride and self-sufficiency, which the British seemed to want to slip back into after the First World War, that Churchill had to work so strenuously to overcome during the 1930s as war approached once more.

Churchill himself saw and experienced firsthand the bravado flourishing in Germany during his trips in 1906 and 1919 to observe the German military.

> In the Review which preceded the manoeuvres 50,000 horse, foot and artillery marched past the Emperor and his galaxy of kings and princes. . . . The very atmosphere was pervaded by a sense of inexhaustible and exuberant manhood and deadly panoply. The glories of this world and force abounding could not present a more formidable, and even stupefying, manifestation.[38]

Meanwhile, in Austria-Hungary, whose empire of façades would provide the detonation for the First World War, there was, in the words of historian and Vienna native Frederic Morton, "a nervous splendor."[39] In the summer of 1888, as Winston Churchill was entering the adventures of adolescence and Adolf Hitler was about to be conceived, "Vienna, that scrollworked bastion, smoldered with more demons of the future than the most forward-minded cities of the West. Its officials were obsessed with the need to continue a great Imperial image."[40]

That obsession meant much bravado, which created tension within the royal family. Emperor Franz Joseph was focused on readying his son, Rudolf, to transport the Austro-Hungarian Empire into the twentieth century. But whereas young Rudolf had developed a vision for reform, his father's solution to the challenges facing the empire was more often to table the discussion or create "a prettier façade to cover the problem."[41]

But the cracks in the façades were becoming too vast for mere cosmetics. "Other empires were approaching modern greatness much faster than Austria,"[42] writes Frederic Morton. To the east, Russia was expanding; in the south, Italy had taken back Lombardy and Venice; to the north and west, Kaiser Wilhelm was dreaming of his Reich and Britain was proving her mastery of the seas. And then there was France, whose magnificent capital city, Paris, bore the "dynamic shadow" of General Boulanger—"The Man on Horseback" who "seemed fated to turn the Third Republic into a united phalanx under his dictatorship."[43]

In the end, all the bravado devolved into the trench-scarred battlefields of the Great War.

By the time Churchill became prime minister in 1940, he had seen enough of bravado—especially that which was displayed by Adolf Hitler and Joseph Goebbels at their grand rallies. It would take real courage to win the battle for Christian civilization. Churchill was certainly not thumping his chest when, just after his appointment as prime minister, he said, "We have before us an ordeal of the most grievous kind . . . many, many long months of struggle and suffering." His solution was to wage war all the way to victory, "with all our might and with all the strength that God can give us."[44]

THE NUREMBERG TRIALS: A CHALLENGE
TO JUDEO-CHRISTIAN CIVILIZATION

By the blessing of God, and with the support of his late-arriving allies, Churchill pressed on to victory. Christian civilization would live to face its next challenge. That test would come early and subtly in the swirl of legal complexities surrounding the Nuremberg trials of the captured Nazi leaders who had worked the levers of the German war machine.

One way to discern what Churchill meant by "Christian civilization" and its "certain way of life" is to study the consensus in the West, in the late nineteenth and early twentieth centuries, regarding morality, ethics, and law—all core components of a civilization. We see these issues writ large in the efforts of the victorious Allies to provide a fair trial for Nazi war criminals. That there would be concern for justice and fairness for the most monstrous people of the twentieth century is a testimony to Judeo-Christian values.

At Yalta, in 1945, Churchill initially told Roosevelt and Stalin that the most appropriate resolution to the problem was simple— summary executions. Roosevelt seemed to agree, but as the trials neared, the American secretary of war, Henry Stimson, "opposed the idea of summary executions and argued for a trial that would reflect democratic notions of justice, in contrast to the tyranny and mayhem the world had just witnessed."[45] A new consensus continued to grow among those who were thinking seriously about the possibility of the trials and what they might look like.

Gordon Dean, who later became press secretary for the Nuremberg trials, prepared a report for the Overseas Section of the Office of War Information detailing why summary executions should not be the outcome. One of the items captured the presuppositional worldview of true Christian civilization regarding justice:

> The concept that guilt should be fairly ascertained is so embedded in the charters of the countries of the civilized that we cannot afford to abandon it here simply because the guilt is great. We fought a war because of what other powers stooped to. Now that victory is here we must not allow ourselves to stoop to their level. In short, we want a just judgment.[46]

Furthermore, "summary execution . . . would only result in the world's forgetting of their major sins, and these sins must never be forgotten."[47]

The whole business must have presented awkward challenges to US Army Colonel Burton Andrus, the commandant of the prison that housed Hermann Goering, chief of Hitler's air force; Hans Frank, the "Jew butcher of Poland"; "gas chamber expert" Ernst Kaltenbrunner; Wilhelm Keitel, chief of staff for the German High Command; Joachim von Ribbentrop, Nazi foreign minister; Alfred Rosenberg, who helped plan the extermination of the Nazis' opponents; and other Nazis.

It must have been extremely difficult for Colonel Andrus to exert the discipline and restraint of a civilized man when he first faced the perpetrators of some of the worst inhumanity seen on the stage of history to that point. When Andrus's army unit had driven through defeated territories in Germany, he had seen firsthand the instruments of their terror. In a letter, Andrus wrote, "Many of their infernal devices have slaughtered innocent maidens, helpless widows, and defenseless orphans. They are making war on the Christian religion and all it stands for."[48]

Yet, in his direct encounters with the men who had plotted and carried out those atrocities, Andrus wanted to reflect the principles of the very Christian civilization they had sought to destroy. Andrus told the prisoners: "Be informed that the considerate treatment you receive here is not because you merit it, but because anything less would be unbecoming to us."[49]

Churchill eventually concluded that the Nuremberg trials were justified. In a speech to the House of Commons in November 1946, he called them "a purgative."[50]

Most of the crimes against civilization and humanity that were exposed in the Nuremberg trials arose from the "perverted science" Churchill had warned about in 1940. However, the twisting and corruption of science by the Nazis was the outgrowth of theories that had been developing for more than a century.

8

Hitler and "Perverted Science"

If we fail, then the whole world, including the United States,
including all that we have known and cared for, will sink
into the abyss of a new Dark Age made more sinister, and
perhaps more protracted, by the lights of perverted science.

WINSTON CHURCHILL, SPEECH TO THE
HOUSE OF COMMONS, JUNE 18, 1940

As EARLY AS 1928, Churchill had recorded his concerns about
"a future catastrophe" that could potentially destroy the human
race.

The organisation of mankind into great States and Empires, and the
rise of nations to full collective consciousness, enabled enterprises
of slaughter to be planned and executed upon a scale and with a
perseverance never before imagined. All the noblest virtues of
individuals were gathered to strengthen the destructive capacity
of the mass. Good finances ... made it possible to divert ... the
energies of whole peoples to the task of devastation. Democratic
institutions gave expression to the willpower of millions. ... Lastly,
Science unfolded her treasures and her secrets to the desperate

demands of men, and placed in their hands agencies and apparatus almost decisive in their character.[1]

A short twelve years later, on June 18, 1940, Churchill was suitably grim as he spoke to the House of Commons. France had just capitulated to the Nazis, leaving Britain to stand alone against Hitler's evil regime. Churchill had been prime minister for thirty-nine days, and the daunting weight of his responsibilities would only increase over the next five years.

In his remarks that day, Churchill not only sounded the alarm for Christian civilization; he also warned that, if the Nazis prevailed, the "whole world" would "sink into the abyss of a new Dark Age made more sinister, and perhaps more protracted, by the lights of perverted science."[2]

In 1940 the scope of atrocities associated with the Nazis' attempts at genocide and racial purification had not yet come to light, but Churchill could see the potential for "enterprises of slaughter," made possible by industrialization and advances in technology.

Today, we might call "perverted science" *scientism*. True science pursues truth wherever it leads, but scientism pursues its own agenda, even if it means denying the truth.

Some today would label those who are concerned about the perversion of science as *anti-science*, but it isn't an either/or proposition. Churchill was certainly not anti-science, but neither was he willing to kowtow to every claim of science.

In his "last great speech . . . in the House of Commons," on March 1, 1955, he offered this warning: "We have antagonisms now as deep as those of the Reformation and its reactions. . . . But now they are spread over the whole world. . . . We have force and science, hitherto the servants of man, now threatening to become his master."[3]

Churchill spoke of two concerns in particular. The first, as we have seen in previous chapters, was the survival of Christian civilization. As a historian, Churchill knew that the roots of true science lay in the rich soil of the Judeo-Christian worldview.[4] He was concerned that the perversion of science in the West would follow its separation from its spiritual roots—a separation that Hitler championed.

Though he began life as a Catholic, Hitler had come to regard Christianity as a religion of "meekness and flabbiness."[5] Furthermore, Hitler viewed the Jews as an inferior race that stood in the way of human evolution, so he had little regard for the virtues of their worldview. He saw the Jews as enemies who would drag humanity to a lower level. Therefore, he tried to sever Germany from its Judeo-Christian roots.

Hitler would destroy those roots by taking over the church and replacing biblical doctrine with Nazi creeds. He sought to establish new roots—poisonous ones that would kill many millions before the war's end.

"Perverted science" would be integral to Hitler's aims. Finding military uses for advancing technology would be front and center. Corruption of scientific practices would be unrestrained. Perverted science would give rise to the sadistic Josef Mengele and other inhumane scientist-physicians, and would sooner invent a better gas chamber for concentration camps than find a cure for cancer.

Some of Churchill's concern about the perversion of science would no doubt have arisen from his reading of *Mein Kampf*, in which Hitler not only provided an autobiography but also described his personal worldview and the philosophy underlying it. In 1948, Churchill reflected on the nature of Hitler's book:

All was there—the programme of German resurrection, the technique of party propaganda; the plan for combating Marxism; the concept of a National-Socialist state; the rightful position of

Germany at the summit of the world. Here was the new Koran of war: turgid, verbose, shapeless, but pregnant with its message.[6]

DISCERNING THE ZEITGEIST

Churchill knew well the forces that had pushed Hitler towards the dark side. His powers of discernment could grasp the "spirit of the age," the *Zeitgeist* in which both he and Hitler had been sired and nurtured. Christa Schroeder, Hitler's secretary throughout the Second World War, said that Hitler "considered the Christian religion to be a hypocritical trap which had out-lived its time" and that the Nazi leader believed that his religion "was the law of nature."[7]

Adolf Hitler was immersed in a *Zeitgeist* full of race-based the-ory and anti-Semitism, and he believed in the Darwinian vision of how life advances towards its highest form. In *From Darwin to Hitler*, professor Richard Weikart explores exhaustively the link between Darwinism and Hitler. His seminal work is an important reference for this chapter.

> Hitler was not even on my radar screen when I began my research. . . . However, the more books, articles, and documents I read by Darwinists and eugenicists in the nineteenth and early twentieth centuries, and the more I read by and about Hitler, the more I became convinced that there were significant historical connections between Darwinism and Hitler's ideology.[8]

Darwin's theory of evolution and its presuppositions were detailed in his book *On the Origin of Species*, first published in 1859. The roots of Darwin's theories found fertile soil in conti-nental Europe, cultivated by racial theorists who had long been tilling the ground: "The influence of Darwinism can be gauged by the outpouring of books and articles in late nineteenth-century Germany, Austria, and Switzerland."[9]

One of those who drank deeply from that flood was the German-born geneticist Richard Goldschmidt, who came to prominence in the twentieth century. In his autobiography, Goldschmidt tells of reading "with burning eyes and soul" the works of Darwinist Ernst Haeckel (who also would have a great influence on Hitler's thinking).[10] The Darwinian worldview as presented by Haeckel "was typical for educated young people of [Goldschmidt's] day."[11]

One of the presuppositions that began to grow (and that would eventually undergird the Nazi worldview) had to do with "biological improvement." Weikart writes:

> Biological improvement of Europeans would give them a greater advantage in the struggle against other races, while biological degeneration—which many eugenicists feared was occurring—might lead to disaster for Europeans in the global struggle for existence.[12]

Important opinion-makers began to realize that Darwinism was not just about biology but was also about society. An entire body of work emerged on "social Darwinism," which Richard Hofstadter defines as "an ideology using a competitive view of nature and Darwin's concept of the struggle for existence as a basis for social theory."[13] Many atheists and other secular Darwinists protest that Darwin intended no social applications from his evolutionary theory. However, in a letter dated July 26, 1872, Darwin himself affirmed that it had certain social implications.[14]

These presuppositions and the resulting worldview characterized not only the societies of continental Europe in the late nineteenth and early twentieth centuries, but also that of the British Isles. Winston Churchill understood these attitudes because they pervaded so much of the British aristocracy prior to 1940. In fact, he and his father had been castigated at times by their peers for including Jews among their friends.

There were many members of the [British] aristocracy who, at least before May 1940, expressed their rather definite sympathies for Hitler—or, at least, for the then Germanophile inclinations of [Prime Minister] Chamberlain. Such tendencies were shared by members of the royal family and, what was more important, by civil servants of considerable influence. One of these was Sir Horace Wilson, who before 1940 was Chamberlain's closest and most trusted adviser.[15]

During the Chamberlain administration, Horace Wilson "sat in a small office outside the prime minister's room in Downing Street, and everyone with an appointment had to pass through this office and have a few minutes' conversation with Sir Horace."[16] One observer called Wilson "the uncrowned ruler of England."[17] But Wilson was also closely tied to the appeasement of Hitler before the war, and "one of the first things that Churchill did [when he became prime minister] was to tell Horace Wilson to get out."[18]

Once Adolf Hitler was firmly in power, with his economic and employment policies in full swing, he was free to focus his attention on what he believed to be the cause of the new Germanic empire's foundational challenges—the Jews. *Mein Kampf* is littered with evidence of Hitler's radical racial beliefs, shaped by what can only be described as "mystical Darwinism"—that is, taking the blind evolutionary processes of natural selection and infusing them with transcendent authority and godlike omniscience and omnipotence.

The Nuremberg Laws, based on the premise of a pure Aryan race of strong and healthy Germans, were utterly anti-Semitic and designed to prevent what Hitler feared would be contamination and defilement of the blood of the superior race.[19]

The Nazi racial doctrine held that intermixing with weak non-Aryans would produce even weaker children, resulting in the inevitable demise of the German race; therefore, it was the duty of the Aryans to ensure that non-Aryans did not infect them with their blood. Once Hitler enacted the Nuremberg Laws, he could easily move forward with his plan to deport the Jews to concentration camps for the purpose of enslaving and murdering them.

THE PERVERSION OF SCIENCE

Churchill's concerns about the corruption of scientific knowledge and its application to the waging of war in the emerging industrial age—"developments and extensions . . . which will be incomparably more formidable and fatal"[20]—were only intensified by what he read in *Mein Kampf*, heard in statements made by Hitler during the prewar period, and saw in the buildup of the Nazi war machine. Let's examine the implications of a few key elements of Nazi ideology.

The "phony war" between reason and revelation, rationality and faith, reality and mystery

Epistemology is the study of how we know what we know. During the period when the principles of modern science were under development, *revelation* and *reason* were linked. Sir Isaac Newton grasped this connection and "explicitly stated that he was investigating God's creation, which was a religious duty because nature reflects the creativity of its maker."[21]

Newton was reaching back into the Middle Ages, a time that has been pilloried as anti-science but that actually represents a more highly integrated approach to philosophy, theology, and the study of the workings of nature.[22] In fact, it was the "natural philosophers" of the Middle Ages (the term *scientist* wasn't coined until 1833) who made modern science possible. Without "their central belief that nature was created by God and so worthy of their attention," writes James Hannam, "modern science would simply not have happened."[23]

During the eighteenth century Enlightenment, *revelation* was pushed out of the epistemological formula. In the minds of some scholars, Darwin's work in the nineteenth century shattered altogether the link between revelation and reason.

Churchill, in his reference to "perverted science," was no doubt conscious of the racial policies already coming to the fore in prewar Nazi society. And Hitler, in measuring scientific truth only on the basis of what appeared to be reasonable inferences drawn from Darwin's theories, contended that he was promoting the science that would help the human race. For Darwin and his followers, "group competition, such as war and racial antagonisms, played a crucial role in the development of human societies, and even in the development of morality."[24] Hitler embraced this theory and pursued "a two-pronged strategy involving both artificial and natural selection: eugenics within German society to improve the health and vitality of the 'Aryan race,' and radical struggle and warfare towards those outside the German racial community."[25]

After Darwin's work was published, the biological sciences grew rapidly. Increasingly, the idea that linked revelation and reason was crushed under the multiplying theories. The result was that "most scientists" in that period began to "advance theories of human inequality as matters of scientific fact," writes professor Henry Friedlander, who himself was held by the Nazis in several concentration camps, including Auschwitz.[26]

Utilitarianism replaces transcendent moral values

Adolf Hitler was no less a child of his times than Winston Churchill. The Darwinist *Zeitgeist* into which Hitler was born was growing rapidly in Austria, Germany, and Britain. In the eighteenth century, the utilitarian philosopher Jeremy Bentham had cast his bread on the waters of British thought, and some in the aristocracy had gobbled it down. According to Bentham, actions are moral in proportion to how much utility they produce, which is measured by material outcomes that produce pleasure and happiness.

Though Churchill had aristocratic roots, he had not taken

Bentham's bait, perhaps because he was not fully received into that social stratum or because he did not think of himself as an aristocrat. Many in the British upper class disdained him, and this may have saved Churchill from adopting a merely utilitarian worldview.

Fifteen years before Hitler was born, Georg von Gizycki and Friedrich Jodl were also thinking about utilitarianism. One outcome of Gizycki's work, writes Richard Weikart, was "rescuing ethics and morality from its connections with religion, creating a this-worldly moral philosophy to replace the prevalent other-worldly conception."[27] Ultimately, this would devolve into the Nazi guidelines for determining whether a person deserved life or death. "One important criterion" for determining whether a person would live or die under Nazi regulations, writes Henry Friedlander, "was utilitarian and based on a patient's level of productivity." Individuals to be executed were "denounced as 'life unworthy of life.'" They were considered "burdensome lives" and "useless eaters."[28]

Utilitarianism has a crushing effect on transcendent values, as Churchill was well aware.

> It would be much better to call a halt in material progress and discovery rather than to be mastered by our own apparatus and the forces which it directs. . . . Without an equal growth of Mercy, Pity, Peace and Love, Science herself may destroy all that makes human life majestic and tolerable.[29]

It is the loss of this transcendence that so captivated Bentham, Hitler, and other utilitarians, with their ethics of raw pragmatics. We still hear the echoes of it today, in the writings of militant atheists such as Richard Dawkins, among many others. In a Twitter exchange with a woman who wrote, "I honestly don't know what I would do if I were pregnant with a kid with Down syndrome,"

Dawkins replied, "Abort it and try again. It would be immoral to bring it into the world if you have the choice."[30]

Reductionism: the mechanization of all things

"Prussian idealism took the heart of flesh and blood from the German and in its place gave him one of iron and paper," wrote Theodor Haecker in 1940.[31] The German educational system that had been the prototype for scholastic excellence in the nineteenth century, and that had drawn students from across the world, had "resurrected in modern garb the most immoral kinds of consciousness, of ethnocentrism and national egotism, apparently now rationally warranted by Darwinian 'racial science.'"[32]

In *The Old Faith and the New*, David Friedrich Strauss, another shaper of the philosophical *Zeitgeist* in which Hitler was raised, tried to displace the Christian worldview with that of naturalistic science. Strauss believed that the human soul was merely the brain and its physical functions and that ethics were developed only to facilitate human existence. "Even the Ten Commandments lose their sanctity," Richard Weikart observes in a discussion about Strauss. "They are merely tools useful to humans in the course of evolutionary competition, rather than divinely ordained commands."[33]

If human beings are nothing more than mechanisms inside a much larger machine, they can be "turned off" if they break down or have inferior parts. According to Nazi philosophy, the only biological mechanism that should be kept running and constantly tweaked through eugenics was the Aryan human.

According to this way of thinking, the Jews were gremlins in the machine. In February 1945, Hitler mused that because the Jews were "parasite[s] which cannot and will not be assimilated," Germany's attempt to eliminate them "has been an essential process of disinfection, which we have prosecuted to its ultimate limit and without which we should ourselves have been asphyxiated and destroyed."[34]

Reductionism: from the ultimate questions to the immediate

The second reduction wrought by scientism has to do with the key issues of life itself. In a mechanistic view, major assumptions about the purpose and meaning of existence are overturned; but a transcendent understanding of humanity is a bulwark against such reductionism.

For Churchill, the ultimate questions could be summed up in three concerns: "Why are we here? What is the purpose of Life? Whither are we going?"[35]

The great schism between revelation and reason shifted the focus away from the ultimate to the immediate. Scientism excused this reductionism by claiming that the ultimate questions were beyond its empirical grasp while at the same time scorning and marginalizing the theology that provides the tools to understand the ultimate questions.

Churchill knew that Hitler hadn't lost sight of the ultimate but that he had formed answers within his own mind, shaped by the spirit of his age. Hitler truly believed he was in the world to advance the Aryan race—the supreme outcome of human evolution—and therefore the empire of the Aryan race. To Hitler's mind, the purpose of life was not merely survival, but the survival of the fittest. And he and the Nazis knew who the fittest would be.

Whither are we going? To the glorious Third Reich, Hitler said, which would usher in, not Augustine's City of God, but the City of Man writ large, the superhuman global empire of the Aryans.

Churchill well knew that the survival of Christian civilization required a dynamic balance between the ultimate and the immediate. Repeatedly he set the big picture before the British people, reminding them why they had to fight on despite the loss of loved ones, homes, and institutions and even despite the risk to their own lives. At the same time, Churchill maintained a focus on the immediate. As minister of defense, he daily assessed the strength of matériel and personnel in all the branches that would "fight on the beaches, . . . on the landing grounds, . . . in the fields and in the streets."

Conflating means and ends

In his speech before the Nuremberg war crimes tribunal, Hitler's chief architect, Albert Speer, said that Hitler's dictatorship "employed to perfection the instruments of technology to dominate its own people."[36] Through such scientific achievements, "eighty million persons could be made subject to the will of one individual."[37]

Most terrifying was the absence of thinking that would have enabled people to use value judgments to distinguish between means and ends. In the absolute realm of scientism, the person who asks questions is marginalized; and when the levers of that scientism are in the hands of a dictator, a critical mind could lead to one's execution. "Telephone, teletype, and radio made it possible to transmit the commands of the highest levels directly to the lowest organs where . . . they were executed uncritically," said Speer.[38]

By contrast, Churchill's actions were challenged constantly, in both the War Cabinet and the House of Commons. There was little room for the conflation of ends and means in the political climate in which Churchill functioned as prime minister. His every recommendation, and every possible motive behind it, was scrutinized repeatedly by his peers, the press, and the British people. Hitler never had to worry about serious internal political resistance because he repressed anyone within Germany who opposed him. Churchill, on the other hand, had to face down votes of no confidence in the House of Commons, as well as disagreements within his coalition War Cabinet. This, however, is the price of a free society, and Churchill gladly bore the cost. During one period of intense battle over his leadership within Parliament, Elizabeth Nel noted the stress on her boss: "I know that despite his lifetime of experience and his enormous strength and self-control in bearing trials, he was still human enough to feel worked up inside."[39]

Removal of transcendent accountability

In a December 1931 article published in *The Strand Magazine*, Churchill wrote: "We have the spectacle of the powers of weapons of man far outstripping the march of his intelligence; we have the march of his intelligence proceeding far more rapidly than the development of his nobility. . . . It is therefore above all things important that the moral philosophy and spiritual conceptions of men and nations should hold their own amid these formidable scientific evolutions."[40]

In his remarks, Churchill describes perfectly the scientism that had infected genuine scientific inquiry.

> There are secrets too mysterious for man in his present state to know; secrets which, once penetrated, may be fatal to human happiness and glory. But the busy hands of the scientists are already fumbling with the keys of all the chambers hitherto forbidden to mankind.[41]

Tyrants always must remove any contrary power that might be perceived to be above them. They rule by fear, and fear is stoked by the shocking truth that the oppressors can do whatever they wish because there is no one to whom they are ultimately accountable. Hitler's minister of propaganda, Josef Goebbels, said, "There is . . . an insoluble opposition between the Christian and a Germanic-heroic worldview."[42] Clearly, if the Nazis had won the war, they would have sought to remove the influence of the church from the European continent.

Europe's spiritual and philosophical soil had long been under cultivation for tyrannical absolutism, and it was well-plowed, in the Germanic territories especially, for the sowing of Hitler's malicious seeds.

Alfred Grotjahn, a professor at the University of Berlin, was among the framers of the *Zeitgeist* into which Hitler was born and through which his thought was shaped. Grotjahn described his own experience of being severed from the idea of the transcendent while reading *Force and Matter* by Ludwig Büchner. Grotjahn said that the influence of Darwinian materialism "swept my brain clear of metaphysical conceptions at an age decisive in the development of my world view and freed me up to receive positivist views and this-worldly ethical values."[43] He went on to become a leading voice in the German eugenics and social hygiene movement that underpinned Nazi philosophy.

THE LOSS OF TRANSCENDENT WONDER

The initial fragmentation of revelation and reason occurred in the philosophy of ancient Greece, which the Nazis intermingled with their own worldview. In the fifth century BC, Protagoras provided what would later become the mantra of scientism: *Man is the measure of all things.* What cannot be subjected to human reason is considered invalid. A major consequence of this philosophy is the limitation of wonder and awe to the observable, measurable world. Ultimately, it means that only that which exists on the scale of human reason can be worshiped. Anything transcendent is ruled out *a priori.*

Charles Taylor, in *A Secular Age,* describes the "disenchantment" of the world that ultimately leads to "a humanism accepting no final goals beyond human flourishing."[44] In a Nazi-controlled Europe, Hitler would decide which humans should "flourish" and which would be considered obstacles to that happy state. Not only would the "fittest" survive, but they would be able to establish the new value codes. It astonishes us now, but both Hitler and Stalin considered themselves and their systems to be *moral.*

The Middle Ages, during which the foundations of modern science were laid, had embraced transcendent wonder. In the seventy-plus cathedrals erected without modern gadgets, Europe is still festooned with evidence of the exuberance for transcendence that characterized the medieval period. The visionaries who gave the world the great structures wanted to lift up the eyes of worshipers to almighty God, who is over all. They saw the confluence of natural philosophy and theology, and the scientifically engineered cathedrals were dazzling testimonies. The words inscribed on the doors of the twelfth-century Basilica of Saint Denis in Paris are revealing:

Whoever thou art, if thou seekest to extol the glory of these doors,
Marvel not at the gold and expense but at the craftsmanship
of the work.
Bright is the noble work; but, being nobly bright, the work
Should brighten the minds, so that they may travel, through
the true lights,
To the True Light where Christ is the true door.
In what manner it be inherent in this world the golden door defines:
The dull mind rises to truth through that which is material
And, in seeing this light, is resurrected from its former submersion.[45]

The biblically minded scholars of the Middle Ages took to heart the words of Psalm 8:3-5:

When I consider your heavens,
    the work of your fingers,
the moon and the stars,
    which you have set in place,
what is mankind that you are mindful of them,
    human beings that you care for them?
You have made them a little lower than the angels
    and crowned them with glory and honor.[46]

These thinkers considered God's handiwork and the place of humanity within this context. They gazed in wonder at the cosmos, and it created a sense of wonder about themselves. But it was not a self-created wonder. Rather, human greatness came from God, just as the glorious splendor of nature was from his hand. John Polkinghorne, a physicist and Anglican priest, writes that one of the experiences "fundamental to the pursuit of science is a sense of wonder."[47]

Hitler's scientists had lost touch with the beautiful balance in Psalm 8 between the divine and the human. They gloried in themselves and saw other human beings as inferior, with no reason for being kept alive except for their utility. When wonder before the transcendent God is removed from the pursuits of science, the restraints are removed and the worst of scientism lies ahead.

This was among the prospects that troubled Winston Churchill the most.

Presumptuous arrogance rather than humble inquiry

The spirit of true science was revealed when Sir Isaac Newton, among the greatest scientists in history, said, "If I have seen a little further then it is by standing on the shoulders of giants."[48]

Scientism knows little of such humility. Austin Hughes, distinguished professor of biological sciences at the University of South Carolina and a veteran of scientific inquiry, writes of "the folly of scientism" and its "temptation to overreach." One aspect of science that attracted Hughes to his career was "the modesty of its practitioners." What made this attitude appealing to him was that the attitude of true science "stood in sharp contrast to the arrogance of the philosophers of the positivist tradition, who claimed for science and its practitioners a broad authority with which practicing scientists were uncomfortable."[49] Hughes continues:

> The temptation to overreach . . . seems increasingly indulged today in discussions about science. Both in the work of professional philosophers and in popular writings by natural scientists, it is

frequently claimed that natural science does or soon will constitute the entire domain of truth. And this attitude is becoming more widespread among scientists themselves. All too many of my contemporaries in science have accepted without question the hype that suggests that an advanced degree in some area of natural science confers the ability to pontificate wisely on any and all subjects.[50]

If overreach is a symptom of arrogant scientism, then Hitler and the Nazis were consumed by the disease. Albert Speer contends that, if observers in Hitler's era had looked more closely at the grand buildings, arenas, and monuments he envisioned for Nuremberg, they would have realized the extent of his megalomania. Primary among the effects of scientism is its presumptuous delusion. Hitler, says Speer, "trusted his inspirations, no matter how inherently contradictory they might be, and these inspirations were governed by extreme contempt for and underestimation of the others."[51]

Hitler would never have acknowledged that he "stood on the shoulders of giants." He was the *only* giant. But he did trust in his science. He had remarkable "communications apparatus at headquarters," writes Speer. He could direct all the theaters of war straight from his table in the situation room. "The more fearful the situation," Speer recalls, "the greater was the gulf modern technology created between reality and fantasies with which the man at the table operated."[52]

As Churchill viewed the rise of Hitlerism, he may have recalled his 1906 visit to review the Kaiser's military might and the "impressive scale of mechanism" he had observed even eight years before the outbreak of the First World War. Between the two wars, Germany was home to some of the most brilliant scientists in history—including Einstein and Heisenberg—as well as masters of other disciplines. Many were Jews who, like Einstein, left Germany before Hitler's policies came to full fruition. Perhaps

Churchill realized that the perversion of science would come through those who remained, whose only restraints would be the delusions foisted on German culture and scholarship from Hitler's corrupted mind.

The Babel mentality

Scientism perverts true science through its haughty presumption and vast overreaching. Its first shadow in human history was cast on the Plain of Shinar, where the ancients gathered to build a tower that would reach to the very heavens. Their motive is stated in Genesis 11:4:

> Then they said, "Come, let us build ourselves a city, with a tower that reaches to the heavens, so that we may make a name for ourselves; otherwise we will be scattered over the face of the whole earth." [53]

The three aims of the Babel agenda are for human beings to (1) reach heaven on their own terms and by their own effort; (2) make a name for themselves; and (3) circumvent God's original intent for humanity to disperse, not cluster.

The first objective is to build a city. The Greek word *polis* (which is part of our English word *metropolis*) refers to a community structured through the order of a particular worldview and set of values. The would-be Babel-builders had lost the City of God and now were seeking to recover paradise, the City of Man, through their own ingenuity.

The city of Nuremberg was very symbolic for Hitler, and he planned for it to be the capital of the Third Reich, *the* world city. There he envisioned a rally site larger than the palace of the Persian kings in Persepolis, with a statue forty-six feet taller than the American Statue of Liberty and a 400,000-seat stadium twice the size of Rome's Circus Maximus. The entire complex would encompass an area three times that which was occupied by the Great Pyramid of Giza.

Looming over everything would be the two all-pervasive symbols of Hitler's regime: a swastika clasped in the talons of a huge eagle.

Once Germany had triumphed and Nuremberg had been established as the crown jewel of the Reich, the entire world would be Hitler's oyster.

> The Führer expresses his unshakeable conviction that the Reich will one day rule all of Europe. . . . And from then on the road to world domination is practically spread out before us. For whoever rules Europe will be able to seize the leadership of the world.[54]

In *The Proud Tower*, Barbara Tuchman titles her chapter on pre-war Germany "Neroism Is in the Air" because many Germans at the time believed that their culture "was the heir of Greece and Rome."[55] Tuchman also shows how war was the natural outcome of Hitler's Darwinian worldview.

> Darwin's findings in *The Origin of Species*, when applied to human society, supplied the philosophical basis for the theory that war was both inherent in nature and ennobling. War was a conflict in which the stronger and superior race survived, thus advancing civilization. Germany's thinkers, historians, political and military scientists, working upon the theory with the industry of moles and the tenacity of bulldogs, raised it to a level of national dogma.[56]

The path of repentance

The mercy of God always invites us to return to God and his truth through repentance, leading to restoration and renewal. At least one high Nazi official seems to have entered into that mercy. Former general field marshal Wilhelm Keitel had been second only to Hitler as the leader of Germany's military command. But in the wee hours of a dank October morning in 1946, he faced execution by order of the Nuremberg war tribunal.

Keitel was trying to maintain stiff composure when US Army captain Henry Gerecke entered his cell. Gerecke was the chaplain selected to minister to the Nazi war criminals who were jailed in Nuremberg. He had visited often with Keitel, and the former German officer felt comfortable with him. Gerecke was carrying a Bible, and he invited Keitel to join him in prayer.

The two men went to their knees, and Gerecke, an American son of German immigrants, prayed in German. Suddenly, it seemed to hit Keitel that he was really about to die. He trembled and "wept uncontrollably" as he "gasped for air." Just before he was hanged, Keitel received Communion, served by Gerecke. As the chaplain later recalled, Keitel, "with tears in his voice," said, "You have helped me more than you know. May Christ, my Savior, stand by me all the way. *I shall need Him so much.*"[57]

As far as we know, Adolf Hitler never repented of his sins or asked God for mercy. Having rejected God's grace again and again, eventually he reaped the consequences of his actions. But until that time, Hitler tramped on, believing devoutly in the technical wonders contrived in the laboratories of his practitioners of scientism.

Hitler knew that at some point he would have to do with the Christians what he was doing with the Jews. The feisty pastors in what was known as the Confessing Church challenged him and dared to preach against Nazism until they were carried off. Eventually, he would need to rid himself of Christians altogether, but first he would co-opt the official German church and make it a servant of Nazi ideology and a legitimizer of its evils.

9

Hitler and the Corruption
of the Church

In Germany the search for a new religion became
an endemic phenomenon, and it is no exaggeration
to describe it as a philosophical psychosis.

LEON POLIAKOV, *THE ARYAN MYTH*

As a SEEDBED OF THE PROTESTANT REFORMATION, Germany was historically a deeply spiritual nation. Josef Goebbels and the other visionaries who created the Nazi pageantry worked hard to tap into the mysticism. They played on wounds in the German soul with their racial theories and visions of Aryan ascendancy. Hitler's followers (without saying so—that would come later) created a modern mythology of the Führer as a new messianic figure, surrounded by "apostles" (his inner circle) and "disciples" (those who took *Mein Kampf* and Hitler's proclamations as revelation).

As Hitler consolidated his power and built his mystique, some leaders in the state church began to fall under the Nazi spell.

PASTOR AND PROPHET

A true and functioning church is crucial for forming and sustaining a healthy Christian society. The authentic church provides both pastoral care and a prophetic voice in a vibrant culture. When the church falls down in either of those two functions or loses the crucial balance between the two, society begins to break down and the culture develops problems.

Even in the midst of tragedy and the abandonment of its true mission by the establishment church, there is always a remnant who remain faithful to God and his revelation. Such passion compelled pastor Dietrich Bonhoeffer both to leave the safe haven that his friends had tried to create for him in America and to return to Germany, where he took up the role of prophetic voice against Hitler.

His fellow clergymen Helmut Thielicke and Martin Niemöller were initially hopeful about Hitler's leadership, but they soon recognized the demonic influence in the Führer. During the war, as Allied bombs fell on their cities, they refused to run, continuing to give pastoral care to their communities.

After the war, Niemöller gave several lectures in which he confessed the complicity of the German church in not speaking up when Hitler began to oppress various groups within society.

First they came for the Socialists, and I did not speak out— Because I was not a Socialist.

Then they came for the Trade Unionists, and I did not speak out— Because I was not a Trade Unionist.

Then they came for the Jews, and I did not speak out— Because I was not a Jew.

Then they came for me—and there was no one left to speak for me.[1]

The Nazis indeed came for Niemöller in 1937. After being jailed for a time and then released, he was arrested again by the

Gestapo in 1938 and imprisoned in concentration camps until the end of the war. Niemöller's quote reflects his view that "Germans—in particular . . . the leaders of the Protestant churches—had been complicit through their silence in the Nazi imprisonment, persecution, and murder of millions of people."[2]

Yet Niemöller and other pastors had confronted Hitler over his efforts to purge "everything un-German . . . from the church."[3] In an intense encounter with Niemöller and several church leaders, the Führer had screamed, "I will protect the German people. You pastors should worry about getting people to heaven and leave this world to me."

As the churchmen were leaving the meeting, Niemöller looked straight at Hitler and said, "A moment ago, Herr Hitler, you told us that you would take care of the German people. But as Christians and men of the church we too have a responsibility for the German people, laid upon us by God. Neither you nor anyone else can take that away from us."[4]

Sadly, not all German pastors had such courage. In fact, after the meeting with Hitler, many of the church leaders were upset with Niemöller.

Heroic Christian leaders during the Nazi era—including Bonhoeffer, Niemöller, and the Catholic philosopher Dietrich von Hildebrand—had a comprehensive vision of Christ's intention for his church. Niemöller had confronted Hitler with the church's pastoral calling, but he also understood its prophetic mission. That mission would see Bonhoeffer executed and Niemöller imprisoned.

CORRUPTING THE CHURCH

What had alarmed church leaders such as Bonhoeffer, Niemöller, and Hildebrand was the nazification of the German church in all its forms. In the eyes of the Nazis, German Christians would constitute "the church of the *Volk*," a fellowship of Aryan purity. In other words, the church would simply become an extension of the Nazi Party and its worldview. Thus proclaimed a banner at a German Christians rally in Berlin in 1931: "One Reich, One People, One Church."

In his biography of Dietrich Bonhoeffer, Eric Metaxas writes that Reinhold Krause, a leader and speaker at the rally, "demanded that the German church must once and for all divest itself of every hint of Jewishness. . . . The New Testament must be revised . . . [to] present a Jesus 'corresponding entirely with the demands of National Socialism.'"[5]

If Churchill was a "flying buttress" in his support of the church from the outside (as he once described himself), Hitler was a wrecking ball. He wanted to demolish the walls so he could build a church more suited to his vision for the world, a church whose doctrine he could use to manipulate and control the spiritual lives of his people.

The true church rests on the authority of the Bible. Hitler's church would have rested on the "authority" of his distorted view of Scripture. In a letter dated April 21, 1939, one of Hitler's secretaries, Christa Schroeder, describes Hitler's distorted view of the Bible and its value and purpose.

> Christianity is founded on knowledge two thousand years old— knowledge blurred and confused by mysticism and the occult (like the Bible parables). The question is: Why can't Christian ideas be updated using the knowledge of the present day?[6]

A closer study of *Mein Kampf* shows that Hitler saw little value in Christian faith at all.

> Christianity also could not content itself with building up its own altar; it was compelled to proceed to destroying the heathen altars. Only out of this fanatical intolerance could an apodictic creed form itself; and this intolerance is even its absolute presupposition. . . .

The individual may state with pain today that with the appearance of Christianity the first spiritual terror has been brought into the much freer old world, but he will not be able to deny the fact that since then the world has been threatened and dominated by this compulsion, and that compulsion is broken only by compulsion, and terror by terror. Only then can a new condition be created by construction.[7]

Hitler's intent in *Mein Kampf* is clear. He proposes the creation of a new, more modern faith based on his own political beliefs.

Hitler openly threatened the church—not only in *Mein Kampf* but also publicly in speeches. On one such occasion, he drew a clear distinction between the responsibilities of the church and the state, professing that the state was to be a law unto itself.

> The National Socialist State will relentlessly deal with those priests who, instead of serving the Lord, see their mission in propagating derisive comments on our present Reich, its institutions, or its leading men. It will bring to their attention the fact that the destruction of this State will not be tolerated. . . . To destroy the enemies of the State is the duty of the State.[8]

Significant voices in the German church attempted to stand against what Hitler was promoting. Many who did, such as Dietrich Bonhoeffer, paid with their lives. In July 1933 Hitler unconstitutionally forced new church elections, and Bonhoeffer made every attempt to muster support for independent, non-Nazi candidates. Sadly, his efforts were in vain. Hitler had rigged the election, and an overwhelming majority of key church positions went to leaders who were firmly in the Nazi camp.

Following the election, Bonhoeffer became involved in the Bethel Confession, which opposed the German Christian movement and affirmed God's faithfulness to the Jews as his chosen people. Bonhoeffer helped to craft the confession, which drew definite distinctions between Christianity and "Germanism," to borrow Bonhoeffer's phrase.[9] The statement was then submitted to a group of prominent theologians for review. What happened next was profoundly disappointing.

"By the time they were through," writes Eric Metaxas, "every bright line was blurred; every sharp edge of difference filed down; and every point blunted. Bonhoeffer was so horrified that he refused to work on the final draft. When it was completed, he refused to sign it."[10]

In September 1933, Bonhoeffer, along with Martin Niemöller, helped to form the Pastors' Emergency League (*Pfarrernotbund*) in an attempt to unite German evangelical theologians, pastors, and church officials against the introduction into the church of the so-called Aryan paragraph, "which called for the exclusion from the church of all Christians with Jewish ancestry . . . [and] had the egregious effect of making race a direct criterion for church membership."[11] The Emergency League became the forerunner of the Confessing Church, which openly promoted Jesus, not the Führer, as head of the church.

The point became moot later that month with the reorganization of the Protestant Church and the establishment of the Nazi-submissive German Evangelical Church, both of which freely adopted the Aryan paragraph, prohibiting non-Aryans from holding parish posts. In the new order, Bonhoeffer was offered a parish post in Berlin, but he bluntly refused in protest of the Aryan policy.

Bonhoeffer saw the danger of Hitler's ideology, and he was aware of the concentration camps springing up all over Eastern Europe. He was determined to warn the world of what Hitler was really up to, hoping to rouse support from the Allies. His brother-in-law, Hans von Dohnányi, helped him by making him a nominal agent in the Abwehr, Germany's military intelligence organization, which exempted him from conscription into the German army and allowed him to travel outside Germany. Within the Abwehr, Dohnányi introduced Bonhoeffer to a group seeking to overthrow Hitler and reverse the damage he had done in Germany.

In April 1943, Bonhoeffer was arrested by the Gestapo, who had become suspicious of his activities within the Abwehr. He was held at a prison in Berlin, where he was interrogated. After a high-level plot to assassinate Hitler failed on July 20, 1944, some documents were discovered linking Bonhoeffer to the plan.

As the war neared its end, Bonhoeffer was transferred to the Buchenwald concentration camp, and then to Flossenbürg, where on April 9, 1945, he was executed by hanging, along with other July 20 conspirators.

Years later, Dr. H. Fischer-Hüllstrung, a Nazi physician at Flossenbürg, remembered what he had observed on the day of Bonhoeffer's execution.

> I saw Pastor Bonhoeffer . . . kneeling on the floor praying fervently to his God. I was most deeply moved by the way this unusually lovable man prayed, so devout and so certain that God heard his prayer. At the place of execution, he again said a short prayer and then climbed the steps to the gallows, brave and composed. His death ensued after a few seconds. In the almost fifty years that I worked as a doctor, I have hardly ever seen a man die so entirely submissive to the will of God.[12]

One of Hitler's great aims was to silence the church's prophetic voice. To mute those who were speaking out against the regime, the Nazis followed a progression that is often still used today in political debate: *caricature* ⟶ *marginalize* ⟶ *vilify* ⟶ *criminalize* ⟶ *eliminate*.

Goebbels's propagandists honed the art of caricature to new levels. Their favorite targets were Jews, whose countenances were depicted with exaggerated features. Any clergy who refused to preach the doctrine reworked by Nazi theologians were depicted as ignorant buffoons who stood in the way of progress.

In 1937 Hans Kerrl, Nazi minister for church affairs, in response to the assertion that "Christianity consists in faith in Christ as the Son of God," said, "That makes me laugh."[13]

"Christianity is not dependent upon the Apostles' Creed," Kerrl continued. "True Christianity is represented by the [Nazi] party, and the German people are now called by the party and especially by the Führer to a real Christianity." Hitler, he proclaimed, "is the herald of a new revelation."[14]

Thus, church leaders who would not bow to the "new revelation" had to be marginalized. They were removed from their pulpits and driven underground. The leaders and church members who followed them were vilified, belittled as people who could not keep up with the times. Followers of Christ were characterized as people who would corrupt the new Nazi-inspired cultural purity. This led to the criminalization of the true church in Germany. Some of its leaders were already in concentration camps before the Holocaust began.

Bruce Walker notes that the primary institutional opposition to the Nazis came not "from universities or science or art or literature or radio or newspapers, but only from religiously serious people."[15]

As part of the Nazis' plan to silence this prophetic voice, Dachau was established in 1933 as the first concentration camp. By 1940, Dachau included a "clergy barracks." More than a thousand Catholic priests and Protestant ministers died at Dachau alone.

Albert Einstein observed firsthand the valiant role played by the genuine church:

Having always been an ardent partisan of freedom, I turned to the Universities, as soon as the revolution broke out in Germany, to find the Universities took refuge in silence. I then turned to the editors of powerful newspapers, who, but lately in flowing articles, had claimed to be the faithful champions of liberty. These men, as well as the Universities, were reduced to silence in a few weeks. I then addressed myself to the authors individually, to those who passed themselves off as the intellectual guides of Germany, and among whom many had frequently discussed the question of freedom and its place in modern life. They are in their turn very dumb. Only the Church opposed the fight which Hitler was waging against liberty. Till then I had no interest in the Church, but now I feel great admiration and am truly attracted to the Church which had the persistent courage to fight for spiritual truth and moral freedom. I feel obliged to confess that I now admire what I used to consider of little value.[16]

The Nazis also tried to use the Bible to force German Christians into line. Some quoted the apostle Paul's words in Romans 13:1-2:

> Let every person be subject to the governing authorities. For there is no authority except from God, and those that exist have been instituted by God. Therefore he who resists the authorities resists what God has appointed, and those who resist will incur judgment.[17]

The National Socialist government of Germany took control of the church and forced their religious leaders to swear the Hitler Oath: pledging allegiance, not to the flag or the government or even to the country, but to Adolf Hitler himself; recognizing Hitler as the supreme authority; and implementing the Aryan paragraph. The Nazis contended that God, as the Creator, had appointed Hitler as Führer; therefore, resistance was in direct violation of God's will. They corrupted Paul's words in Romans 13:3-5.

> For rulers are not a terror to good conduct, but to bad. Would you have no fear of him who is in authority? Then do what is good,

and you will receive his approval, for he is God's servant for your good. But if you do wrong, be afraid, for he does not bear the sword in vain; he is the servant of God to execute his wrath on the wrongdoer. Therefore one must be subject, not only to avoid God's wrath but also for the sake of conscience.[18]

The Nazis saw this as divine sanction to exact justice on those who either refused to take the oath or who dared to say anything against the new regime.

AUTHORITY VERSUS AUTHORITARIANISM

The Nazi distortion occurred because of their ignorance—or willful disregard—of the differences between *authority* and *power*. They confused authoritarianism with true authority. Lucifer was the first to discover that being cut off from God means losing one's authority, and he was the first to undertake a perpetual quest for raw power in an attempt to fill the void and remain significant.[19]

Since Eden, the human race, created in the very image of God himself, was intended to use its God-granted authority to bless the entire creation. The rebellion in the Garden severed humanity from its right relationship with God. Cain, exerting raw power without the sanction of authority, killed Abel and was driven into the land of Nod, where he became terrified of the power that others might use against him.

Therein lies the contrast between the kingdoms: The Kingdom of God is the realm of *true authority*; the kingdom of Satan is seen in the tyranny of *raw power*. Churchill and Hitler, in their time, were primary characters in this ongoing parable of authority and power. Though Hitler clearly did not understand the importance of transcendent authority, Churchill did. In 1931, as Churchill contemplated the future "fifty years hence," he fretted about the dangers of power in human hands.

Without an equal growth of Mercy, Pity, Peace and Love, Science herself may destroy all that makes human life majestic and tolerable. There never was a time when the inherent virtue of human beings required more strong and confident expression in daily life; there never was a time when the hope of immortality and the disdain of earthly power and achievement were more necessary for the safety of the children of men.[20]

Authority shows itself in constructive power, whereas raw power is inevitably destructive, as Hitler and the Nazis amply demonstrated. Authority is granted from the higher to the lower, but power is seized. Authority is given to the humble, those under authority; power is snatched by the proud, who acknowledge no authority over themselves. Authority is sustained through relationship, which is why Churchill devoted so much time to communicating and to being among the people. Raw power, on the other hand, is sustained through four control mechanisms: *manipulation*, *condemnation*, *intimidation*, and *domination*, skills that Hitler and the Nazis honed to a sharp point.

As we have seen, Nazism crushed the German soul that had once given the world spiritual treasures. Churchill knew that heartless humanity was its own greatest threat. "A nation without conscience is a nation without a soul," he said. "A nation without a soul is a nation that cannot live."[21]

Management guru Jim Collins sums up the difference between the authority of true leadership and the coercive nature of raw power: "If I put a loaded gun to your head, I can get you to do things you might not otherwise do, but I've not practiced leadership; I've exercised power. *True leadership only exists if people follow when they have the freedom not to.*"[22]

Governments are given authority to establish order. Without true authority, nations fall into chaos. The church, in God's plan, is a conduit of grace. When the church tries to become the enforcer of law, it moves away from this high calling. God grants authority to governments to enact and enforce justice and extend mercy by protecting the innocent. Only then is civil government truly authoritative and not merely authoritarian.

We see this in the Old Testament with Israel and its first king, Saul. God gave Saul the same mandate that every leader has: the right to govern within the confines of God's Ten Commandments.

1. I am the LORD your God. Do not worship any other god but me.
2. Do not make idols of any kind.
3. Do not misuse the name of the LORD your God.
4. Remember to observe the Sabbath day by keeping it holy.
5. Honor your father and mother.
6. Do not murder.
7. Do not commit adultery.
8. Do not steal.
9. Do not testify falsely against your neighbor.
10. Do not covet your neighbor's house. Do not covet your neighbor's wife . . . or anything that belongs to your neighbor.[23]

The Ten Commandments are foundational for civilized nations. Hitler's regime brazenly broke every one of them. Once the Nazis severed themselves from God's universal laws, all they had left was the naked abuse of power.

10

Nazism and the German Disaster

Another time of testing has come. Another day of
reckoning is here. This is a testing and a reckoning . . .
that could prove even more decisive than earlier trials.

OS GUINNESS, *A FREE PEOPLE'S SUICIDE*

HOW DID GERMANY, a nation with such a rich theological and
cultural heritage, come to such disastrous ruin? Given the similarities between Churchill's age and our own, we must consider
how a nation steeped in theology, art, and scientific and technical achievement could collapse at the feet of Hitler and Nazism.
Why did important segments of the church ignore the warning
signs? Why did so many in the church allow themselves to be
led astray?

Today, many people believe that Christian civilization is once
again being weighed in the balance. Mary Eberstadt, senior fellow at the Ethics and Public Policy Center in Washington, DC,
describes the situation like this:

Some time back, the great majority of people living in what still broadly can be called Western civilization believed in certain things: *God created the world; He has a plan for humanity; He promises everlasting life to those who live by His Word;* and other items of faith that Judeo-Christianity bequeathed to the world. Today . . . no great majority continues to believe in all such particulars.[1]

Harvard sociologist Samuel Huntington refers to "the fragility of nations," as "national identities, like other identities, are constructed and deconstructed, upgraded and downgraded, embraced and rejected . . . with a growing gap between . . . cosmopolitan and transnational commitments and . . . highly nationalist and patriotic values."[2]

Anthony Daniels (writing under the pseudonym Theodore Dalrymple), a retired psychiatrist and physician who spent his career working in emerging nations and serving institutions in Britain's social welfare system, ties the destruction of civil society to a progressive breakdown in the "constitutional, traditional, institutional, and social restraints on . . . evil."[3] Being "unconventional," breaking taboos, and opposing traditional social rules are now "terms of the highest praise in the vocabulary of modern critics."[4] Yet the consequences of this breakdown in moral restraint are simple and obvious: "When the barriers to evil are brought down, it flourishes."[5]

Daniels also notes that the locus of control has moved from the external to the internal. "In the worst dictatorships, some of the evil that ordinary men and women do, they do out of fear of not committing it. There, goodness requires heroism." But now, in our current postmodern culture, "instead of one dictator, . . . there are thousands, each the absolute ruler of his own little sphere. . . . Perhaps the most alarming feature of this low-level but endemic evil . . . is that it is unforced and spontaneous."

After everything he observed, Daniels concluded, "Never again will I be tempted to believe in the fundamental goodness of man, or that evil is something exceptional or alien to human nature."[6]

Prime Minister Margaret Thatcher, addressing the Church of Scotland General Assembly in 1988, said, "I think back to many discussions in my early life when we all agreed that if you try to take the fruits of Christianity without its roots, the fruits will wither. And they will not come again unless you nurture the roots."[7] Far from nurturing the roots of Christian civilization in our day, much of what our culture now embraces seems more like an herbicide.

Prime Minister David Cameron, expressing his desire "in this ever more secular age" that Britain be regarded as a "Christian country," has called for "expanding the role of faith-based organisations" in the nation. "People who . . . advocate some sort of secular neutrality fail to grasp the consequences of that neutrality," he said in remarks that reflect almost Churchillian insight.[8]

Seeing that people such as Churchill and other civilization-saving leaders have seemed to appear at just the right time throughout history gives us hope that God has such leadership in the wings in our critical hour.

The Bible has a phrase for these timely occurrences: *the fullness of time.* Jesus, for example, was born "when the fullness of time had come," according to the apostle Paul.[9] In line with God's purpose, human history builds to climactic moments. God often positions human leaders strategically to keep the course of history on track and prevent the derailing of his ultimate purpose.

It can be discouraging when those leaders are not readily apparent, but noted historian Will Durant expressed optimism in his day that "the very excess of our present paganism may warrant some hope that it will not long endure."[10] That hope rests on the shoulders of leaders whom God may raise up with the qualities of a Winston Churchill.

Many observers of our contemporary situation draw parallels

between the present array of crises imperiling Western civilization—and all orderly societies everywhere—and those of the Nazi era, though most seem to focus primarily on jihadist terrorism as the present image of Nazi cruelty. In Churchill's day, many wondered if they would continue to live under the freedoms of Judeo-Christian civilization or fall under the tyranny of the Third Reich. In our day, the question is whether the world will live according to Christ's Kingdom of love and grace or under a caliphate of legalism enforced by terror. But it's not as simple as that. We find broader resemblances between the contemporary forces of repression and that of the Nazis.

THE FOUR Ds

When the Second World War ended, the Allied task force charged with restoring German liberty, order, and culture had to look at the broader picture. Shutting down the military machine that had slaughtered and terrorized millions was only part of the problem. The seeds for Nazism had been sown deeply into the German soul since at least the 1920s, and the spiritual, moral, and philosophical malignancies that had fed the cancer of Nazism had been growing and spreading for more than a century. The Nazi worldview had shaped family, education, law, entertainment, media, government, business, and even theology and the church, as we have seen.

In order to address the problem holistically, Great Britain, the United States, and the Soviet Union instituted the 1945 Potsdam Agreement to establish categories for German restoration. There were variations in the precise wording, but the general agreement encompassed four major groupings:

- Demilitarization—disarming and disbanding German military forces
- Denazification—rooting out Nazi doctrine from German institutions

- Decartelization—eliminating cartels and monopolies that had provided such a facile tool in Nazi hands for the construction of their war machine
- Democracy—returning the German government to a democratic foundation

Why were the Four Ds necessary? How had Germany, once a land of such promise, veered so far from its highest ideals?

Germany had been the seedbed of the Protestant Reformation, the nesting place of deep spiritual movements and a verdant forest of biblical study. By the time the Nazis came along to scour the landscape, deforestation was already well underway through forces that, in some ways, parallel those in Jesus' parable of the farmer scattering seed in Matthew 13:1-9. As the sower went along casting his seed, some of it "fell among thorns that grew up and choked out the tender plants."" In the late nineteenth and early twentieth century in Germany, as Christians hurled the good seed of the gospel throughout the land, the ravenous ideologies of racialism, militarism, Teutonic mythology, and a distorted messiah complex quickly swallowed it up.

Spiritual, moral, ethical, social, cultural, and political deforestation resulted. By examining the steps through which nazification occurred in Germany, we can see how similar devastation might arise in our contemporary culture.

Knocking down the windbreaks

People living on the prairies in the United States and Canada in the 1930s knew how to appreciate windbreaks. Dust storms during that time were so intense that the era became known as the Dirty Thirties. However, the problem wasn't merely the gritty sting of flying topsoil but the fact that the winds reduced fertile land to barren ground. Farmers soon learned how to raise hedge barriers that would limit the impact of the gales.

Johann Sebastian Bach, born in 1685, could be the poster child for all that was good in the soul of German Christianity. "The aim and final end of all music," he said, "should be none other than the glory of God and the refreshment of the soul."[12] He inscribed most of his compositions with the letters *SDG*, representing the Latin words, *soli Deo gloria* (to God alone be glory).

Bach lived long enough to see the early incursions of the spiritual-cultural desert as the reductive-destructive forces of the Enlightenment began to batter the windbreaks. Taking Bach's transcendent vision of music for God's glory, Enlightenment theoreticians such as Charles Burney whittled it down to "the art of pleasing," "an innocent luxury," and a "gratification of the sense of hearing."[13] Immanuel Kant was even more demeaning when he said that instrumental music is an art that "merely plays with the sensations."[14] It was no longer all about God but all about human experience.

Bach worked hard in his day to build up the windbreaks that sheltered the arts and nourished the German soul.

> Bach knew that the times were changing. In [his] later works, he was erecting monuments upholding the high view of music bequeathed to him by his ancestors: music as a "refreshment of spirit" for his neighbor, a tool for the proclamation of the gospel, and a way of giving glory to God. In the world around him, that view was rapidly giving way to a lower view of music spawned by the Enlightenment.[15]

In attempting to make music pleasing to the German ear, the new Enlightenment composers actually contributed to the withering of the German soul. Wagner's operas, though musically rich, were philosophically and spiritually devastating. It's no wonder that he was Hitler's favorite composer and that listening to a Wagner opera stirred a sinister call in the young Adolf. It was the siren song of the Valkyries, not the call of the Holy Spirit, that summoned Hitler to his destiny.

The same reductive theories that struck the arts also began to blow at gale force against the windbreak of sound theological doctrine, and by the late nineteenth century, Germany's theological windbreaks had largely been uprooted. Eventually, the arid tenets of theological scientism—that matters of the human spirit can be evaluated empirically, that any idea of transcendent causality should be summarily dismissed, that the primary ethic of scientific research and application should be mere utility, and that anyone challenging such ideas deserves no place in secular institutions—stretched across the landscape. In fact, one might argue that the perversion of science, which Churchill found to be so distressing and such a threat to civilization, resulted from the perversion of theology, the "queen of sciences."

German theologian J. S. Semler played a key role in the assault on theology. Milton Terry refers to Semler as "the father of the destructive school of German Rationalism" in hermeneutics (biblical interpretation) and theology, though he also says that Semler "was surprised at the use others made of his critical principles." Semler regarded the Bible's reporting of miracles and the ideas of sacrificial atonement, Christ's resurrection, the existence of angels, and the coming of a final judgment as "an accommodation to the superstitious notions, prejudices, and ignorance of the times. The supernatural was thus set aside."[16]

Semler fragmented biblical scholarship by severing the sacred text from the Holy Spirit's inspiration and by separating religion and theology. Religion was a private matter, "largely a matter of personal taste, and should be cultivated as individual feeling and the dictates of reason prompted."[17]

Germany was not the only place where Semler's ideas took root. As William Wilberforce crusaded in the British Parliament for the end of the slave trade, Lord Melbourne reportedly said that "things have come to a pretty pass when religion is allowed to invade public life."[18] But we should not blame it all on Semler, writes Milton Terry. Some German theologians "were thoroughly infected with the leaven of English deism and French infidelity, and . . . writings [that] breathed the most offensive spirit of hostility to all accepted Christian doctrine."[19] Semler's work, in the hands of others, turned into "instruments for the destruction of all faith in divine revelation."[20]

The concepts of rationalism crescendoed in the nineteenth century, reaching an explosive pitch with the publication of Darwin's theories and shaping the *Zeitgeist* into which Adolf Hitler was born and educated. Nineteenth-century German theologians widened the divide between the Old and New Testaments forged by their Enlightenment predecessors. Thus, writes Leon Poliakov in *The Aryan Myth*, "the fathers prepared the ground for the heresies of the children."[21]

The German psyche, fueled by Teutonic myths, yearned for the mystical and the supernatural. Even if the Bible could be dismissed, the mystical longings could not. Hitlerism celebrated the demotion of biblical authority wrought by theological scientism, but it also sought to fill the spiritual void for which the German soul hungered and thirsted.

The devastating gales of Wagnerism, Nietzscheism, and Darwinism

RICHARD WAGNER

Hitler acknowledged that Richard Wagner, the nineteenth-century Bayreuth composer, was the source of his worldview and the inspirer of his destiny. In *Mein Kampf*, Hitler declares that he was "captivated" by the composer. Hitler's "youthful enthusiasm for the master of Bayreuth knew no bounds."[22] He retained that enthusiasm for the rest of his life. "Wagner's line of thought is intimately familiar to me," Hitler said. "At every stage of my life I come back to him."[23]

Part of Wagner's appeal to the Nazi leader lay in the composer's racialist undertones. Among the ideas that informed Wagner's art were Schopenhauer's anti-Jewish metaphysics and Gobineau's racial theories. As Leon Poliakov notes, Wagner's work "was a mixture of musical, ideological, theatrical and religious themes" that "could not have been better suited to the needs of the time." Furthermore, "in a society searching for new myths and avid for undiscovered thrills," Wagner's compositions and productions "aroused a frenzy of enthusiasm."[24]

Thus, Wagner's music "unleashed the savagery of the Nazis," in the words of Thomas Mann.[25] Spiritually, writes Mann, "Wagner's work was a clear proclamation of that 'metapolitical' movement which today terrorizes the world."[26]

Listening to Wagner propelled Adolf Hitler and his devotees towards sheer triumphalism in their conviction that Aryan beliefs and cultural forms had every right to sweep the entire world into its superior civilization. Millions were under the spell that Wagner, long-dead, had helped weave. "Under the Third Reich," writes Geoffrey Wheatcroft, "Bayreuth became a temple of National Socialist art."[27]

Hitler met the Wagner family in Bayreuth in 1923 when he came "to pay homage to the composer's memory" and to meet Wagner's son-in-law, Houston Stewart Chamberlain (who, incidentally, was also Neville Chamberlain's cousin). Houston Chamberlain's "sub-Darwinian eugenics, mystical championing of pure Aryan blood, and hatred of Jews" appealed to Hitler and would later cause him to be seen by many Nazis as "the seer and herald of the Third Reich."[28] Within a year of Hitler's 1923 visit, "some devotees of Wagner's music were already claiming that it was being hijacked for unsavoury political purposes."[29]

Thereafter, Hitler made annual pilgrimages to Bayreuth. As members of the Wagner family and the Bayreuth community learned more about Hitler and his vision, they began to view him as akin to Wagner's *Parsifal* redeemer, who would save Germany.

In response to this adulation, Hitler reportedly declared, "From *Parsifal* I build my religion, a sacred service in ceremonial form without theological trappings."[30]

Thus, through Nazism's appropriation of his work, Wagner provided the hymnody and vast orchestrations for the emerging liturgies of neopaganism, of which the spectacular Nazi rallies were prime examples.

FRIEDRICH NIETZSCHE

As a young man, Nietzsche idolized Wagner; but later in life, he turned against him with an attitude approaching violence—especially as Nietzsche's mind deteriorated. Part of the problem was religious: While Wagner continued to use mystical imagery in his operas, Nietzsche had become a militant atheist for whom "belief in God [was] no longer possible, due to such nineteenth-century factors as the dominance of the historical-critical method of reading Scripture, the rise of modern science (and thus the rise of incredulity towards anything miraculous), the growing sense that Scripture is merely a human product, and the idea that God is the creation of wish projection."[31] As Nietzsche himself wrote:

> God is dead. God remains dead. And we have killed him.
>
> How shall we comfort ourselves, the murderers of all murderers? What was holiest and mightiest of all that the world has yet owned has bled to death under our knives: who will wipe this blood off us? What water is there for us to clean ourselves? What festivals of atonement, what sacred games shall we have to invent? Is not the greatness of this deed too great for us? Must we ourselves not become gods simply to appear worthy of it?[32]

The Nazis created a god in their own image and used him to manipulate and control the masses. Hitler's disciples wrote new scriptures supportive of Nazi thought, and they force-fed the hungry German soul with their newly revealed insights into ancient wisdom.

Another of Nietzsche's ideas added to the poison: *the will to power*. According to Nietzsche, the passion for power over others drives every human thought and behavior. No matter how noble or how seemingly altruistic an action is, the motive is always to impose one's will on other people. For Nietzsche, every individual is an egotist.

From this, the Nazi theoreticians deduced that power is the justification for all things because it is simply the way things are.

Nietzsche had a passionate vision of the future in which the message of Christ would be eradicated from Europe and European society and culture would be freed from its "enslavement" to Christianity. This would lead to Nietzsche's apocalyptic hope—the coming of the *Übermensch* (superman)—the ultimate expression of the will to power. Because, for Nietzsche, God is dead, humanity is left as the loftiest form of being. However, even within the human race, there would arise a manifestation of mankind that would be superior to all—the *Übermensch*.

The *Übermensch* would be free from the restraints and accountability that belong to the notion of absolute truth because, ultimately, power determines truth. There is no "higher self"; the greatest self is that which lives fully and interacts with existential reality, which is all that exists and thus all that matters.

In the pages of *Mein Kampf*, Hitler built on Nietzsche's concepts:

A stronger race (*Geschlecht*) will supplant the weaker, since the drive for life in its final form will decimate every ridiculous fetter of the so-called humaneness of individuals, in order to make place for the humaneness of nature, which destroys the weak to make place for the strong.[33]

CHARLES DARWIN

We have already examined in detail the link between Hitler and Darwinism. Here, we will simply summarize the Darwinian presuppositions that most affected Hitler and his Nazi ideology.

In the first edition of *On the Origin of Species*, Darwin used the term *natural selection* to explain his theory of evolution. But he was somewhat ambivalent about the term, "as it seems to imply conscious choice."[34] He came to prefer the phrase "survival of the fittest," which he adapted from Herbert Spencer's *Principles of Biology* (1866) and introduced to *On the Origin of Species* in the 1869 edition.

Darwin found Spencer's term more appealing because it emphasized the mechanical (impersonal, automatic) processes of nature rather than the teleological (which implies purpose or design—and thus a designer). Darwin had abandoned the notion of the transcendent, and he found that Spencer's label meshed well with *natural* selection but said it better.

Hitler, on the other hand, was teleological in his theorizing. He believed that evolution was indeed moving towards a grand purpose—the crowning emergence of the Aryan *Übermensch*. Thus, the survival of the fittest necessitated the classification of the human species to distinguish the "superior" from the "inferior." The superior would then assume responsibility for weeding out the inferior through eugenics and extermination so that these people would not weaken the human gene pool and complicate the path to the emergence of the perfect Aryan.

Spencer was also instrumental in laying a foundation for social Darwinism. In *The Man versus the State*, he describes how, through the survival of the fittest, "the militant type of society becomes characterized by profound confidence in the governing power, joined with a loyalty causing submission to it in all matters whatever."[35] Hitler interwove Darwinian biological evolution with Spencerian social evolution in building the Third Reich.

There must tend to be established among those who speculate about political affairs in a militant society, a theory giving form to the needful ideas and feelings; accompanied by assertions that the law-giver if not divine in nature is divinely directed, and that unlimited obedience to him is divinely ordered.[36]

Hitler regarded himself as the vessel chosen by the gods, or by the primal evolutionary forces, to intervene in the pace of evolution and to be its guardian and accelerator. "In a 1923 speech," writes Richard Weikart, "Hitler explained the relationship between struggle and right."

Decisive [in history] is the power that the peoples (*Volker*) have within them; it turns out that the stronger before God and the world has the right to impose its will. . . . All of nature is a constant struggle between power and weakness, a constant triumph of the strong over the weak.[37]

Some scholars have sought to reason through Darwinism to its logical conclusion. Ultimately, the outcome of "natural selection" or "survival of the fittest" is that "only from death on a genocidal scale could the few progress."[38]

Ultimately, the issue of who should die and who should live came down to decisions about who was "productive" or "unproductive." Humans who could not produce according to Nazi standards would be eliminated. "Productivity" was not merely about nuts and bolts, manufacturing and construction, but about society itself. Those races that diminished society and cultural creativity—as defined by the Nazis—should die, along with the mentally and physically disabled.

According to the Nazis' eugenic morality, weeding out obstacles to the advancement of human evolution was the most responsible and humane thing to do and would contribute to a greater quality of human life.

With eugenics as the driving impulse and genocide as the inevitable outcome, war, among other means, was seen as essential to the struggle for evolutionary progress.

In the years between the two World Wars, Hitler enlarged on his "ethic." As he gained power in Germany, he justified his brutality on the basis of moral necessity. Preserving the races that produced high culture "is tied to the iron law of necessity," he wrote in *Mein Kampf.* Even though it might call for "harsh" methods, "it is simply the way it is!"[39] In this he echoed Nietzsche as well as Darwin.

A BOILING STEW

We began this chapter with the question of how Germany, with its rich Christian history, could fall into such a spiritual disaster. Historian Konrad Heiden believes that it's not surprising.

> Germany was the perfect place for this development. In almost no other country were so many "miracles" performed, so many ghosts conjured, so many illnesses cured by magnetism, so many horoscopes read, between the two World Wars.[40]

Flavored by the bitter herbs of Wagnerism, Nietzscheism, and Darwinism, and spiced with seeds of resentment left over from the First World War, Hitler's Nazi ideology became a boiling stew of mysticism, spiritism, scientism, evolutionism, triumphalism, and nationalism.

Churchill observed these phenomena in Germany with a sharp eye. A diagnostician of nations, he detected the malignancy growing in the German soul. If it were not stopped, he knew it would metastasize until it consumed not only the European continent and Britain, but Western civilization itself.

11

Churchill's Urgent Concern— and Ours

Civilisation is hideously fragile, you know that. There's
not much between us and the horrors underneath.
Just about a coat of varnish, wouldn't you say?

C. P. SNOW, *A COAT OF VARNISH*

WINSTON CHURCHILL had good cause to be concerned about the survival of Christian civilization. The Aryan cancer growing in Germany was affecting British society as well. Churchill believed in the exceptionalism of the Judeo-Christian worldview that had gifted Britain with its finest values. Therefore, in Churchill's mind at least, Hitler had to be defeated at all costs for the sake of Christian civilization.

> Civilisation will not last, freedom will not survive, peace will not be kept, unless a very large majority of mankind unite together to defend them and show themselves possessed of a constabulary power before which barbaric and atavistic forces will stand in awe.[1]

As a student of history, Churchill would have known the work of one of his contemporaries, Oxford historian Arnold Toynbee, who theorized about the inevitability and process of civilizational decline and death. As Churchill pondered the fate of his own nation, he might have been especially concerned about Toynbee's idea that civilizations commit suicide rather than perishing through murder.

Churchill knew there could be no ambiguity in his policy towards the Nazis. It was clear-cut: order or chaos, light or dark, good or evil. The contemporary doctrines of equivalency by which all things are of equal truth—then popular among British intellectuals—were unthinkable. Equivalency fosters ambiguity; ambiguity gives birth to confusion; and confusion breeds disaster, as the early twenty-first century has already shown. This is surely part of what Harvard political scientist Samuel Huntington means when he writes: "Efforts to define national interest presuppose agreement on the nature of the country whose interests are to be defined. . . . National interest derives from national identity. *We have to know who we are before we can know what our interests are.*"[2] Equivalency doesn't know what to fight for or where. Foreign policy and the defense of a nation and its civilization can get lost in relativistic fog.

John Maynard Keynes, the economist who gave the world Keynesian economics, commented on the prevailing intellectual climate of his time.

> The thinness and superficiality, as well as the falsity, of our view of man's heart became, as it now seems to me, more obvious. . . . Our comments on life and affairs were bright and amusing, but brittle . . . because there was no solid diagnosis of human nature underlying them. [Bertrand Russell] in particular sustained simultaneously a pair of opinions ludicrously incompatible.[3]

Winston Churchill did not dawdle about in an obscuring haze of "opinions ludicrously incompatible," searching for a policy. He knew who he was, and he knew the identity of his nation. Therefore, he understood clearly what the struggle with the Nazis was about—the survival of Christian civilization. As far as Churchill was concerned, one does not negotiate with the devil and hell.

> We have but one aim and one single irrevocable purpose. We are resolved to destroy Hitler and every vestige of the Nazi regime. From this nothing will turn us. Nothing. We will never parley; we will never negotiate with Hitler or any of his gang. We shall fight him by land; we shall fight him by sea; we shall fight him in the air, until, with God's help we have rid the earth of his shadow and liberated its peoples from his yoke. Any man or State who fights on against Nazism will have our aid. Any man or State who marches with Hitler is our foe.[4]

Churchill loathed Nazism because he recognized that it would destroy the rich fruit arising from Christian civilization that had blessed many nations. He recognized that Hitler's aim was to hack down the very tree that had borne the healthy fruit and to replace it with another, bearing only thorns and thistles.

THEN AND NOW

There are broad similarities between the assault on Christian civilization in Churchill's day and in ours.

A fierce militaristic foe with a vision for global hegemony

Before most of the world grasped the implications of Hitler's ideology, Churchill saw into the nihilistic core of Nazism. Speaking in Devonshire in 1933, Churchill termed the Nazis "the most formidable people in the world, and now the most dangerous, a people who inculcate a form of blood-lust in their children, and lay down the doctrine that every frontier must be the starting point for invasion."[5]

Churchill equated the rise of Nazism with a return to the Dark Ages in a speech to the United States and Britain, broadcast on October 16, 1938.

> We are confronted with another theme. It is not a new theme; it leaps out upon us from the Dark Ages—racial persecution, religious intolerance, deprivation of free speech, the conception of the citizen as a mere soulless fraction of the State. To this has been added the cult of war. Children are to be taught in their earliest schooling the delights and profits of conquest and aggression. A whole mighty community has been drawn painfully, by severe privations, into a warlike frame.[6]

Many in the twenty-first century have been shocked at the intensification of global chaos. From the constant threat of terrorist attacks, to randomly exploding roadside bombs, to mass kidnappings of innocent schoolgirls, to increasing insurgencies by the stateless Islamic State, whose proponents record and post to the Internet images of beheadings and other murders, the threats to what Churchill termed Christian civilization are again growing.

In fact, the peril may be even greater than in Churchill's day. During the Second World War, the Allies faced an enemy who waged conventional warfare with identifiable lines and rules of engagement. The lines would shift, but they could always be located; and they provided clear points for the concentration of force. The conflict in the twenty-first century has become amorphous. The fury of terrorism or guerrilla warfare can erupt anywhere at any moment. And the battle lines are now spiritual, moral, ethical, and intellectual as well as brutally physical.

Internal forces that were antinomian and anti-civilizational
In Britain during the 1930s, socialism and communism veered in the direction of atheism. In our day, we've seen the rise of a mili-

tant atheism across Western culture. From the perspective of British tradition, the movements in Churchill's day were afflicted with powerful antinomian and anti-civilizational trends, as measured by Britain's traditional canons.[7]

The Bloomsbury-Cambridge elites gave intellectual affirmation to societal rejection of traditional cultural restraints. Many were hedonists who lived according to their own ethical sanctions. They distinguished between "intrinsic value" and "instrumental value." What mattered was the *intrinsic*—action taken for its own sake. Thus they were able to justify, on autocratic moral grounds, whatever brought them pleasure.

Such intellectualism troubled Winston Churchill as Hitler's power grew. Among other things, the intelligentsia in the Bloomsbury-Cambridge group disdained and scorned British tradition at precisely the time when the people of Britain needed to recognize both the rich heritage of their society and the threat that Hitler posed to it. Thus, on St. George's Day in 1933, Churchill said, "Our difficulties come from the mood of unwarrantable self-abasement into which we have been cast by a powerful section of our own intellectuals. They come from the acceptance of defeatist doctrines by a large proportion of our politicians. But what have they to offer but a vague internationalism, a squalid materialism, and the promise of impossible Utopias?"[8]

After the war, Churchill had not changed his opinion. If anything, it was stronger. During a debate in the House of Commons on October 28, 1948, he spoke of a mood in the nation "encouraged by the race of degenerate intellectuals . . . who, when they wake up every morning have looked around upon the British inheritance, whatever it was, to see what they could find to demolish, to undermine, or cast away."[9]

In 2012, Os Guinness identified a present-day mind-set that springs from what he called "a soft though decadent nihilism that devours tradition, destroys social cohesion, cheapens cultural standards, hollows moral convictions and in the years to come will produce its own dark harvest of social consequences."[10]

"The recovery of moral control and the return of spiritual order have now become the indispensable conditions of human survival," said British cultural scholar Christopher Dawson in the 1947 Gifford Lectures at Edinburgh University.[11] Christianity, said Dawson, "is the soul of Western civilization. . . . When the soul is gone, the body putrefies."[12]

A public consensus that was uninformed and naive about the threats

Richard Langworth writes that "Churchill found a natural ally in Franklin Roosevelt, . . . whose clear-sightedness regarding Hitler was more appealing to Churchill than the imaginings of his own British colleagues."[13]

Some, even among the British elites, saw Hitler as the symbol of a new dynamism taking shape in the world. Robert Boothby, an ally of Churchill's in the House of Commons, described the mood in a secret memorandum to the War Cabinet on March 20, 1940. Hitler and his followers represented to some "the incredible conception of a *movement*—young, virile, dynamic, and violent—which is advancing irresistibly to overthrow a decaying old world."[14] Hitler's open admirers in pre-war Britain ranged from Oswald Mosley, founder of the British Union of Fascists; to trendy, avant-garde writers such as Wyndham Lewis, Enid Bagnold, and Philip Gibbs; to media mogul Lord Rothermere.

Others who were not so outspoken thought that Britain could use a dose of whatever had energized Germany under the Nazis. A quarter century after the end of the First World War, the war's absurdities and horrors had been washed in a romantic light, and some in Great Britain felt that "the Germans had been gallant and brave fighters."[15] Some believed that parliamentary government, coupled with a constitutional monarchy, was a cumbersome relic and that what the British people needed was the dynamism and efficiency of the Nazis. The Cliveden Set, an influential pro-appeasement group that often met at the estate of Lady Nancy Astor in the Buckinghamshire countryside, became a symbol of the notables in British society who tilted towards Hitler in the 1930s.

Sometimes such people even found their way into Winston Churchill's home. Sisters Diana and Unity Mitford, Hitler enthusiasts, were related to Clementine Churchill. The "Mitford tribe."— as Mary Soames, the Churchills' youngest daughter, put it—was on "pleasant" terms with Winston and Clementine. My (Jonathan's) grandmother, Diana Churchill, was a bridesmaid at Diana Mitford's 1929 wedding. Diana Mitford would leave her husband later in life and pursue an open affair with Oswald Mosley. (Ironically, during the early days of the war, especially in 1940 when a German victory seemed inevitable, Mosley, as a leading fascist, was a likely candidate for prime minister once the Nazis conquered Britain.)

Mary Soames notes that Diana and Unity Mitford "went to the first of the Nuremberg rallies [staged by Josef Goebbels], where their ardour for the Führer was predictably fanned." Their parents, on the other hand, regarded Hitler and the Nazis "as a murderous gang of pests" and were "absolutely horrified" by their daughters' association with the Nazi leaders. It wasn't until 1935 that Unity Mitford met Hitler in person, "and she and Diana became part of his accepted circle." But when she introduced her mother to Hitler, Unity was disappointed when her mother wasn't impressed by him. She "does not feel his goodness and wonderfulness radiating out like we do."[16]

Diana and Unity again attended the Nuremberg rallies in 1933, the very year that Churchill was becoming increasingly vocal about Nazi rearmament and British complacency.

In 1936, after returning from the Olympic Games in Berlin, Diana Mitford dined with the Churchills at Chartwell. Just back from Germany, Diana encouraged Churchill to meet Hitler. "She thought they would get on well together—but Winston would not entertain the idea," Mary Soames recalled years later.[17]

Even as late as 1942, the midpoint of the war, Churchill was distressed by division in British society over the war. Elizabeth Nel, one of his secretaries during that period, observed that Churchill "felt our losses deeply, and threw himself anew into hitting back." But "it was the lack of complete unanimity at home that troubled him as much as anything."[18]

A complacent public that had forgotten the importance of its founding values

It wasn't only highly visible members of the aristocracy who influenced the policy of appeasement in the years leading up to the Second World War. Public opinion was also largely in favor. But the attitude of many in the 1930s—that Hitler was providing a model for energizing a nation—was a stark contradiction to the democratic principles that had developed in Britain since the thirteenth century. Hitler's vision and plan were diametrically opposed to the most cherished historical values on which British freedom rested.

Nevertheless, in 1933 students at Oxford University adopted a motion proposing *not* to go to war for king and country in the future. Apparently, the young scholars found nothing in their society worth fighting for. Voters in East Fulham handed a major defeat to the Conservative Party candidate, who was a vocal supporter of rearmament, and elected instead his opponent, who supported disarmament. Thus, as Hitler accelerated German rearmament in 1936—at a point when he could have been stopped—the British government, with heavy public support, was reducing its own military capabilities.

Much of the British press helped to mold public opinion, and though Hitler openly elaborated on his worldview and goals, many saw no need to slow him down. Among a majority of the British public, and also in Parliament, a desire to avoid another world war prevailed.

Today, there is a troubling level of historical illiteracy throughout America and Europe. Historian David McCullough raised the alarm in 1995 at a National Book Awards ceremony.

> We, in our time, are raising a new generation of Americans who, to an alarming degree, are historically illiterate. The situation is serious and sad. And it is quite real, let there be no mistake. It has been coming on for a long time, like a creeping disease, eating away at the national memory. While the clamorous popular culture races on, the American past is slipping away, out of sight and out of mind. We are losing our story, forgetting who we are and what it's taken to come this far.[19]

"What it's taken to come this far" is a commitment to the Judeo-Christian worldview that has shaped the best of the history we are now in danger of forgetting, and that has produced the fruit of Christian civilization that Churchill was so passionate about defending.

However, the source of all that good fruit is now under attack from all sides. Meanwhile, proponents of other worldviews and belief systems across the globe are zealously advancing their own causes and are committed to spreading their ideology to every nation, just as Hitler was in the 1930s.

Just as nature abhors a vacuum, so too does the human soul. As we forget who we are and where we've come from, a great void is being carved out in the soul of the West—and many other belief systems are seeking to fill the vacuum. In the ever-expanding marketplace of ideas, it's no surprise that "ancient paganism and idolatry are making a strong comeback in the midst of Western civilization."[20]

In our time, the loss of the vision for the preservation of Christian civilization that was so central to Churchill's thinking has also resulted in the devaluation of history. As Theodore Dalrymple (Anthony Daniels) observes, "Critics of social institutions and traditions . . . should always be aware that civilization needs conservation at least as much as it needs change."[21] In his time, Churchill sought to practice historical conservation, and he highlighted the importance of defeating the Nazis and other movements that might in the future imperil that civilizational order.

THE RHYME OF HISTORY

Someone once said that history doesn't repeat itself, but it does rhyme.[22] Many observers of the current global situation hear familiar chords from the age of Churchill—especially from the rise of Nazism and the run-up to the Second World War.

Military historian Victor David Hanson warns that American and European leaders "are repeating the mistakes of their 1930s predecessors."[23] Writing in *The Atlantic*, Graeme Wood says, "The Islamic State partisans have much the same allure" as Hitler did prior to the Second World War—"project[ing] an underdog quality, even when his goals were cowardly or loathsome."[24] The young ISIS fighters "believe that they are personally involved in struggles beyond their own lives, and that merely to be swept up in the drama, on the side of righteousness, is a privilege and a pleasure— especially when it is also a burden."[25] Meanwhile, *Mein Kampf* is enjoying renewed readership in Europe and elsewhere.

In the "rhyming" of history, we face once again the issues of internal decay and a fierce set of external adversaries, fired by ideology at the very moment when the Western democracies seem rudderless in a sea of doubt and ambiguity.

Multitudes are now asking the same question posed by those whom Winston Churchill awakened in the 1930s and 1940s: *Is there any hope?*

PART IV

HOPE FOR OUR TIME

12

How Churchill Kept Calm and Carried On

Laugh a little, and teach your men to laugh. . . . If you can't smile, grin. If you can't grin, keep out of the way till you can.

WINSTON CHURCHILL, TO HIS OFFICERS
IN THE TRENCHES IN FRANCE, 1916

CONTEMPORARY GLOBAL CONDITIONS have made us starkly aware of the fragile nature of civil order and the need for humanity to unite against the "barbaric and atavistic forces" mentioned by Winston Churchill.[1]

We are living in a stressful age that *New York Times* columnist Roger Cohen calls a "time of unraveling."[2] Cohen imagines a future conversation about the grim situations of the present, and writes: "It was the time of unraveling . . . a time of beheadings . . . a time of aggression . . . a time of breakup . . . a time of weakness . . . a time of hatred . . . a time of fever . . . a time of disorientation" in which "the fabric of society frayed."[3]

Democracy looked quaint or outmoded beside new authoritarianisms. Politicians, haunted by their incapacity, played on the fears of their populations, who were device-distracted or under device-driven stress. Dystopia was a vogue word, like utopia in the 20th century. The great rising nations of vast populations held the fate of the world in their hands but hardly seemed to care . . . until it was too late and people could see the Great Unraveling for what it was and what it had wrought.[4]

How, then, can we remain steady and unruffled in the civilization-battering turbulence all around us? Many people are wondering about that, as evidenced by the recent popularity of posters, T-shirts, and other objects bearing a message that symbolized British pluck during the fiery storms of the Second World War: "Keep Calm and Carry On."

For many, Winston Churchill epitomized the attitude those words convey. His life, as we have seen, was pummeled by heavy waves of adversity that could have capsized him many times, but he stayed on beam and sailed ahead.

On September 1, 1939, as Nazi troops invaded Poland, Churchill again found himself at the helm of the British navy, at the invitation of Prime Minister Neville Chamberlain. As first lord of the Admiralty, he also had a seat on the War Cabinet.

By now sixty-four years old, Churchill probably thought that his career had already crested. However, as he took up residence in Admiralty House, where he had last lived a quarter century earlier, it was really only the beginning. His destiny—the day for which his entire life had been preparing him—was yet ahead. As he scanned the rooms so familiar to him, he could still see the maps depicting positions of ships in 1915, when he had left the Admiralty after the Gallipoli disaster.

This time, however, he would meet with only acclaim. When word of his appointment reached the Admiralty Board, the order was given to send a message to all British naval stations and ships: "WINSTON IS BACK."

The last time Churchill had helmed the British navy, he had sailed into the storm of the Dardanelles controversy. This time, the first lord of the Admiralty would voyage with all his "shipmates" into a typhoon of even greater proportions. And this time Churchill would come out the victor. However, it would be a frightening and arduous journey.

The great question before him initially was how to keep his naval forces afloat amid the turbulence of the early days of the war. In less than a year, his great concern would turn to holding the British ship of state on an even keel as it was pounded by Nazi assaults. To do that, he would need to keep the nation calm, a goal he would accomplish with his speeches and his demeanor of relentless optimism and composure.

His own personality and character would be a crucial element in this enterprise. He would have to demonstrate personally how to "keep calm and carry on." The challenges he faced in forming a new government reveal the enormity of the task.

For starters, he had to put together a coalition consisting of various political parties and their leaders, all of whom he had managed to offend at some point in his long career. When he walked into the House of Commons for the first time as prime minister, his own party, the Conservatives, gave him a tepid response, not even offering a standing ovation—though they heartily applauded Neville Chamberlain.

"Meanwhile events across the Channel were moving fast," writes Churchill's daughter Mary Soames.[5] Four days after Churchill became prime minister, Nazi military forces blitzed through French defenders at Sedan. The next day, May 15, the Luftwaffe leveled Rotterdam in the Netherlands, and the Dutch army capitulated. On May 28, Belgium collapsed, and Hitler's forces surged to the Channel coast, with many of his officers eager to invade Britain. Churchill, meanwhile, had to focus on the task of getting more than 330,000 of his own troops and their allies off the French coast and back to England.

On top of all that, an even greater nightmare was taking shape in Paris, where there were signs that the French were going to cave in to the Nazis' military might and abandon the fight. Over the next few weeks, Churchill and his advisors made five perilous flights to France to try to persuade the French leaders not to give up. But their efforts were futile. The Germans captured Paris on June 14, and by June 22 the French government had signed a surrender agreement with the Nazis.

Not long after moving into the prime minister's residence at No. 10 Downing Street, Churchill invited David Margesson, the government chief whip in the House of Commons, to lunch. Margesson, a fellow Conservative, had sometimes opposed Churchill, and he had been an appeaser during the Chamberlain administration. Now, however, he was a Churchill ally, and his change of heart seemed genuine.

Clementine, however, was not so ready to forgive and forget. She had strongly opposed the appeasement policy and could still taste the gall of those years. She felt that people like Margesson had put Britain in its present precarious position.

As they sat at table, Clementine could finally no longer contain her indignation. She exploded at David Margesson, and, in Mary Soames's words, "flayed him verbally before sweeping out" of the room, with Mary in tow. Mary was "most ashamed and horrified," but she later concluded about her mother, "This outburst from the normally immaculately well-mannered Clementine is indicative of the tensions in her life at that time."[6]

Considering the huge load that both Winston and Clementine Churchill bore during this period, they could be forgiven an occasional lapse in their composure. But as the war ground on for another five grueling years, together they became a shining example of how to "keep calm and carry on."

ORIGINS AND MEANING

Posters bearing the "keep calm and carry on" slogan had been created by the Ministry of Information in 1939 as preparations for war began in earnest. More than two million placards were printed, but they were "never officially seen by the public" because the intended use was "only upon the invasion of Britain by Germany," which never happened.[7] It wasn't until 2000, when Stuart Manley, a bookstore owner in Northumberland, discovered one of the original posters while sorting through a box of old books, that the posters, and the slogan, came to public attention. Manley and his wife framed and hung the placard over their cash register, and they eventually began printing and selling copies.[8] In recent years, variations on the basic message have popped up all over, to the point of near-ubiquity.

Susannah Walker, a design historian, explains the contemporary significance of the message as "not only a distillation of a crucial moment in Britishness, but also an inspiring message from the past to the present in a time of crisis."[9]

Though Winston Churchill may never have seen one of the "keep calm and carry on" posters during his lifetime, during the Second World War he epitomized the message. Amid the greatest of upheavals, he showed that composure is a choice, an act of the will that subdues terrible thoughts and steadies frazzled emotions.

Churchill also modeled *endurance* that arose from a larger vision. He intuitively grasped the ancient truth of Solomon that people without a vision will cast off restraint and give way to chaos, through which they will ultimately perish.[10] As Churchill demonstrated during his years on the backbenches in the House of Commons, vision should inspire all of us, not just our leaders.

As London mayor Boris Johnson says of Churchill, "The point . . . is that one man can make all the difference."[11]

How, then, did Churchill "keep calm and carry on" at the very epicenter of the Allied war effort? For one thing, he believed that his entire life—with all its character-forming lessons, tempering experiences, and attitude-shaping challenges—was preparation for that destiny. The character revealed in the great moments had been formed in the small moments. Those character traits enabled Churchill to stay on an even keel and stabilize the nation through the turmoil of war.

Moreover, the spiritual lessons he had learned from Elizabeth Everest were lodged in his heart and guided his actions. As a testimony to the importance of her role in his life, Mrs. Everest's picture was still at Churchill's bedside when he died in 1965 at the age of ninety.

THE UNDERPINNINGS OF CHURCHILL'S COMPOSURE
Faith

Winston Churchill was not an overtly religious man, but he was a man of faith. He believed in God's ultimate providential care—for himself and for his nation. Such a faith was foundational to his internal fortitude when all external signs pointed to disaster.

Churchill referred often to Providence, as he did in a February 1941 broadcast appeal to the United States:

> Put your confidence in us. Give us your faith and your blessing, and, under Providence, all will be well. We shall not fail or falter; we shall not weaken or tire. Neither the sudden shock of battle, nor the long-drawn trials of vigilance and exertion will wear us down. Give us the tools, and we will finish the job.[12]

When his bodyguard, Walter Thompson, complained that Churchill was placing himself at risk, Churchill replied that he would not die because he had "important work to do." Churchill had faith that God would keep him safe all the way to the accomplishment of that "important work." He believed that he would fulfill the destiny he had foreseen in 1891 at the age of sixteen, and that Providence would protect and preserve him for his life's mission.

Churchill did not regard Providence as an impersonal force; he saw it as the guiding hand of God. In his very first speech as prime minister, Churchill said that the policy of his new government would be to wage war against Hitler "with all our might and with all the strength that God can give us."[13] Speaking on Trinity Sunday 1940 about the eventual outcome of the war, Churchill quoted from the Bible and concluded, "As the Will of God is in Heaven, even so let it be."[14]

Churchill's faith was not a rigid sectarianism, but it encompassed a high view of Jesus Christ. One day in May 1952, he was strolling on a hill overlooking Chequers, the prime minister's country retreat, with Field Marshal Bernard Montgomery, a Christian of deep conviction. They were talking about human greatness. John Colville, Churchill's private secretary, accompanied the men and later recorded his memory of the conversation.

[Montgomery] would fire questions at the Prime Minister as from a machine gun, loving to act the part of Grand Inquisitor. How did Churchill define a great man? Was Hitler great? Certainly not, said Churchill; he made too many mistakes. How could Churchill maintain that Napoleon was great when he was the Hitler of the nineteenth century? He was not, Churchill replied. Surely the only really great men were the religious leaders? Churchill's reply to that interested me, for he seldom spoke of religion. He said that their greatness was undisputed, but it was of a different kind: Christ's story was unequalled and his death to save sinners unsurpassed.[15]

When Churchill's grandson and namesake was born, in May 1952, Churchill proposed a toast to "Christ's new faithful soldier and servant."[16]

Churchill's faith was personal and private, but it was foundational to his character and all that he did.

Confidence

Churchill's faith in God's providence was at the core of his confidence. "Strength is granted to us all when we are needed to serve great causes," he said in 1946.[17] Through the strength of that confidence, he was able to reassure the British people during the darkest days of the war.

Confidence is forged by adversity, and Churchill had seen plenty of that. A person, he believed, "must never be discouraged by defeats in one's youth, but continue to learn throughout one's whole life."[18] Churchill knew people who had been hobbled by reversals, mistakes, and failings early in life. But the way to rise above them and gain confidence was to learn from them.

Vision

"I see further ahead," Churchill told his friend Murland Evans in 1891 at Harrow. During the 1930s, Churchill's vision enabled him to see clearly the threat posed by Hitler and the Nazis. More importantly, he was also able to grasp what it would take to defeat the growing German war machine.

Churchill was not an idealistic visionary, soothing the British people with empty platitudes. He wasn't like the prophets described in Jeremiah 6:14 who offered "superficial treatments" for the nation's "mortal wound" and gave "assurances of peace when there is no peace." Rather, he was like the leaders of the tribe of Issachar mentioned in the book of 1 Chronicles, who "understood the signs of the times and knew the best course . . . to take."[19]

Churchill's oratorical gifts were put to use casting a vision for the British people and their allies and encouraging them to practice the disciplines necessary for victory. He spoke of the long, hard, bloody road ahead, but the dark elements of that vision were always tinted with hope. Because he had not concealed the difficulties, his words had integrity when he spoke of his vision for victory.

Churchill scholar John Lukacs connects "Churchill's vision with a suggestion about his place in history":

> He knew that . . . perhaps an entire era in the world that had begun about four hundred years before his birth was moving toward its end. In sum, he was the defender of civilization at the end of the Modern Age. . . . At a dramatic moment in the twentieth century God allowed Churchill the task of being [civilization's] principal defender.[20]

Honesty

Churchill had a realistic understanding of human nature. In his acceptance speech for the Nobel Prize in Literature in 1953, he said, "The power of man has grown in every sphere except over himself."[21] While Churchill eschewed religious labels, he believed that honesty about human nature and his own personality and capacities hinged on a spiritual understanding. "Man is spirit," he said.[22]

Churchill's honest self-appraisal also reflected his awareness that, despite the acclaim that accompanied his leadership skills, he still needed help. People called him their hope, the embodiment of strength and courage, the man who could win the war. Yet he knew he could not go it alone—in contrast to Hitler's megalomania. "There is only one thing worse than fighting with allies," he said, "and that is fighting without them."[23]

He was also brutally honest about his nation's policies. On May 2, 1935, he spoke of "inertia" regarding the British response to the expanding Nazi threat, and especially after Britain and its allies at that time had failed in their commitment to help Austria maintain its independence.

> When the situation was manageable it was neglected, and now that it is thoroughly out of hand we apply too late the remedies which then might have effected a cure.
>
> There is nothing new in the story. It is as old as the Sibylline Books. It falls into that long, dismal catalogue of the fruitlessness of experience and the confirmed unteachability of mankind. Want of foresight, unwillingness to act when action would be simple and effective, lack of clear thinking, confusion of counsel until the emergency comes, until self-preservation strikes its jarring gong—these are the features which constitute the endless repetition of history.[24]

Churchill's assessment was disturbing, yet it demonstrated that someone in leadership understood the situation and had the boldness to address it.

Courage

"Courage," said Churchill, "is rightly esteemed the first of human qualities because, as has been said, it is the quality which guarantees all others."[25] Churchill expected those closest to him to embrace and display such courage and toughness. In 1940, as bombs rained on London, Churchill added a "wry remark" in a secret speech: "Learn to get used to it. Eels get used to skinning."[26]

Churchill's visits to bombed areas took great courage because there was always the danger of assassination when he was in public. However, as he walked among the ruins and talked to people who had lost loved ones, homes, businesses, and much more, his courage was passed on to them. He lifted his fingers in the V-for-victory sign and modeled for the nation how to be courageous under fire.

Determination

In the minds of many Britons, Winston Churchill was the personification of the "British Bulldog." Churchill himself admired the feisty animal. "The nose of the bulldog has been slanted backwards so that he can breathe without letting go," he said.[27] Indeed, Churchill's determination was relentless when others were pushing for appeasement and even surrender. That character quality also inspired the nation not to turn Hitler loose until he was defeated.

In his biography of Churchill, Lewis Broad describes the situation that Churchill faced when he assumed leadership of the British government:

> Never did a PM assume office in such an hour. The blitzkrieg had opened as a tornado. Every message gave tidings of disaster from Holland, from Belgium, and from France. The Germans were sweeping all before them. They had broken out at the Ardennes gap. It was on the shortest route to Paris.[28]

"If you are going through hell, keep going" is a quote often attributed to Churchill, though there is no indication that he ever actually said it. Still, it reflects his dogged determination to get his nation to the other side of the hellish road it now traveled. "For defeat there is only one answer—victory," he proclaimed.[29]

Churchill rallied the nation to carry on by drawing inspiration from their long history: "Persevere towards those objectives which are lighted for us by all the wisdom and inspiration of the past."[30] In fact, one of his mottoes was "We must just KBO." *KBO* stood for "Keep Buggering On"—that is, keep on plodding even when you are too tired to run.[31]

Churchill once asked one of his hardworking secretaries, Elizabeth Nel, if she was tired. When she said that she wasn't, Churchill replied, "We must go on and on like the gun-horses, till we drop."[32]

Churchill drew inspiration from Moses in the Old Testament. Very broadly interpreting Exodus 3–4, he writes:

> God spoke to Moses from the Burning Bush. He said to him in effect: "You cannot leave your fellow-countrymen in bondage. Death or freedom! Better the wilderness than slavery. You must go back and bring them out. . . . No more let them be chained in the house of bondage. . . . I will endow you with superhuman power. There is nothing that man cannot do, if he wills it with enough resolution. Man is the epitome of the universe. All moves and exists as a result of his invincible will, which is My Will." [33]

Churchill says of the burning bush that it was "now surely inside the frame of Moses."[34] Such a spirit of fire was clearly inside Churchill's "frame" as well, and it contributed greatly to his ability to "keep calm and carry on."

Moral balance

"From his earliest days, Churchill was absorbed with a moral vision for his life," writes Steven Hayward.[35] He did not exclude personal behavior from his consideration of morality, though he was not a romantic idealist like the utopians who denied the fallen nature of humanity.

He knew that maintaining moral equilibrium was essential for individuals and their societies. "Civilization," he said, "is the state of society when moral forces begin to escape the tyranny of physical forces."[36] In this, Churchill reflected the Bible's view of the law, which the apostle Paul says serves as a "guardian" to keep things in check until the principles can be internalized.[37] The law places necessary restraints on our behavior for the safety and well-being of society. To Churchill, the necessity of moral balance was clearcut: "Human life is presented to us as a simple choice between right and wrong."[38]

In his essay on Moses, Churchill reflects on Pharaoh's seesaw-ing promises, which reveal the Egyptian leader's lack of moral balance. Each day when Moses appeared before him, Pharaoh "hardened his heart and took back in the morning what he had promised the night before."[39] Churchill knew he could not equivo-cate; that he had to maintain the balance of integrity. He could be wily, which had contributed to the perception by some that he could not be trusted. But now the nation's resolve to press on depended on his trustworthiness.

Realistic optimism

Sir Charles Wilson was Churchill's personal physician, and he knew Churchill's disposition well. He attributed Churchill's resil-ience to his "buoyant temperament."[40]

That "buoyancy" lifted many in Britain and beyond. Churchill's optimism could be trusted because it was couched in reality. For example, as war loomed in January, 1940, he said, "Certainly, it is true that we are facing numerical odds; but that is no new thing in our history."[41] As he said at another time, "The threat of adversity is a necessary factor in stimulating self-reliance."[42]

Foresight

Churchill gave people the sense that he could look at the past through the lessons of history, had a clear view of the present, and could peer far ahead into the future. He calculated present situa-tions based on historical precedents and future impacts.

Churchill's foresight arose from his personal philosophy: "Plant a garden in which you can sit when digging days are done."[43] He was preparing his nation not only to defeat the enemy in the pres-ent but also to preserve their long-term quality of life. Victory was incomplete unless people could enjoy its fruits. Churchill intended to take his people all the way, sowing the garden, as it were, for their children, grandchildren, and great-grandchildren.

Perspective

Churchill learned much from painting. As he studied perspective in art, he saw the application of those principles to life in general: "The glory of light cannot exist without its shadows."[44] That was the attitude that helped Britain and the Allies carry on with hope.

His perspective was also sharpened by his sense of the historic: "The future is unknowable, but the past should give us hope."[45] His passion for this type of perspective was revealed in an admonition he gave to a young student: "Study history, study history. In history lies all the secrets of statecraft."[46]

Churchill dealt with large-scale issues, but he had high regard for the little things as well. In the words of the Old Testament prophet Zechariah, he did not "despise the day of small things."[47] He was a calming influence because his staff and the British people knew there was little that escaped his attention. They had also learned that he could read between the lines and discern the actual meanings behind pompous diplomatic statements, warlike threats, and inflated statistics.

Churchill was the rare leader in whom all three leadership essentials combined: *vision*, *strategy*, and *tactics*. There was much he missed and wrongly estimated, but there was a great deal he properly discerned. In 1933, when Churchill was still out of favor with many in the British establishment, former Prime Minister and Liberal Party leader David Lloyd George referred to him as one of "the most remarkable and puzzling enigmas of his time. . . . His fertile mind, his undoubted courage, his untiring industry, and his thorough study of the art of war, would have made him a useful member of a War Cabinet."[48]

That "thorough study of the art of war" coupled with discernment was what enabled Churchill to see the potential of the tank as a weapon. Though he did not invent it, he certainly contributed to its development. Indeed, during the First World War, "Churchill's natural interest in scientific gadgetry deepened."[49]

Highly visionary people sometimes fail because they neglect to consider the small details and hidden facts, which can be swallowed up in their big-picture thinking. But Churchill realized that "the veils of the future are lifted one by one, and mortals must act from day to day."[50] Such a perspective keeps the visionary from being blindsided by the fine print.

Perspective is also vital in holding back the urge to panic under pressure. "When danger is far off we may think of our weakness; when it is near we must not forget our strength."[51]

Churchill believed that perspective aided by discernment would give the complete picture necessary for success. "Life is a whole," he said, "and good and ill must be accepted together."[52] But always one's view must be based on reality, because even man's "greatest neglects or failures may bring him good. Even his greatest achievements may work him ill."[53]

Agility

In his early life, especially when he changed political parties, Churchill was viewed as inconsistent. No doubt there were times in his youth when such an allegation carried some truth. However, instead of becoming stodgy and inflexible as he matured, he continued to embrace the importance of flexibility and adaptability.

"In life's steeplechase," he said, "one must always jump the fences when they come." Necessary change was a good thing, he thought. "To improve is to change, so to be perfect is to have changed often."[54] Churchill may have smiled a bit when he wrote those words.

His frustrations mounted, however, when he was unable to persuade Parliament and the prime minister—first Stanley Baldwin and then Neville Chamberlain—to change their policies towards Hitler and to rearm Britain as the Nazi threat intensified.

On May 2, 1935, Baldwin made a confession in Parliament that stunned Churchill. The British leader revealed that the Germans had achieved air parity with Great Britain—something that the prime minister had promised six months earlier he would never allow to happen.

Churchill rose to respond. He gave Parliament a brief history lesson:

> I pause to ask the Committee to consider what these facts mean and what their consequences impose. I confess that words fail me. In the year 1708, Mr. Secretary St. John, by a calculated Ministerial indiscretion, revealed to the House the fact the battle of Almanza had been lost in the previous summer because only 8,000 British troops were actually in Spain out of the 29,000 that had been voted by the House of Commons for that service. When a month later this revelation was confirmed by the Government, it is recorded that the House sat in silence for half an hour, no Member caring to speak or wishing to make a comment upon so staggering an announcement. And yet how incomparably small that event was to what we have now to face.[55]

Churchill understood the importance of being agile enough to "jump the fences," and he was distressed at the government's intransigence, inability to see the reality of Nazi Germany's threats, and lack of the flexibility needed to take action.

When at last he became prime minister, he knew he had to move quickly to shift Britain's policy to wartime status—and he hoped it was not too late.

Grace

Despite his frustrations both with his country's leadership before the war and with his opponents throughout his political career, Churchill understood the importance of grace. This character quality also inspired his countrymen to "keep calm and carry on," especially in the face of betrayal and accusation.

Churchill was a great giver of grace, which is what enabled him to work successfully with his coalition War Cabinet, even though the sailing was not always smooth. Just as Churchill came to power, his most somber warnings were now coming true, and the unwillingness of so many to take him seriously was laid bare. "No man on earth has such good reason today to say, I told you so," René Kraus observes. "He never says it."[56]

There was good reason for Churchill to show such grace. "Hatred plays the same part in government as acids in chemistry," he said.[57] That understanding governed Churchill's actions after the Germans had been defeated, and it may have saved Europe from repeating the catastrophic situation created by the Versailles Treaty after the First World War. "As we have triumphed, so we may be merciful; as we are strong, so we can afford to be generous."[58]

Rest

Between 1940 and 1945, Churchill had the most demanding, stressful job in the world. It was overwhelming and wearying, and yet he flourished. His energy was reassuring to his own people and to those nations who fought at their side. Despite being run over by a car in New York in 1931, suffering a heart attack in 1941, and having a bout with pneumonia while visiting the North African front in 1943, Churchill was able to plow on.

He lived to the ripe old age of ninety.

One of his secrets was understanding the importance of rest. So many leaders, it seems, try to impress others with their heavy schedules, as if the entire world would collapse if they paused and rested. Churchill needed to impress no one, starting with himself. He scheduled time away from London at Chequers, the rural retreat of British prime ministers that his daughter Mary called "a true haven . . . from outer storms."[59] Chartwell, Churchill's family home in the rolling countryside of Kent, was his favorite site for relaxation. He felt that "a day away from Chartwell [was] a day wasted."[60]

Mary Soames describes her father resting during a 1942 visit to President Franklin Roosevelt's home at Hyde Park, New York.

> Papa presented a charming sight . . . flat on his back in a patch of sun. . . . I lay near him and we gazed up at the very blue sky & the green leaves dancing against it—flecked with sun.[61]

Such relaxation eased Churchill's much-burdened mind, and he began to muse about the colors he would use if he were painting the scene: "[He] commented on the wisdom of God in having made the sky *blue* and the trees *green*. 'It wouldn't have been nearly so good the other way round.'"[62]

Churchill believed that cultivating "a hobby and new forms of interest is . . . a policy of first importance to a public man."[63] He discovered such a hobby at the age of forty in his love for painting. "Painting came to my rescue in a most trying time," he said.[64] Churchill described how, after he left the Admiralty in 1915, he was still a member of the prime minister's Cabinet and War Council. However, the sudden change in pace from the intensity of the Admiralty to the "narrowly measured duties of a counsellor left me gasping."[65] But Churchill also felt "great anxiety and no means of relieving it" as he listened to discussions and watched developments regarding the First World War from a position where he "knew everything and could do nothing."[66]

Then, one Sunday in the country, he took a paint box belonging to his children, experimented with it, and decided "to procure the next morning a complete outfit for painting in oils." Years later, he recalled of those days that "the Muse of Painting came to my rescue—out of charity and out of chivalry."[67]

The lazy afternoon he spent at Hyde Park with Mary, thinking about God, the sky, and colors, may have seemed trivial against the immense issues that would be the primary topic of his later conversation with Franklin Roosevelt. However, that moment with his daughter showed how Churchill's mind expanded to the true scale of reality and found calmness there. In that frame, he was able to shoulder the nearly unbearable burden of giving leadership to his nation in a time of war and persevering until victory was achieved.

13

Churchill and the Character
of Leadership

Now with the help of God, and with the conviction
that we are the defenders of civilisation and
freedom, we are going to persevere to the end.
WINSTON CHURCHILL, OCTOBER 1, 1939

IF WE SEE SIMILARITIES between Churchill's times and our own,
then we ought to be able to examine his leadership style for insights
about the kind of leadership we need today.

> The story of Churchill . . . is about the indomitability of the human
> spirit. He may seem horribly unfashionable in his views to us today,
> but in his essential character he is a source of eternal—and perhaps
> growing—inspiration.[1]

The character attributes that steadied and strengthened Churchill
and enabled him to inspire his people to "keep calm and carry on"
were also central to his leadership style.

> A Statesman in contact with the moving current of events and
> anxious to keep the ship of state on an even keel and steer a steady
> course may lean all his weight now on one side and now on the

other. . . . A Statesman should always try to do what he believes is best in the long view for his country, and he should not be dissuaded from so acting by having to divorce himself from a great body of doctrine to which he formerly sincerely adhered.[2]

Now we examine how these elements of Churchill's personality worked out practically as he led Britain and the Allies during the great battle for the survival of Christian civilization.

Churchill's critics during his backbench period could never have envisioned him as prime minister. They considered him a joke. And indeed he was, but in a way they did not comprehend. As we examine how God may have raised up Winston Churchill for just such a time as the one he faced, it's helpful to remember that God often confounds our greatest wisdom and uses the least likely person that we might choose.

We don't often think of the Bible as a funny book, probably because it has for so long been read to us in such pompous, stentorian tones. . . . But if you read it with the eye of a comic, you will have to admit it is filled with some sublimely ridiculous moments. . . .

Think of Isaiah, who ran around naked in the desert for three years; Jeremiah, the grumpy potter . . . wearing an ox-yoke around his neck; Jonah, the reluctant prophet . . . in the belly of [the fish]. . . . Think of Peter, the bumbling, big-talking backwater fisherman . . . or Zacchaeus, the pint-sized tax collector. . . . If you were writing the script, are these the characters you would pick for heroes? . . .

There are three things that occasion humor: a sense of the incongruous, a relaxed, light-hearted attitude, and suddenness or surprise. Any God who chooses a carpenter from the one-horse town of Nazareth as his redeemer of the universe certainly has a sense of the incongruous.[3]

Winston Churchill falls into that "incongruous" category—a perpetual reminder that God has a sense of humor and that his ways are not our ways. Indeed, "God chose the foolish things of the world to shame the wise; God chose the weak things of the world to shame the strong."[4]

We have explored the incongruities of life that formed Churchill's character and prepared him for his destiny. Leadership style cannot be separated from a person's character. Essence precedes function; what we *do* arises from *who we are*. Maurice Hankey, Cabinet secretary during the First World War, remembered the impact of Churchill's personality during that trying period.

> We owed a good deal in those early days to the courage and inspiration of Winston Churchill who, undaunted by difficulties and losses, set an infectious example. . . . His stout attitude did something to hearten his colleagues.[5]

LEADERSHIP, CHURCHILL-STYLE

This brings us to a vital question: Has God placed a "Churchill" among us in our turbulent times, when once again the survival of Judeo-Christian civilization is at stake?

Those in Europe with sufficient historical perspective may lament the devastation of the cultures that sowed the world with high ideals. Americans with broad insight fret over the loss of fundamental liberties that were once a beacon to oppressed people everywhere. Moreover, the assaults on Western civilization now come not through conventional warfare with set fronts and boundaries and weapons that can be outclassed. The contemporary battle is spiritual, moral, and philosophical. It is often a guerrilla war of intangibles. The front lines intrude into every institution. It is a battle that involves anarchy, terrorism, warped worldviews, and twisted behaviors. Its storm troopers take no prisoners. There is a foreboding sense of cataclysm, an often-indefinable *angst*, and people are searching for leaders to show us the way through.

Such a state of affairs demands a certain quality of leadership.

Churchill's style provides examples of what is now needed across the globe.

We need leaders with a sense of destiny

"I lift up my eyes to the mountains—where does my help come from?"[6] In his time of trouble, King David scanned the slopes of Mount Zion and the crest of Mount Moriah, drawing inspiration from the primary symbols of his nation's heritage and destiny. Others would have lifted their eyes to the high places where idols had been erected. But whether it was Mount Zion or a pagan high place, the real locus of hope was in God himself.

The key to David's effectiveness as a leader was not just in the seeing but in the very process of lifting up his eyes. Elevating our vision aligns our focus with transcendent meaning and purpose, without which a sense of destiny is impossible. Churchill had the vertical perspective that enabled him to see the lofty significance of the things he fought for on the horizontal plane.

Thus, Churchill believed in the destiny of his nation and of Christian civilization before he believed in his own destiny. He knew that his personal horizons were set within the context of a greater goal: the preservation of a civilization that had already given much to the world. This vision of his own destiny in the context of a larger purpose was what kept him from becoming a tyrant when he was granted unprecedented powers as Britain's wartime leader.

In the present multicultural fervor of Western society, emerging voices have begun to question whether Judeo-Christian civilization deserves to have a future. Others have already declared it null and void. According to the doctrine of equivalency, every society is of equal value and benefit, simply by virtue of being (or by numbers of population), and no single civilization can dare assert itself as superior at any point.

We understand the concerns that have arisen from the age of manifest destiny that propelled British imperialism and American hemispheric and global hegemony. But now we live in an age of overcorrection; equivalency is as distorted a view as the worst of the imperialistic impulses. The hard fact of life in our fallen, dangerous world is that there will always be dominant powers. Our times are no different from all previous history, except in one respect: The capacities for enslavement and destruction are much greater today in our Internet-woven, atomic world. Therefore, the critical determinant is the quality of the nation—its worldview and values—that becomes a global hegemon. Will its immense powers be used for destructive purposes or to help secure peace and prosperity and preserve the best values for all cultures?

Britain, the United States, and other nations that have long been repositories of values that enhance civilization must have leaders who believe in the merits of Western/Christian culture and its destiny.

We need leaders who recognize the Destiny-Giver as bigger than themselves

A sense of accountability to God prevents national destiny from deteriorating into raw imperialism.

Churchill was a God-conscious man who believed that Providence had assigned him his destiny. And Churchill felt himself accountable to God for the execution of that role. As powerful as he was in the realm of human affairs, the sense that he was accountable to someone greater than himself—greater, even, than the British monarchy—was a major factor in his basic humility.

We need leaders with a long-range focus

Churchill led from the rare equipoise between grim reality on one hand and confident hope on the other. He demonstrated how visionary leaders can gauge their present sufferings by the value of the outcomes they desire for the future.

Jesus displayed this same balance in the days and hours leading up to his crucifixion. When he told his disciples that the time had come for him to go to Jerusalem and "suffer many terrible things," Peter "began to reprimand him for saying such things."' But Jesus immediately rebuked Peter's shortsightedness. Jesus saw the Cross and its horror; but he also saw beyond it to his resurrection and ascension, and he declared that the sacrifice was worth it all.[8]

Whenever Churchill had to put the hard facts before the British people, he also continually held out hope. People learned that they could trust him to tell them the truth while at the same time directing their eyes upward to the hope of victory. They grew in their confidence that Churchill could lead them all the way home because that was his focus.

On May 13, 1940, in his first address to Parliament after becoming prime minister, Churchill uttered the famous line, "I have nothing to offer but blood, toil, tears, and sweat." Then came the inspiring counterbalance: "But I take up my task with buoyancy and hope. I feel sure that our cause will not be suffered to fail among men."[9]

Roger Parrott, president of Belhaven University, describes the perspective needed by transformational leaders:

> The short view doesn't work, but it will continue to permeate our society, direct our actions, and be the gold standard for "success" until purposeful, visionary, and determined leaders pull us back to a longview outlook that seeks lasting value.[10]

In talking to the US embassy staff in Ethiopia about "a number of different cross-currents of modernity that are coming together to make things even more challenging" in Africa, John Kerry, secretary of state during President Barack Obama's second term, said, "Some people believe that people ought to be able to . . . live by their interpretation of something that was written down a thousand plus, two thousand years ago. That's not the way I think most people want to live."[11]

In Kerry's remarks, he essentially dismisses the long view—that which values the lessons of history and the richness of culture arising from religious faith and long-standing sacred values—as "not the way most people want to live." But if we throw those things away, all we have left is the "short view"—which, as Parrott notes, is lacking in "lasting value."

The "short view" in Britain in the 1930s failed to take seriously Churchill's warnings about Hitler's ultimate intentions. Churchill emerged as the "purposeful, visionary, and determined" leader who sometimes had to pull others back to see the long view, with all its terrors and challenges.

We need leaders who can link the future with the past and present

One characteristic of our current age is a disregard or disdain for history. Deconstructionist academics, infused with principles of existentialism—or, worse, nihilism—have trained the upcoming generation to see history as either meaningless or unimportant. For others, it is a past easily rewritten and squeezed into the mold of modern times.

Churchill, however, was a true historian. He was not content with a view of history as nothing more than an assemblage of dates, places, and names. He understood history as a repository of treasures. As he contemplated London during the Blitz, he called it "this strong City of Refuge which enshrines the title-deeds of human progress and is of deep consequence to Christian civilization."[12]

Winning the battle for our civilization requires leaders who know and respect the best of their historical heritage and believe it is worth saving.

We need leaders who will tell the truth, no matter how ridiculous they may appear

"The greatest lesson in life is to know that even fools are right sometimes," said Churchill.[13] He had learned this lesson the hard way.

By 1938, his persistent warnings about the German threat had led others in the government to attack and ridicule him. By this point, Prime Minister Chamberlain had tired of Churchill's voice and was weary of Churchill's constant criticism of the government's inaction. Yet within two years Churchill's foresight and wisdom would be amply vindicated.

We need leaders who have the courage to pay
a hard price for the greater good

On March 25, 1938, Churchill rose in Parliament to challenge the disarmament policy the British government had followed since the end of the First World War. He saw clearly through Hitler's veiled intentions and realized Britain's vulnerability. The only result of the disarmament policy had been that one nation—Germany— had built up its arsenals while Britain had steadily disarmed. Rearmament was one of Churchill's many talking points that lodged themselves in Neville Chamberlain's craw. Chamberlain was convinced that Churchill's persistent calls for military strength would only intensify Hitler's desire to make war.

It was well known that Churchill was not wealthy and that he relied on an income from his books and his column in the *Evening Standard*. However, the day after Churchill's March 25 speech, he received a letter from R. J. Thompson, editor of the *Evening Standard*: "It has been evident that your views on foreign affairs and the part which this country should play are entirely opposed to those held by us."[14] Thompson summarily fired Churchill from his column, which was a tremendous blow to Churchill personally and to his finances.

Churchill was financially broken and forced into a corner. Profits from his books and speeches had been invested in American stocks and lost in the 1929 Wall Street crash. The income from the *Evening Standard* had enabled him to remain in Parliament, lower his debts, and sustain him while he completed his books on the Marlborough family. Now faced with certain bankruptcy, Churchill had to make a choice: either to stay in Parliament and continue to speak out, which would cause continuing financial hardship for his family; or to leave the center of action in Parliament and seek a position as a journalist—as an observer rather than a shaper of events. The situation sickened him.

Eventually, however, he began writing for London's *Daily Telegraph* on a six-month trial, which became an ongoing engagement. In the pages of the *Telegraph*, which had a predominantly Conservative readership, Churchill continued to fight against the government. It soon became clear that the only people who disagreed with Churchill were those in government. His readers loved him. Fourteen months later, Churchill was offered better terms with the *Daily Mirror*, and he began to write a larger, more prominent column.

The newspaper column secured an income for Churchill, but he still faced mounting debt. His only asset was the family home at Chartwell, and he knew its sale would enable him to continue his fight against the government without fear of financial reprisals. Heartbroken at the prospect, Churchill paid for a full page in the London *Times*, offering Chartwell for sale. Knowing how much I (Jonathan) love Chartwell, I can only imagine the pain my great-grandfather must have felt to see the advertisement. Selling Chartwell would have been to him the ultimate sacrifice for king and country.

Churchill believed that selling his home "might merit a discreet paragraph in the *Times*' 'Londoner's Diary.'"[15] What happened instead was a vile example of those who use the media to peddle their own agendas. Lord Beaverbrook, who owned both the *Evening Standard* and the *Daily Express* and who was also aligned with Chamberlain in the appeasement camp, ran a story that "managed to insinuate that Churchill was irresponsible" and was "auctioning off his home while attempting to sabotage Chamberlain's thrifty budgets."[16] The *Times* was even crueler. As it took Churchill's money for the advertisement, the paper simultaneously published a full article on the first news page, informing the world that Churchill was selling his home. The article included sensationalized personal information, which upset Churchill.

Embarrassed, Churchill approached Brendan Bracken, one of his staunchest allies. Churchill knew little about finance, but Bracken did; he helped to resolve Churchill's embarrassing debt crisis, which had become a hot gossip item. Churchill proposed that he would leave Parliament while he focused on generating a better income, but Bracken was horrified at the idea that Churchill would not be able to continue his fight in Parliament—especially since Austria had recently fallen to Germany. Bracken immediately approached Sir Henry Strakosch, who was happy to loan Churchill the money he needed, on the repayment terms that Churchill had proposed. Strakosch would have happily given Churchill the money, but Churchill was an honorable man and would have felt it wrong to accept such a large sum with no return for the donor.

Strakosch managed the securities purchased from Churchill for three years, and made investments to repay the debt on Churchill's behalf. Churchill's only stipulation was that he accumulate no further debts. Strakosch honored the agreement, and it brought great relief to Churchill, enabling him to continue his stance in Parliament against Chamberlain's appeasement policy. Although it came at great personal cost, Churchill was dogged in his determination to see Britain take the right course of action in response to German rearmament.

We need leaders who see threats realistically but not hysterically
Churchill, as we have seen, understood the threat of Nazi Germany because he stoked himself with information. He was armed with

statistical data when he sought to raise Parliament's awareness of the growing peril. Yet, even though he intensely felt the urgency of the situation, Churchill carefully measured his words.

When Prime Minister Baldwin confessed on May 22, 1935, that he had been "completely wrong" and was "completely misled" regarding future estimates of German air power, Churchill's emotions boiled over. When his turn came to speak, Churchill pulled out all the rhetorical stops.

> For the first time for centuries we are not fully equipped to repel or to retaliate for an invasion. That to an island people is astonishing. Panic indeed! The position is the other way round. We are the incredulous, indifferent children of centuries of security behind the shield of the Royal Navy, not yet able to wake up to the woefully transformed conditions of the modern world.[17]

Churchill knew that the way to avoid hysteria and panic was through a frank assessment of the situation, followed by the development and execution of plans to respond to the crisis.

Within five years, Churchill would be the country's leader as Nazi warplanes—whose pace of construction Baldwin had woefully miscalculated—were setting British cities ablaze. Churchill had to employ his skills as an orator not only to tell the people the facts but also to reassure them, even as they dodged bombs, slept in subway tunnels, and grieved over lost loved ones.

The hysteria had begun to build in 1939, when people living in the south of England along the Channel were told to burn their maps, secure their food supplies, and take other measures to prevent invading Nazis from seizing the advantage. By the time Churchill became prime minister, in May 1940, multitudes throughout the British Isles were terribly afraid. But as he took to the airwaves in his new leadership role, Churchill's resonant voice had a calming effect, even when he had to deliver distressing news.

Though the balance, he said, was sometimes hard to strike, "it is very much better sometimes to have a panic feeling beforehand, and then be quite calm when things happen, than to be extremely calm beforehand and to get into a panic when things happen."[18]

We need leaders who don't need the spotlight

Churchill's ego was forged through his trials and challenges. His early arrogance was noteworthy. Recall the letter he wrote to his mother after the Battle of Omdurman, in which he said, "I do not believe the gods would create so potent a being as myself for so prosaic an ending."[19]

But the furnace of adversity that Churchill entered in ensuing years seared the edge off that arrogance and produced humility. Part of his effectiveness as prime minister was that he saw himself as one of the people—no better, no worse. This galvanized his supporters and made them love him. Many assume that one must be aloof to be a leader, but Churchill believed otherwise. In the crisis of war, he realized that his reassuring presence among the anxious people of Britain was needed.

The root of Britain's victory over Adolf Hitler may lie in the contrast between arrogance and humility. "Pride goes before destruction," says Proverbs 16:18. Pride was at the core of the Nazis' stance: pride in Hitler as their leader, pride in their race, pride in their right to world dominance. In fact, as we have seen, Hitler's appeal to his nation was to overcome the humiliation wrought by the Versailles Treaty. In a sense, Hitler and the Nazis were all about pride.

Churchill, on the other hand, spoke honestly of the weaknesses to overcome, the hardships to be borne, and the near-impossible task of winning the war. In doing so, he and the British people who rallied behind him proved that "God opposes the proud, but gives grace to the humble."[20]

We need leaders who recognize the difference between authority and power and who function in that knowledge

Over the year that followed the collapse of the Munich Agreement and the onset of war, Churchill stood firmly with Neville Chamberlain. He had every opportunity to criticize Chamberlain's leadership or to bring up the failures of the past. At any time, he could have said, "I told you so." But he didn't. Churchill was not a man like Hitler, who sought office for his own gain. Churchill truly served those he represented. People who had waited to see the showdown between Churchill and Chamberlain after the change in leadership must have been very disappointed to witness the two working together as if nothing had gone before. The war needed to be fought and won—that was all that mattered. Magnanimity was called for, and Churchill proved by his actions that he believed it.

Churchill proved to the British people and to his parliamentary colleagues that they had misjudged him. In 1939, every slur that had been spoken against Churchill was replaced with the greatest respect. Churchill quickly rebuilt the trust he had lost when he switched political parties in 1904 and then in 1924. He reestablished the confidence in him that had been shattered by the 1915 Gallipoli disaster and the economic failure of returning Britain to the gold standard in 1925. In the early days of the war, he served at the pleasure of the prime minister, focused on his job, and offered his best advice.

The secret of Churchill's leadership was his instinctive understanding of the difference between power and authority, as we've already seen. Rather than use his growing influence to lead a coup, Churchill submitted to authority and was granted power. "At last I had the authority to give directions over the whole scene," he later wrote of his appointment as prime minister.[21] True power is granted only to those under authority. Churchill kept himself under Chamberlain's authority, and therefore he could be trusted with power.

Hitler was a mere authoritarian who, in the end, had to

sequester himself in an underground lair. The only power he had left was expressed in his own suicide. Churchill, on the other hand, continues to speak with leadership-shaping authority even today.

We need leaders mature enough to have overcome past failures

There is a narrow zone in which all of us can function with remarkable excellence. It is bounded by our God-intended identity and purpose; the gifts he has given us to accomplish our high purpose; the functional talents and skills we have that lend themselves to the task; and the quality of our inner core, which is formed by the way we respond to our trials and learn from them.

Winston Churchill most definitely entered his personal "zone of excellence" when the king summoned him to Buckingham Palace and asked him to form a new government and lead the nation through the war. This was when Churchill realized that his previous hardships and successes had prepared him for that moment. The purpose he had felt as a teenager at Harrow; the awakening of his gift of exhortation in his extraordinary speaking ability; the sharpening of his leadership skills; and the toughening of his character through dealing with rejection, failure, and his own "besetting sins" all came together in a grand confluence. He had to overcome immense challenges to his character and reputation, but even these hardships contributed to bringing him into his personal zone of excellence.

Earlier, we saw how young Winston overcame his educational limitations by taking advantage of a lull in the action to read and study after he arrived in India to join his regiment. And yet that wide array of knowledge would have proven useless without the wisdom to understand and apply the principles he had learned. Overcoming his doubts about God during his time in India brought Churchill to the "foundation of wisdom," which is "fear [reverence and respect] of the LORD."[22]

"Wisdom shouts in the streets," says Proverbs 1:20, and "cries out in the public square." Churchill's wisdom, gained by acquiring knowledge and learning from his own disappointments and failures, thundered in the House of Commons, the streets, and the great public square.

Rarely in history have all the elements of greatness converged so quickly, and with such completeness in a crucial moment, as they did in Winston Churchill. As the book of Proverbs says:

> [God] stores up sound wisdom for the upright;
> He is a shield to those who walk in integrity,
> Guarding the paths of justice,
> And He preserves the way of His godly ones.[23]

As previous chapters have shown, Winston Churchill's way was preserved so remarkably that it constitutes a miraculous protection from God himself. Churchill's role was indeed to guard "the paths of justice." Now, more than seventy years after the end of the Second World War, we are not enjoying the fruits of that civilization simply because of *luck*. Rather, we enjoy them because God intervened in history through a remarkable man, Winston Churchill.

The example of Churchill and his times can give us hope in our present circumstances. If God was engaged in human history back then, we can be certain that he is guiding its course today as well.

14

Help and Hope for Our Times

On this day of Sabbath the British people mourn a great David-like figure who is buried with the pomp and reward of a great Old Testament Patriarch. . . . He was a new King Cyrus. . . . He rose like a hero, highest in those months in 1940 when the future of human decency was at stake, and when Jewry and Christianity were on the same side, which was the side incarnated by him. . . . [Churchill] succeeded: because of his resolution and—allow me to say this—because of God's will, of which, like every human being, he was but an instrument. He was surely no saint, he was not a religious man, and he had many faults. Yet so it happened.

JOHN LUKACS

WE BEGAN OUR RESEARCH into the life and times of Winston Churchill with an eye towards discovering the "hidden something" behind his singular role in world history. What we found, ultimately, was a testimony not as much to Churchill's spirituality as it was to God's sovereignty. What we've endeavored to show in these pages is not that Churchill had particular beliefs about God but that God, in his wisdom, was able to use this ordinary human being for extraordinary purposes.

What eventually brought us together was our common belief that God had raised up Churchill in the crucial hour to stand in

the gap and preserve the future of Christian civilization for generations to come. In that way, Churchill takes his place among the
ranks of those who have emerged at key points in history to defend
and preserve their civilizations.

A brief, and admittedly incomplete, survey shows that these
leaders were often unlikely candidates for heroic work—Moses,
stuttering his way through the deliverance of his people while
trying to control his anger; Cyrus, the Persian king, freeing the
Jews from exile to return to Jerusalem and rebuild the Temple;
Abraham Lincoln, scorned and oft-defeated, rising to the role of
Great Emancipator; and Winston Churchill—sometimes lacking judgment and insight, seemingly capricious and waffling in
his early years—ultimately becoming the resolute champion who
overcame the Nazi threat to humanity.

If God has intervened through such flawed individuals throughout history, it gives us hope for our own lives and for the dreadful
hour through which we are now passing.

WHAT IF?

Some have wondered what might have happened if Winston
Churchill had never been born or if he hadn't emerged on the
stage of world history at the precise moment that he did.

Churchill biographer (and current mayor of London) Boris
Johnson, for example, provides a scenario for a "non-Churchill
universe":

> [If we] take Churchill out of the equation . . . we leave the fate of
> Britain and the world in the hands of Halifax, Chamberlain, and
> the representatives of the Labour and Liberal parties. Would they
> have treated with Hitler, as the Foreign Secretary was proposing?
> It seems overwhelmingly likely. . . .
>
> It was Churchill—and only Churchill—who had made
> resistance to the Nazis his political mission. . . .

If you end British resistance in 1940, you create the conditions for an irredeemable disaster in Europe.[1]

As interesting as these speculations might be, a more intriguing question from our perspective is, *Why Winston Churchill?* Why did this particular man show up on history's stage at the precise moment to become the antithesis to Adolf Hitler and save Christian civilization?

We believe that Churchill's life is an example of how God dynamically engages with human events by intervening at critical junctures to guide the course of history towards its *telos*—its ultimate end, purpose, or goal. We believe Churchill intuitively recognized that he had a destiny tied to a greater historical purpose and that his life at times was preserved because, as he told his bodyguard, Walter Thompson, he had "important work to do."

THE PURPOSE OF HISTORY

Jesus taught that the purpose of history is the advancement and full manifestation of God's Kingdom in the world. In one of his great apocalyptic messages, Jesus told his followers that the "gospel of the kingdom will be preached in the whole world as a testimony to all nations, and then the end [*telos*] will come."[2] The ultimate goal of history will have been reached.

Jesus set this prediction in its historical context, speaking of Daniel's time, the days of Noah, seasons of upheaval in nature, and a constancy of "wars and rumors of wars."[3] There is a pattern to the unveiling of God's Kingdom in history—advancement followed by resistance through human attempts to build rival empires. Perhaps Churchill, knowing the Bible as he did, saw Hitler's dream of the Third Reich as one of these rival empires to Jesus' Kingdom of love, grace, goodness, peace, and joy.[4] He muses on similar themes in his *Thoughts and Adventures*:

Many centuries were to pass before the God that spake in the Burning Bush was to manifest Himself in a new revelation, which nevertheless was the oldest of all the inspirations of the Hebrew people—as the God not only of Israel, but of all mankind who wished to serve Him; a God not only of justice, but of mercy; a God not only of self-preservation and survival, but of pity, self-sacrifice, and ineffable love.[5]

WHERE IS GOD?

Despite Churchill's conviction that God intervenes in history, there were many who suffered in Hitler's concentration camps who asked a different question: *Where is God?* To all appearances, from inside the barbed wire, Nietzsche was right when he declared that "God is dead."

One cannot respond casually to such spiritual and psychic pain. And the question persists today. Where is God?

When asked in a 1968 interview if he was saying that God had actually died, Dr. Thomas Altizer, one of the leading proponents of God-is-dead theology, explained that he was not speaking of *death* as we understand it but of the existential sense some felt of God's "absence."[6] His idea seemed to be an extreme form of *deism*—that God the Creator, the First Cause, had withdrawn from the world to such an extent that he may as well have been dead. God was not engaged with history but had left things to humanity. Some other God-is-dead theologians saw this absence as a central element—even a necessity—of God's love. If he created us to be free, then he must pull back so that we can be truly free.

Those who look for God's direct intervention in human history as proof of his existence will one day have all the evidence they need—though it may not be in the way they desire. In the meantime, in his inscrutable and infinite wisdom, he has chosen to work through frail and fallible human beings to achieve his purposes. Thus, even as millions languished in the Nazi death camps, seemingly without hope, God was present and active, working through people like Churchill to bring liberation. In fact, even before Hitler and his murderous regime came to power, God was preparing those who would bring down the tyrants, restore peace, and accomplish his will.

Churchill himself made note of God's timely intervention in the affairs of history. In his essay on Moses in *Thoughts and Adventures*, he observes how the Egyptians "sought to arrest the increase of male Israelites" in their midst. Their "final solution"—to borrow a phrase from Hitler—was to slaughter the male babies. "There was evidently at this time a strong tension between the principle of Jewish life and the ruthless force of established Egyptian civilization," Churchill observed. *"It was at this moment that Moses was born."*[7]

Here again we see the concept of "a certain day" or a momentous time, those pivotal moments in history that occur in relation to God's purpose and plan. Chronological time involves the ticking of the clock or the progression of the calendar. Momentous time refers to periods of special opportunity or significance. Thus, Scripture speaks of *times* and *seasons*. Within the cycles of chronological time (that is, the bounds of human history), God interacts with humanity at key moments to maintain the historical course that will ultimately arrive at the intended destination: the fully revealed Kingdom of Heaven. But he allows for variations in the unfolding of history for the sake of human freedom.

Still, in every chronological sequence, there is a buildup towards the momentous time identified by Jesus in Matthew 24—the culmination of chronological history and the full revelation of the Kingdom of God. Everything that happens in history—whether by God's intentional will (the blessings that come to people and nations) or by God's permissive will (which, again, makes allowance for human freedom)—is tied to that great end, or goal, of history.

THE GREAT RIVER

Think of the movement of a great river such as the Nile, which flows more than four thousand miles from the heart of Africa to the Mediterranean. Though countercurrents, swirls, and cross-currents at times move against or athwart the main current, nothing alters the central flow. Sailors can steer against the mighty current, but they are ultimately carried downriver to the sea.

With respect to human freedom, God's permissive will allows us to steer ourselves, our nations, our institutions, and our cultures against the current, but even then we are still in the all-encompassing flow of history that will take us inevitably to the Great Encounter with Christ at the end of time. As the Lord of history, God will not allow any occurrence along the chronological flow to sink our vessels. He always raises up a deliverer to grab hold of the tiller and get us back into the main current. Thus, the prophet Daniel was able to write:

> Praise be to the name of God for ever and ever;
>   wisdom and power are his.
> He changes times and seasons;
>   he deposes kings and raises up others.[8]

Every human deliverer who has appeared throughout history is simply a type of the Grand Deliverer who will come at the destination-point of history to establish the rule of God's Kingdom of "righteousness, peace, and joy in the Holy Spirit" everywhere.[9]

There is, then, a clear historical pattern in the Bible that has moved within the channels of God's crucial interactions with his people—a relationship into which everyone can choose to enter. The "cycle of nations" is especially apparent in the book of Judges.

1. **A nation is founded on values and principles centered on God (Judges 2:7).** During the time of Joshua and the leaders

who immediately succeeded him, the nation of Israel enjoyed a period of clear truth. Their culture was anchored to a solid belief system whose values formed the consensus for the key institutions undergirding the society's infrastructure. In our contemporary society, the most graphic evidence of this phase is in the scriptural inscriptions and references to God on old public buildings (which many powerful groups now want declared unconstitutional and removed).

2. A "lapse of memory" phase follows (Judges 2:10). When the old "values regime" dies, a new one emerges.[10] Often a new consensus forms around values that are alien to those of the previous regime. In the United States and other Western nations, this stage began in the 1920s and emerged even more intensely in the 1960s.

3. As the memory of God as the source of national blessings fades, there is a season of rebellion (Judges 2:11-12). Influential cultural elites rebel against the founding vision and its underlying truths and values. A critical mass of other people in the society join with them.

4. Next comes the age of the refiner's fire (Judges 2:14-15). The consequences of rebellion from God's ways fall on the society. The ruin of society-stabilizing institutions, such as the family and centers of worship, become the kindling for the conflagration that begins to burn the very core of the civilization.

5. This crisis sparks a desire for remembrance, and recovery begins to grow among insightful people within the society (Judges 3:9). Prophets arise in the initial phase of this period, calling people back to fundamental values. They are persecuted at first, but eventually they are heeded by enough legitimizers to begin a slow restoration.

6. A critical mass of leaders and the populace repent and seek to turn themselves, their institutions, and their nation back to

God and his revealed truth (Judges 10:15-16; 2 Chronicles 7:14). Repentance means a radical change of direction. In a biblical context, it means a turn back to God and his ways. In a society founded initially on biblically revealed Judeo-Christian principles, the remnant community is the critical facet of society whose repentance blesses the whole.

7. **Revival winds begin to blow across the national landscape** (Judges 5:1-3). Substantial numbers of people within the society join the movement of repentance and turn back to foundational beliefs and principles. In the mid-1940s, revival began stirring in the United States. All the way through the 1950s, local churches were often packed for revivals that lasted for up to two weeks. Billy Graham's ministry touched millions across the world.

8. **There is a restoration of God's Kingdom principles among many within the culture** (Judges 5:9-11). The society's fundamental truths are again revered, there is a return of respect for institutions promoting the original values, and the culture is restored to its roots. In 1740, during the age of the Great Awakening, Benjamin Franklin wrote the following reflection after a visit by evangelist George Whitefield: "It was wonderful to see the change soon made in the manners of our inhabitants. From being thoughtless or indifferent about religion, it seem'd as if all the world were growing religious; so that one could not walk thro' the town in an evening without hearing psalms sung in different families of every street."[11]

9. **The land has "rest" until a new generation arises that forgets God** (Judges 3:11). *Rest* is not the same thing as a national malaise. Rather, it is a period characterized by stability, peace, productivity, and prosperity. The 1950s boomed across the West and in many other quarters, as the focus was on recovery and restoration. "One nation *under God*" was added to the American pledge of allegiance in 1954. In Germany, a

massive effort transformed school textbooks and other tools that the Nazis had used to sow their poison into society. West Germany became one of the world's most prosperous nations. And then came the 1960s, and another "lapse of memory" began.

THE DESTROYER-DELIVERER MOTIF

Within these cycles of history, we observe another biblical theme: the destroyer-deliverer motif. The book of Revelation refers to an apocalyptic being at the end of time as "Apollyon—the Destroyer."[12]

Though Hitler was not the figure foreseen in Revelation, he was certainly the face of Apollyon in his time, "possessed of a demonic personality."[13] The apostle John, in his writings, speaks of "the spirit of the antichrist, which . . . even now is already in the world."[14] The apostle Paul seems to identify this spiritual being as the "lawless one."[15]

The antichrist spirit, then, manifests itself across history in all who seek to undermine the peace, order, and well-being of civilization. Many Bible interpreters believe this spirit will be incarnate in a particular world tyrant towards the end of time. Until then, Hitler and those like him will appear across the historic cycles of nations, threatening their unraveling, as noted in a previous chapter. This is why Catholic philosopher Dietrich von Hildebrand often referred to Hitler as an antichrist.

However, in every period of unraveling (historical stages in which it seems God's historical purpose is about to be undone by human causes), a deliverer emerges. Will Durant writes of "heroes of history," and David Aikman of "great souls." This is certainly what John Lukacs has in mind when he refers to Winston Churchill as "a great David-like figure" and a new "King Cyrus." All the human deliverers who have saved the world and their societies from evil, tyranny, and the threat of extinction lead up to the ultimate Deliverer, Jesus Christ.

Our contention is that Winston Churchill was a deliverer prepared and brought onto the human scene through a sovereign act of God to counteract the work of Adolf Hitler, who manifested the dark power he worshiped and was its agent in his historical moment and geographical sphere. We have not tried to cast Churchill as a religious pietist. But he was a *willing* and *available* leader with an intuitive sense of divine destiny. As we have shown, Churchill grew in his understanding that his destiny was set by God himself. He is a wonderful example of how God "looks at the heart," not at "the outward appearance."[16]

A NEW "CHRISTENDOM"

Both Churchill and Hitler believed there were propitious moments when destiny-defining events occurred. However, a major difference between Churchill and Hitler was in their view of the Jews and their place in history.

For Hitler and the Nazi eugenicists, Jewish blood weakened the human species, subverted the rise of Aryan superiority, and needed to be eliminated. Churchill, on the other hand, saw that through the Jews the foundations had been set for the "highest forms of human society."[17] In his *Thoughts and Adventures*, he writes, "This wandering tribe, in many respects indistinguishable from numberless nomadic communities, grasped and proclaimed an idea of which all the genius of Greece and all the power of Rome were incapable."[18]

Churchill saw the West in his day as benefiting from the values of Judeo-Christian civilization, but he did not view "Christian civilization" as the exclusive property of the West. Today, given the shift of the center of world Christianity to the global South, it is even less accurate to conflate "Christian civilization" and "Western civilization." According to religious historian Philip Jenkins, "Christendom . . . may well re-emerge as [a primary cultural reference] in the Christian [global] South—as a new transnational order in which political, social, and personal identities are defined chiefly by religious loyalties."[19]

Churchill's internationalist vision and fervor meant that he did not see himself or his mission as narrowly restricted to the survival of Western societies. He sought their preservation as a crucible for principles that would benefit the entire world. Though, like all mortals, he suffered prejudices—especially in his early life—he genuinely believed the British Empire helped to bring progress in what today would be called "developing nations."

Churchill understood himself as an instrument of God's intervention, which is why he sensed a mission to save "Christian civilization" from the threat of Nazism. Here, then, is our hope for the cataclysmic time in which we live: *The same God who brought forth Winston Churchill (and other deliverers) still rules over history, and he has a deliverer—or deliverers—for our season as well.*

It might even be the ultimate Deliverer.

THE "ODDITY" OF CHURCHILL

"How odd of God to choose the Jews," quipped British journalist William Ewer. Poet Ogden Nash is said to have replied: "It wasn't odd; the Jews chose God." We might also say, in light of what we've seen of Winston Churchill's life, "How odd of God to choose Churchill."

Odd, indeed, for Churchill was sometimes a stranger to his own class and their worldview. For one thing, he had a different perspective of hope than did many of his contemporaries. "Material progress," he said, "in itself so splendid, does not meet any of the real needs of the human race."[20] Future development, "even though it takes shapes we cannot now conceive, or however it may expand the faculties of man, [cannot] bring comfort to his soul." But in that very fact lies "the best hope that all will be well."[21]

Through many tribulations and mistakes, Churchill came to

realize the source of help and hope for all people. He was an orator and not a pulpiteer, yet through his orations and life's example, Churchill was able to "give the reason for the hope" that was in him, to borrow a phrase from the apostle Peter.[22] Often, he returned to the truth in one of the Scriptures that Elizabeth Everest had instilled in him:

> God is our refuge and strength, a very present help in trouble.
> Therefore will not we fear, though the earth be removed, and
> though the mountains be carried into the midst of the sea;
> Though the waters thereof roar and be troubled, though the
> mountains shake with the swelling thereof.[23]

As God was Winston Churchill's "very present help in trouble," so God will be for us. The promise is not just for prime ministers and presidents but for all who will humble themselves and seek God's help. Through the prophet Isaiah, God says, "I live in a high and holy place, but also with the one who is contrite and lowly in spirit, to revive the spirit of the lowly and to revive the heart of the contrite."[24]

Winston Churchill had every reason to be arrogant, but he learned contriteness in the dangers and humiliations through which he passed. It takes such trials for most of us to come down from trying to usurp God's "high place" so that we are instead positioned to receive his help and hope. Isaiah also reminds us that "people walking in darkness have seen a great light."[25] Churchill found that the greater the darkness, the brighter the light.

The source of what Sir Charles Wilson termed Churchill's "buoyancy" arose from his Judeo-Christian worldview. It sustained him all the way to the end. Despite the sorrows and challenges he faced, the journey was full of meaning and purpose, undertaken with exuberance and always with hope.

It seems fitting to allow Churchill the final word, instructing and inspiring us in our times of danger and darkness as he did the people of his era:

> Let us be contented with what has happened to us and thankful for all we have been spared. Let us accept the natural order in which we move. Let us reconcile ourselves to the mysterious rhythm of our destinies, such as they must be in this world of space and time. Let us treasure our joys but not bewail our sorrows. The glory of light cannot exist without its shadows. Life is a whole, and good and ill must be accepted together. The journey has been enjoyable and well worth making—once.[26]

NOTES

INTRODUCTION

1. Winston Churchill, speech in the House of Commons, April 22, 1926, in Winston S. Churchill, *Never Give In!: Winston Churchill's Speeches* (London: Bloomsbury, 2013), 73–74.
2. Proverbs 21:1, RSV.
3. See Daniel 2:21.

CHAPTER 1: A VISION OF DESTINY

1. Winston S. Churchill, "Finest Hour, Man of the Millennium," *Finest Hour*, no. 104, Autumn 1999, 12–15. The full text of the article can be found online at www.winstonchurchill.org/images/finesthour/pdf/Finest_Hour_104.pdf.
2. Ibid.
3. Martin Gilbert, *Churchill: The Power of Words* (Boston: Da Capo Press, 2012), 8.
4. Winston S. Churchill, *A Roving Commission: My Early Life* (New York: Charles Scribner's Sons, 1930), 5.
5. Ibid.
6. Cited in Gertrude Himmelfarb, *The Moral Imagination* (Rowman & Littlefield, 2012), 255.
7. William Manchester, from his Introduction to Winston Churchill, *My Early Life: 1874–1904* (New York: Touchstone, 1996), ix.
8. Ibid.
9. Martin Gilbert, *Churchill: A Life* (New York: Henry Holt, 1991), 6.
10. Ibid., 9.
11. Manchester, introduction to Winston S. Churchill, *My Early Life*, x.
12. Gilbert, *Churchill: A Life*, 22.
13. Ibid.
14. Winston Churchill, *My Early Life: 1874–1904* (New York: Touchstone, 1996), 5.
15. Randolph S. Churchill, *Winston S. Churchill: Youth, 1874–1900* (New York: Houghton Mifflin, 1966), 255.
16. Winston Spencer Churchill, *Savrola: A Tale of the Revolution in Laurania* (London: Longmans Green, 1899), 44.
17. Stephen Mansfield, *Never Give In: The Extraordinary Character of Winston Churchill* (Nashville: Cumberland House, 1995), 39.

18. Winston Churchill, *My Early Life*, 13.

19. Retrieved from http://www.churchill-society-london.org.uk/garter.html.

20. "Mr. Churchill Declines High Honour," *Sydney Morning Herald,* July 31, 1945.

21. Gilbert, *Churchill: A Life*, 19.

22. Ibid., 20.

23. Ibid., 22.

24. Ibid.

25. Ibid., 38. Some suggest that Lord Randolph Churchill did not have syphilis. However, the statement regarding the physicians' diagnosis is cited by Gilbert.

26. Ibid.

27. Richard M. Langworth, "Cover Story: From Dream to Reality," *Finest Hour,* no. 56, 1987, 8; http://www.winstonchurchill.org/images/finesthour/pdf/Finest_Hour_056 .pdf.

28. Richard Langworth's introduction to Winston S. Churchill, *The Dream,* electronic edition: RosettaBooks LLC, 2014.

29. Richard M. Langworth, ed., *Churchill by Himself: The Definitive Collection of Quotations* (New York: Public Affairs, 2008), 73.

30. Winston S. Churchill, *The Dream,* electronic edition: RosettaBooks LLC, 2014.

31. Winston S. Churchill, *A Roving Commission: My Early Life* (New York: Charles Scribner's Sons, 1930), 36.

32. Ibid., 43.

33. Ibid., 59.

34. Ibid.

35. Ibid.

36. Ibid., 77.

37. Ibid., 106.

38. Ibid., 109.

39. Ibid., 107–108.

40. Violet Bonham Carter, *Winston Churchill: An Intimate Portrait* (New York: Konecky & Konecky, 1965), 19.

41. Winston S. Churchill, *A Roving Commission*, 115.

42. Ibid., 166.

43. Carter, *An Intimate Portrait*, 22.

CHAPTER 2: SURVIVING DESTINY'S PERILOUS PATHS

1. Randolph S. Churchill, *The Churchill Documents, Volume 2: Young Soldier, 1896–1901* (Hillsdale, MI: Hillsdale College Press, 2006).

2. Winston S. Churchill, *A Roving Commission: My Early Life* (New York: Charles Scribner's Sons, 1930), 191.

3. Martin Gilbert, *Churchill: A Life* (New York: Henry Holt, 1991), 82.

4. Randolph S. Churchill, *The Churchill Documents, Volume 2*, 784.

5. Celia Sandys, *Churchill Wanted Dead or Alive* (New York: Carroll & Graf, 1999), 38.

6. Ibid., 39.

7. Richard M. Langworth, ed., *Churchill by Himself: The Definitive Collection of Quotations* (New York: Public Affairs, 2008), 273.

8. Martin Gilbert, *Winston S. Churchill, Volume 6: Finest Hour, 1939–1941* (Hillsdale, MI: Hillsdale College Press, 2011), 420.

9. Martin Gilbert, *Winston S. Churchill, Volume 1: Youth, 1874–1900* (Hillsdale, MI: Hillsdale College Press, 2006), 462.

10. Winston S. Churchill, *A Roving Commission*, 244.

11. Ibid., 245.

12. Ibid.

13. Ibid., 250.

14. Ibid., 252.

15. Langworth, *Churchill by Himself*, 214.

16. Winston S. Churchill, *A Roving Commission*, 258.

17. Ibid.

18. Randolph S. Churchill, *The Churchill Documents, Volume 1: Youth, 1874–1900* (Hillsdale, MI: Hillsdale College Press, 2006), 465.

19. "Warm Tribute to Mr. Winston Churchill," *Daily Telegraph*, issue 9721, March 22, 1900, 7; http://paperspast.natlib.govt.nz/cgi-bin/paperspast?a=d&d =DTN19000322.2.24.

20. "The Victoria Cross," History Learning Site, www.historylearningsite.co.uk /victoria_cross.htm.

21. Randolph S. Churchill, *Churchill Documents, Volume 1*, 467.

22. Winston S. Churchill, *A Roving Commission*, 259–260.

23. Ibid.

24. Celia Sandys, *Churchill Wanted Dead or Alive*, 86.

25. Ibid., 94–95.

26. Winston S. Churchill, *A Roving Commission*, 271–272.

27. Ibid., 274.

28. Ibid.

29. Ibid.

30. Ibid., 279.

31. Ibid., 280.

32. Winston S. Churchill, *The Boer War: London to Ladysmith via Pretoria and Ian Hamilton's March* (London: Bloomsbury, 2013), 77.

33. Winston S. Churchill, *A Roving Commission*, 280.

34. Ibid.

35. Ibid.

36. Ibid., 281.

37. Ibid., 282.

38. Ibid.

39. Ibid., 297.

40. Ibid.

41. Winston S. Churchill, *A Roving Commission*, 354.

42. Winston S. Churchill, speech to Joint Session of US Congress, in Robert Rhodes James, ed., *Churchill Speaks 1897–1963—Collected Speeches in Peace and War* (Atheneum, 1981), 781.

43. Gilbert, *Churchill: A Life*, 148.

44. Winston Churchill, *Thoughts and Adventures* (London: Thornton Butterworth, 1932), 304.

45. Violet Bonham Carter, *Winston Churchill: An Intimate Portrait* (New York: Konecky & Konecky, 1965), 184.

46. *Daemon* is an ancient Greek term for a spirit or supernatural being.

CHAPTER 3: FROM THE ADMIRALTY TO THE TRENCHES

1. René Kraus, *Winston Churchill: A Biography* (Philadelphia: J. B. Lippincott, 1940), 100.

2. A. E. Housman, "A Shropshire Lad," xxxv, quoted in Violet Bonham Carter, *Winston Churchill: An Intimate Portrait* (New York: Konecky & Konecky, 1965), 186. Bonham notes that Churchill slightly altered Housman's original second line, "Sleepy with the flow of streams," to "Sleepy with the sound of streams."

3. Winston S. Churchill, *The World Crisis, 1911–1918* (New York: Free Press, 2005), 41.

4. Ibid.

5. Carter, *An Intimate Portrait*, 186.

6. Ibid.

7. Ibid., 187.

8. Ibid., 188.

9. Winston S. Churchill, *The World Crisis, 1911–1918, Volume I* (London: Oldham's Press, 1938), 49.

10. Ibid.

11. Ibid.

12. Deuteronomy 9:1-5, KJV.

13. René Kraus, *Winston Churchill: A Biography,* 141.

14. Winston S. Churchill, *World Crisis,* 48.

15. Ibid., 319.

16. Ibid., 320.

17. Spencer C. Tucker, ed., *World War I: The Definitive Encyclopedia and Document Collection* (Santa Barbara, CA: ABC-CLIO, 2014), 445.

18. Ibid.

19. Winston S. Churchill, *World Crisis,* 327.

20. Carter, *An Intimate Portrait,* 289.

21. Admiral Sir Roger Keyes, *Naval Memoirs, 1910–1915* (London: Thornton Butterworth, 1934), 186.

22. Cited in Carter, *An Intimate Portrait,* 304.

23. Martin Gilbert, *Churchill: A Life* (New York: Henry Holt, 1991), 321.

24. Martin Gilbert, *Winston S. Churchill: Volume 3: The Challenge of War, 1914–1916* (Hillsdale, MI: Hillsdale College Press, 2008), 564.

25. Kraus, *Winston Churchill: A Biography,* 201.

26. Ibid.

27. Mary Soames, ed., *Winston and Clementine: The Personal Letters of the Churchills* (New York: Mariner, 2001), 111.

28. Winston Churchill, *The Power of Words,* ed. Martin Gilbert (Boston: De Capo Press, 2012), 115.

29. Gilbert, *Winston S. Churchill, Volume 3,* 566.

30. Ibid., 574.

31. Winston Churchill, *Thoughts and Adventures* (London: Thornton Butterworth, 1932), 69.

32. Ibid.

33. Ibid.

34. Winston Churchill, *Thoughts and Adventures*, 71.

35. Gilbert, *Winston S. Churchill, Volume 3*, 584.

36. Ibid., 585.

37. Ibid.

38. Mary Soames, *Winston and Clementine*, 119.

CHAPTER 4: HITLER'S VISION

1. The History Place; "Hitler in World War I." http://www.historyplace.com/worldwar2/riseofhitler/warone.htm.

2. Ibid.

3. Sherree Owens Zalampas, *Adolf Hitler: A Psychological Interpretation of His Views on Architecture, Art, and Music* (Bowling Green, OH: BGSU Popular Press, 1990), 132.

4. August Kubizek, *The Young Hitler I Knew: The Memoirs of Hitler's Childhood Friend* (Frontline Books, 2011), 116. Kubizek's credibility has been called into question, most notably by Franz Jetzinger in his 1958 book titled *Hitler's Youth* but also by Ian Kershaw in his introduction to the 2011 Frontline Books edition of Kubizek's book that we used in quoting Kubizek's account. Though at first we were concerned about these critiques, we ultimately decided to trust the conclusions drawn by the Austrian historian Brigitte Hamann (*Hitler's Vienna: A Dictator's Apprenticeship* [1998]), who writes, "Altogether, Kubizek is reliable. His book is a rich and unique source for Hitler's early years" (*Hitler's Vienna*, 56). Also, Ian Kershaw, though critical of Kubizek in many respects, ultimately concludes in his introduction, "Kubizek's book rings true in the portrait of Hitler's personality and mentality" (*The Young Hitler I Knew*, 14). Both of these quotations can also be found in Ben Novak, *Hitler and Abductive Logic: The Strategy of a Tyrant* (Lexington Books, 2014). Novak, who earned a doctorate in history and philosophy and also practiced law for thirty years, concludes that "Kubizek's uncontradicted eyewitness account of Hitler's conduct on that occasion is strongly corroborated by multiple independent sources, justifying the conclusion that it meets the normal common law standard for primary evidence worthy of *prima facie* acceptance" (*Hitler and Abductive Logic*, 212). See also Ben Novak, "Hitler's Rienzi Experience: Factuality," in *Revista de Historia Actual*, vol. 5, no. 5 (2007): 105–116, cited in *Hitler and Abductive Logic*.

5. Kubizek, *Young Hitler*, 117.

6. Ibid., 117–118.

7. Ibid., 118.

8. Thomas S. Grey, ed., *The Cambridge Companion to Wagner* (Cambridge: Cambridge University Press, 2008), 36.

9. W. George Scarlett, "Spiritual Pathology: The Case of Adolf Hitler," *Religions* 2012, 3, 391; http://www.mdpi.com/2077-1444/3/2/389/htm.

10. George Scarlett, quoting Fritz Redlich, in W. George Scarlett, "Spiritual Pathology: The Case of Adolf Hitler," *Religions* 2012, 3, 391; http://www.mdpi.com/2077-1444/

3/2/389/pdf. Redlich's quote is taken from Fritz Redlich, *Hitler: Diagnosis of a Destructive Prophet* (New York: Oxford University Press, 1998), 341.

11. W. George Scarlett, "Spiritual Pathology: The Case of Adolf Hitler," *Religions* 2012, 3, 391; http://www.mdpi.com/2077-1444/3/2/389/pdf.

12. See, for example, Exodus 8:22; 1 Samuel 7:10; Isaiah 11:11; Jeremiah 30:8; Ezekiel 29:21; Haggai 2:23; Mark 4:35; Luke 5:17; Luke 8:22; 2 Thessalonians 1:10; Hebrews 4:7.

13. Adolf Hitler, *Mein Kampf* (New York: Reynal & Hitchcock, 1941), 7–8. Italics added.

14. This quotation is from a translation of Wilhelm Dahm's biography of Lanz von Liebenfels, *Der Mann, der Hitler die Ideen gab* (Munich, 1985), cited on the *Occult History of the Third Reich* blog; http://thirdreichocculthistory.blogspot.com/2013/02/atlantis-und-das-dritte-reich.html.

15. Emmanuel Faye, *Heidegger: The Introduction of Nazism into Philosophy in Light of the Unpublished Seminars of 1933–1935* (New Haven, CT: Yale University Press, 2009), 242.

16. Ibid., 316.

17. Tom Rockmore, *On Heidegger's Nazism and Philosophy* (Berkeley, CA: University of California Press, 1991), 60.

18. John Lukacs, *Five Days in London: May 1940* (New Haven, CT: Yale University Press, 1999), 10.

19. Ibid., 6.

20. Ibid., 128.

21. Ibid.

22. William L. Shirer, *The Rise and Fall of the Third Reich* (New York: Simon and Schuster, 2011), 193.

23. Ibid., 194.

24. Ibid.

25. Winston S. Churchill, speech in Amsterdam, May 9, 1948.

26. Shirer, *Rise and Fall of the Third Reich*, 227.

27. Robert G. L. Waite, *The Psychopathic God Adolf Hitler* (Boston: Da Capo Press, 1993), 31.

28. Ibid.

29. Winston S. Churchill, "Painting as a Pastime," in *Thoughts and Adventures: Churchill Reflects on Spies, Cartoons, Flying, and the Future* (Wilmington, DE: Intercollegiate Studies Institute, 2009), 323.

30. Ibid.

31. Daniel 5:27, KJV.

CHAPTER 5: PRIME MINISTER AT LAST

1. Martin Gilbert, *Churchill: A Life* (New York: Macmillan, 1992), 543.

2. Winston S. Churchill, speech to the House of Commons (London, April 13, 1933).

3. Winston Churchill, speech to the House of Commons in debate, November 28, 1934, vol. 295, cc857-983; retrieved from http://hansard.millbanksystems.com/commons/1934/nov/28/debate-on-the-address.

4. Winston S. Churchill, "Air Parity Lost" (speech to the House of Commons, London, May 2, 1935). The full text of this speech can be found online at www.winstonchurchill.org/resources/speeches/1930-1938-the-wilderness/air-parity-lost.

5. Stanley Baldwin, speech to the House of Commons in debate, March 8, 1934, vol. 286, cc2027-89; retrieved from http://hansard.millbanksystems.com/commons /1934/mar/08/air-estimates-1934#column_2078.

6. Cabinet Minutes, May 1, 1935. Retrieved from nationalarchives.gov.uk.

7. Ibid.

8. John Lukacs, *Five Days in London: May 1940* (New Haven, CT: Yale University Press, 1999), 23.

9. Ibid.

10. Ibid.

11. David Cannadine, quoted in John Lukacs, *Five Days in London: May 1940* (New Haven, CT: Yale University Press, 1999), 21.

12. David Cannadine, *Aspects of Aristocracy: Grandeur and Decline in Modern Britain* (New Haven, CT: Yale University Press, 1994), 132, 147. John Lukacs thought that "these generalizations by David Cannadine have the mark of a heavy pen; they are somewhat exaggerated, but they are not without substance" (*Five Days in London*, 21).

13. Cannadine, *Aspects of Aristocracy*, 118.

14. Ibid., 147.

15. John Lukacs, *Five Days*, 22.

16. Ibid., 23.

17. John Lukacs, *The Duel: The Eighty-Day Struggle Between Churchill and Hitler* (New Haven, CT: Yale University Press, 2001), 23.

18. Martin Gilbert, *Churchill: A Life*, 603.

19. Ibid.

20. Winston S. Churchill, *The Gathering Storm* (Boston: Houghton Mifflin, 1948), 665.

21. Martin Gilbert, *Winston S. Churchill, Volume 6: Finest Hour, 1939–1941* (Hillsdale, MI: Hillsdale College Press, 2011), 314.

22. Ibid., 667.

23. Winston Churchill, "Their Finest Hour" (speech to the House of Commons, London June 18, 1940). The full text of this speech can be found online at www .winstonchurchill.org/resources/speeches/1940-the-finest-hour/their-finest-hour.

24. Winston Churchill, "Blood, Toil, Tears and Sweat" (speech to the House of Commons, London, May 13, 1940). The full text of this speech can be found online at www.winstonchurchill.org/resources/speeches/1940-the-finest-hour /blood-toil-tears-and-sweat.

25. Gilbert, *Finest Hour*, 333.

26. John Colville, *The Fringes of Power: The Incredible Inside Story of Winston Churchill During World War II* (London: Hodder & Stoughton, 1985), 129.

27. Ibid., 135.

28. Cited in Lukacs, *Five Days in London*, 25. The Butler Papers are held at Trinity College, Cambridge.

29. Winston Churchill, "We Shall Fight on the Beaches" (speech to the House of Commons, London, June 4, 1940). The full text of this speech can be found online at www.winstonchurchill.org/resources/speeches/1940-the-finest-hour /we-shall-fight-on-the-beaches.

30. Winston Churchill, "Be Ye Men of Valour," BBC broadcast, May 19, 1940. The full text of this speech can be found online at www.winstonchurchill.org/resources /speeches/1940-the-finest-hour/be-ye-men-of-valour.

31. Judges 6:12, 14, KJV.

32. Richard M. Langworth, ed., *Churchill By Himself: The Definitive Collection of Quotations* (New York: Public Affairs, 2008), 6.

33. Ibid., 596.

34. Ibid.

CHAPTER 6: CHURCHILL AND THE SERMON ON THE MOUNT

1. Winston Churchill, "The Gift of a Common Tongue" (speech at Harvard University, Cambridge, MA, September 6, 1943). The full text of this speech can be found online at www.winstonchurchill.org/resources/speeches/1941-1945-war-leader/the-price-of-greatness-is-responsibility.

2. Stephen Mansfield, "Why Winston Churchill?" stephenmansfield.tv, November 30, 2009. For background, see also Stephen Mansfield, *Never Give In: The Extraordinary Character of Winston Churchill* (Cumberland House, 1997).

3. Winston Churchill, "The Munich Agreement" (speech to the House of Commons, London, October 5, 1938). The full text of this speech can be found online at www.winstonchurchill.org/resources/speeches/1930-1938-the-wilderness/the-munich-agreement.

4. Richard M. Langworth, ed., *Churchill by Himself: The Definitive Collection of Quotations* (New York: Public Affairs, 2008), 170.

5. Winston Churchill, "War of the Unknown Warriors," BBC broadcast, July 14, 1940. The full text of this speech can be found online at www.winstonchurchill.org/resources/speeches/1940-the-finest-hour/war-of-the-unknown-warriors.

6. Winston S. Churchill, speech at the Pilgrims Society luncheon for ambassador-designate Lord Halifax, London, January 9, 1941. See Robert Rhodes James, ed., *Winston S. Churchill: His Complete Speeches 1897–1963* (New York: Bowker, 1974), vol. 6, 6327–6328.

7. Winston Churchill, "The Sinews of Peace" (speech at Westminster College, Fulton, MO, March 5, 1946). The full text of this speech (also commonly known as the "Iron Curtain" speech) can be found online at www.winstonchurchill.org/resources/speeches/1946-1963-elder-statesman/the-sinews-of-peace.

8. Winston Churchill, "A Property-Owning Democracy" (speech at the Conservative Party Conference, Blackpool, October 5, 1946), in Winston S. Churchill, *Never Give In! The Best of Winston Churchill's Speeches* (New York: Hyperion, 2003), 431.

9. Winston Churchill, keynote address (MIT Mid-Century Convocation, Cambridge, MA, March 31, 1949). The full text of this speech can be found online at https://libraries.mit.edu/archives/exhibits/midcentury/mid-cent-churchill.html.

10. Langworth, *Churchill by Himself*, 461.

11. Stephen Mansfield, "The Hidden Calling," *The Christian Post*, July 19, 2012; http://blogs.christianpost.com/in-our-time/the-hidden-calling-10923.

12. Ibid.

13. Winston Churchill, "The Defence of Freedom and Peace (The Lights Are Going Out)," broadcast to the United States and to London, October 16, 1938. The full text of this speech can be found online at www.winstonchurchill.org/resources/speeches/1930-1938-the-wilderness/the-defence-of-freedom-and-peace.

14. Editor's explanatory note in Langworth, *Churchill by Himself*, 476.

15. Matthew 5:1-10, KJV.

16. Winston Churchill, "We Shall Fight on the Beaches" (speech to the House of

Commons, London, June 4, 1940). Italics added. The full text of this speech can be found online at www.winstonchurchill.org/resources/speeches/1940-the-finest-hour/we-shall-fight-on-the-beaches.

17. Elizabeth Nel, *Mr. Churchill's Secretary* (New York: Coward-McCann, 1958), 73.

18. Ibid.

19. Edmund Burke, quoted in Drew Maciag, *Edmund Burke in America: The Contested Career of the Father of Modern Conservatism* (Ithaca, NY: Cornell University Press, 2013), 133.

20. Langworth, *Churchill by Himself*, 369.

21. Proverbs 2:15, NIV.

22. Winston Churchill, speech to the Royal Society of St. John (London, April 24, 1933). The full text of this speech can be found online at www.winstonchurchill.org/publications/finest-hour/finest-hour-133/churchill-on-england.

23. Langworth, *Churchill by Himself*, 23.

24. Winston Churchill, "War of the Unknown Warriors, 1940," BBC broadcast, July 14, 1940. The full text of this speech can be found online at www.nationalchurchillmuseum.org/war-of-the-unknown-warriors-speech.html.

25. Winston S. Churchill, eulogy for Neville Chamberlain, November 12, 1940. The full text of this eulogy can be found online at www.winstonchurchill.org/resources/speeches/1940-the-finest-hour/neville-chamberlain.

26. Spiros Zodhiates, ed., *The Hebrew-Greek Key Word Study Bible* (Iowa City, IA: World Bible Publishers), 1699.

27. James 4:8, NIV.

28. Kenneth W. Thompson, *Winston Churchill's World View: Statesmanship and Power* (Baton Rouge: Louisiana State University Press, 1983), 20.

29. Winston Churchill, speech to the House of Commons (London, December 3, 1936).

30. "Peace and Solvency," *The Times* (London), November 10, 1951, 7. Cited in Thompson, *Winston Churchill's World View*, 22.

31. Thompson, *Winston Churchill's World View*, 22.

32. Andrew Roberts, "Churchill Proceedings—Winston Churchill and Religion—A Comfortable Relationship with the Almighty," *Finest Hour* 163, Summer 2014, 52.

33. John Colville, *The Fringes of Power: The Incredible Inside Story of Winston Churchill During World War II* (London: Hodder & Stoughton, 1985), 648.

34. Matthew 5:13-14.

35. Elizabeth Nel, *Mr. Churchill's Secretary*, 8.

36. Ibid., 137.

37. Winston S. Churchill, "Prime Minister to Minister for Works and Buildings," January 6, 1941, in *The Second World War, Volume 3: The Grand Alliance*. (Boston: Houghton Mifflin, 1950), 723. Cited in Thompson, *Winston Churchill's World View*, 102.

38. Winston Churchill, "The Defence of Freedom and Peace (The Lights Are Going Out)," broadcast to the United States and to London, October 16, 1938. The full text of this speech can be found online at www.winstonchurchill.org/resources/speeches/1930-1938-the-wilderness/the-defence-of-freedom-and-peace.

39. Winston Churchill, *Thoughts and Adventures* (London: Thornton Butterworth, 1932), 5.

40. Matthew 5:17-19.

41. Winston Churchill, speech at Birmingham Town Hall, November 11, 1903.

42. Ibid.

43. Winston Churchill, memo to General Ismay for the Chiefs of Staff Committee, July 6, 1944, cited in Martin Gilbert, *Churchill: A Life.* (New York: Henry Holt, 1991), 782–783. The full text of the memorandum can be found online at www.information clearinghouse.info/article999.htm.

44. Matthew 23:23, KJV.

45. Winston Churchill, *Thoughts and Adventures*, 299–311.

46. Matthew 5:21-22, 25.

47. Churchill, *Thoughts and Adventures*, 225.

48. Ibid.

49. Ibid.

50. Winston S. Churchill, *Amid These Storms: Thoughts and Adventures* (New York: Charles Scribner's Sons, 1932), 203–204.

51. Matthew 5:23-24.

52. Churchill, *Amid These Storms*, 225–226.

53. Matthew 5:31-32.

54. Alexandra Sifferlin, "Top 10 Famous Love Letters," *Time*, Lifestyle, February 9, 2012.

55. Ibid., 34.

56. Ibid., 35.

57. From an Associated Press report, October 24, 1963.

58. Matthew 5:33-37.

59. Churchill, *Thoughts and Adventures,* 306.

60. Ibid.

61. Winston S. Churchill, speech to the House of Commons (London, March 26, 1936). The full text of the debate can be found online at http://hansard. millbanksystems.com/commons/1936/mar/26/european-situation# S5CV0310P0_19360326_HOC_344. Mr. Churchill's remarks are just before 9:52 p.m. and just past marker 1530.

62. Matthew 5:38-40.

63. Churchill's remarks cited in Martin Gilbert, *The Second World War: A Complete History* (New York: Henry Holt, 1989), 441. See also Christopher C. Harmon, "Are We Beasts? Churchill and the Moral Question of World War II 'Area Bombing,'" Newport Paper #1, December 1991, Naval War College, Newport, RI, 3.

64. Cited in Harmon, "Are We Beasts?" 5.

65. Ibid.

66. Herman S. Wolk, *Cataclysm: General Hap Arnold and the Defeat of Japan* (Denton: University of North Texas Press, 2010), 53.

67. Harmon, "Are We Beasts?" 4.

68. Ibid.

69. Winston S. Churchill, *The Gathering Storm* (Boston: Houghton Mifflin, 1948), 35.

70. Ibid., 35, 37.

71. Matthew 5:43-45.

72. Churchill, *Thoughts and Adventures*, 224.

73. "August 10, 1941: Churchill and Roosevelt Pray Together," World War II Today; http://ww2today.com/10th-august-1941-churchill-and-roosevelt-pray-together.

74. Mary Soames, *A Daughter's Tale: The Memoir of Winston Churchill's Youngest Child* (New York: Random House, 2011), 6.

75. Matthew 6:19-21.

76. Churchill, *Thoughts and Adventures,* 308.

77. Ibid., 292–293.

78. Ibid., 311.

79. Winston Churchill, quoted in Kenneth W. Thompson, *Winston Churchill's World View* (Baton Rouge: Louisiana State University Press, 1983), 9.

80. Winston Churchill, keynote address at MIT Mid-Century Convocation, (Cambridge, MA, March 31, 1949). The full text of this speech can be found online at https://libraries.mit.edu/archives/exhibits/midcentury/mid-cent-churchill.html.

81. Churchill, "The Defence of Freedom and Peace (The Lights Are Going Out)."

CHAPTER 7: PRESERVING A "CERTAIN WAY OF LIFE"

1. Winston S. Churchill, *A History of the English-Speaking Peoples, Volume 1: The Birth of Britain* (New York: Dodd, Mead, 1956), 120, 122.

2. Ibid., 122.

3. Ibid., 121. Churchill's attribution for this quote is as follows: "Quoted in Hodgkin, *History of the Anglo-Saxons,* p. 609."

4. Ibid., again quoting from Hodgkin.

5. Matthew 12:35.

6. Edmund Burke, quoted in Drew Maciag, *Edmund Burke in America: The Contested Career of the Father of Modern Conservatism* (Ithaca, NY: Cornell University Press, 2013), 133.

7. Winston Churchill, *Thoughts and Adventures* (London: Thornton Butterworth, 1932), 310.

8. Darrell Holley, *Churchill's Literary Allusions* (Jefferson, NC: McFarland, 1987), 7. Italics in the original.

9. Ibid.

10. Paul Addison, *Churchill: The Unexpected Hero* (Oxford: Oxford University Press, 2005), 217.

11. Churchill, *Thoughts and Adventures,* 293.

12. Ibid., 304.

13. Ibid., 288.

14. Ibid.

15. Ibid., 294.

16. Ibid.

17. Richard M. Langworth, ed., *Churchill by Himself: The Definitive Collection of Quotations* (New York: Public Affairs, 2008), 76.

18. Ibid., 75.

19. Ibid., 91.

20. Kenneth W. Thompson, *Winston Churchill's World View: Statesmanship and Power,* (Baton Rouge: Louisiana State University Press, 1983), 67.

21. Winston Churchill, "Army Reform," speech to the House of Commons (London, May 13, 1901). The full text of this speech can be found online at www.winstonchurchill.org/resources/speeches/1901-1914-rising-star/army-reform.

22. Ibid.

23. Winston Churchill, "War of the Unknown Warriors," BBC broadcast, July 14, 1940. The full text of this speech can be found online at www.winstonchurchill.org/resources/speeches/1940-the-finest-hour/war-of-the-unknown-warriors.

24. Winston Churchill, *The Story of the Malakand Field Force* (Mineola, NY: Dover, 2010), 29.

25. Ibid.

26. Edmund Burke, "Reflections on the Revolution in France" (1790), in *Burke, Select Works* (Oxford: Clarendon, 1888), vol. 2, 290–291.

27. Winston Churchill, "War of the Unknown Warriors," BBC broadcast, July 14, 1940. The full text of this speech can be found online at www.winstonchurchill.org/resources/speeches/1940-the-finest-hour/war-of-the-unknown-warriors.

28. Langworth, *Churchill by Himself*, 76.

29. Churchill, *Thoughts and Adventures*, 283.

30. Patrick Sawer, "Sir Winston Churchill's family feared he might convert to Islam," *The Telegraph*, December 28, 2014, www.telegraph.co.uk/news/religion/11314580/Sir-Winston-Churchill-s-family-feared-he-might-convert-to-Islam.html.

31. Warren Dockter, *Churchill and the Islamic World* (London: I. B. Tauris, 2015), 12.

32. Winston Spencer Churchill, *The River War: An Historical Account of the Reconquest of the Soudan* (London: Longmans, Green, 1899), vol. 2, 248–250.

33. Ibid.

34. Spencer Warren, "In the Ranks of Honor," review of *Winston S. Churchill: Finest Hour, 1939–1941*, by Martin Gilbert, *Commentary*, July 1, 1984, www.commentarymagazine.com/article/winston-s-churchill-finest-hour-1939-1941-by-martin-gilbert.

35. Joshua 1:9.

36. Barbara W. Tuchman, *The Proud Tower: A Portrait of the World before the War, 1890–1914*, trade paperback edition (New York: Random House, 2014), xv.

37. Ibid., 33–34.

38. Winston S. Churchill, *Amid These Storms: Thoughts and Adventures* (New York: Charles Scribner's Sons, 1932), 76–77.

39. Frederic Morton, *A Nervous Splendor: Vienna, 1888/1889* (New York: Penguin, 1979).

40. Ibid., 17–18.

41. Ibid., 9.

42. Ibid., 11.

43. Ibid.

44. Winston Churchill, "Blood, Toil, Tears and Sweat" (speech to the House of Commons, London, May 13, 1940). The full text of this speech can be found online at www.winstonchurchill.org/resources/speeches/1940-the-finest-hour/blood-toil-tears-and-sweat.

45. Tim Townsend, *Mission at Nuremberg: An American Army Chaplain and the Trial of the Nazis* (New York: HarperLuxe, 2014), 193.

46. Ibid., 200.

47. Ibid., 199.

48. Colonel Burton C. Andrus, letter to the San Diego Commandery of the Masonic Order of the Knights Templar, cited in Townsend, *Mission at Nuremberg*, 98. Andrus also wrote his own account of the Nuremberg trials: *I Was the Nuremberg Jailer* (New York: Coward-McCann, 1969).

49. Townsend, *Mission at Nuremberg*, 153.
50. "Churchill on War Crimes Trials," *Opinio Juris*, January 23, 2006. Retrieved from http://lawofnations.blogspot.com/2006/01/churchill-on-war-crimes-trials_23.html.

CHAPTER 8: HITLER AND "PERVERTED SCIENCE"

1. Winston S. Churchill, *The Gathering Storm* (Boston: Houghton Mifflin, 1948), 35–36.
2. Winston Churchill, "Their Finest Hour" (speech to the House of Commons, London, June 18, 1940). The full text of this speech can be found online at www.winstonchurchill.org/resources/speeches/1940-the-finest-hour/their-finest-hour.
3. Winston S. Churchill, "Never Despair" (speech to the House of Commons, London, March 1, 1955).
4. See, for example, James Hannam, *God's Philosophers: How the Medieval World Laid the Foundations of Modern Science* (London: Icon Books, 2009).
5. Albert Speer, *Inside the Third Reich* (New York: Simon & Schuster, 1970), 96.
6. Churchill, *Gathering Storm*, 50.
7. Christa Schroeder, *He Was My Chief: The Memoirs of Adolf Hitler's Secretary* (Barnsley, UK: Frontline Books, 2009), Kindle edition.
8. Richard Weikart, *From Darwin to Hitler: Evolutionary Ethics, Eugenics, and Racism in Germany* (New York: Palgrave Macmillan, 2004), x.
9. Ibid., 11.
10. Richard Goldschmidt, *Portraits from Memory* (Seattle: University of Washington Press, 1956), 34. Cited in Weikart, *From Darwin to Hitler*, 11.
11. Weikart, *From Darwin to Hitler*, 11.
12. Ibid., 196.
13. Richard Weikart, "The Origins of Social Darwinism in Germany, 1859–1895," *Journal of the History of Ideas*, July 1993, 469.
14. Richard Weikart, "A Recently Discovered Darwin Letter on Social Darwinism," Isis 86 (1995): 609–611; www.csustan.edu/sites/default/files/History/Faculty/Weikart/Recently-Discovered-Darwin-Letter.pdf
15. John Lukacs, *Five Days in London: May 1940* (New Haven, CT: Yale University Press, 1999), 56.
16. Ibid., 58
17. Ibid., 57.
18. Ibid., 58.
19. See Adolf Hitler, *Mein Kampf* (New York: Reynal & Hitchcock, 1941), 406.
20. Churchill, *Gathering Storm*, 37.
21. James Hannam, *God's Philosophers* (London: Icon, 2009), 340–341.
22. Ibid., 337–342.
23. Ibid, 336.
24. Weikart, *From Darwin to Hitler*, 212.
25. Ibid.
26. Henry Friedlander, *The Origins of Nazi Genocide: From Euthanasia to the Final Solution* (Chapel Hill: University of North Carolina Press, 1995), 1.
27. Weikart, *From Darwin to Hitler*, 31.

28. Friedlander, *Origins of Nazi Genocide*, 81.

29. Winston Churchill, "Fifty Years Hence, 1931," www.nationalchurchillmuseum.org /fifty-years-hence.html.

30. Jenn Selby, "Richard Dawkins on babies with Down Syndrome," *The Independent*, August 20, 2014, www.independent.co.uk/news/people/richard-dawkins-on -babies-with-down-syndrome-abort-it-and-try-again-it-would-be-immoral-to -bring-it-into-the-world-9681549.html.

31. M. D. Aeschliman, "Theodor Haecker," *Crisis Magazine*, April 9, 2012.

32. Ibid.

33. Weikart, *From Darwin to Hitler*, 33.

34. Francois Genoud, ed., *The Testament of Adolf Hitler: The Hitler-Bormann Documents, February–April, 1945*, trans. R. H. Stevens (London: Icon, 1962). Cited in Weikart, *From Darwin to Hitler*, 213.

35. Winston Churchill, *Thoughts and Adventures* (London: Thornton Butterworth, 1932), 295.

36. Albert Speer, *Inside the Third Reich*, 520.

37. Ibid.

38. Ibid., 520–521.

39. Elizabeth Nel, *Mr. Churchill's Secretary* (New York: Coward-McCann, 1958), 82.

40. Winston Churchill, "Fifty Years Hence, 1931."

41. Ibid.

42. Ian Kershaw, *Hitler: A Biography* (New York: WW Norton, 2008), 661.

43. Alfred Gortjahn, quoted in Weikart, *From Darwin to Hitler*, 12. (In general, positivism is the theory that any assertion that claims to be rational can be verified scientifically, logically, or mathematically. Theism—truth based on deity and revelation—is considered invalid as a source of rational truth. Social-legal positivism holds that there is no absolute truth that might restrain the laws of a particular society, but rather that judgments are authoritative in the context of prevailing culture and precedent.)

44. Charles Taylor, *A Secular Age* (Cambridge, MA: Belknap, 2007), 18.

45. "Abbot Suger of Saint-Denis: the Patron of the Arts," in Teresa G. Frisch, *Gothic Art 1140–c. 1450: Sources and Documents* (Toronto: University of Toronto Press, 1987), 7.

46. Psalm 8:3-5, NIV.

47. John Polkinghorne, *Exploring Reality: The Intertwining of Science and Religion* (New Haven, CT: Yale University Press, 2005), 5.

48. Isaac Newton, letter to Robert Hooke, February 5, 1676. Cited in James Hannam, *God's Philosophers*, 1.

49. Austin L. Hughes, "The Folly of Scientism," *The New Atlantis: A Journal of Technology & Society*, no. 37, Fall 2012, www.thenewatlantis.com/publications /the-folly-of-scientism.

50. Ibid.

51. Speer, *Inside the Third Reich*, 165.

52. Ibid., 357.

53. Genesis 11:4, NIV.

54. Josef Goebbels, diary entry, May 8, 1943. Cited in Albert Speer, *Inside the Third Reich*, 160. Exactly two years after he wrote this entry, Germany surrendered.

55. Barbara Tuchman, *The Proud Tower*, trade paperback edition (New York: Random House, 2014), 323, 326.

56. Ibid., 278.

57. Tim Townsend, *Mission at Nuremberg: An American Army Chaplain and the Trial of the Nazis* (New York: HarperLuxe, 2014), 11. Italics added.

CHAPTER 9: HITLER AND THE CORRUPTION OF THE CHURCH

1. Quoted in "Martin Niemöller: 'First they came for the Socialists . . .'," *Holocaust Encyclopedia*, United States Holocaust Memorial Museum, Washington, DC, http://www.ushmm.org/wlc/en/article.php?ModuleId=10007392.

2. Ibid.

3. Charles Colson, *Kingdoms in Conflict* (Grand Rapids: Zondervan, 1987), 138.

4. Ibid., 140.

5. Eric Metaxas, *Bonhoeffer: Pastor, Martyr, Prophet, Spy* (Nashville: Thomas Nelson, 2010), 193.

6. Christa Schroeder, *He Was My Chief: The Memoirs of Adolf Hitler's Secretary* (Barnsley, UK: Frontline Books, 2009), Kindle edition.

7. Adolf Hitler, *Mein Kampf* (New York: Reynal & Hitchcock, 1941), 675–676.

8. Max Domarus, ed., *Hitler: Speeches and Proclamations, 1932–1945*, trans. Mary Fran Gilbert (Wauconda, IL: Bolchazi-Carducci, 1990), 1451.

9. Metaxas, *Bonhoeffer*, 185.

10. Ibid.

11. "Introduction to the Theological Declaration of Barmen," *Book of Confessions*, study edition (Louisville, KY: Geneva Press, 1996), 303.

12. H. Fischer-Hüllstrung, cited in Metaxas, *Bonhoeffer*, 532.

13. Hans Kerrl, cited in William L. Shirer, *The Rise and Fall of the Third Reich: A History of Nazi Germany* (New York: Simon & Schuster, 1959), 239.

14. Ibid.

15. Bruce Walker, "Christian Opposition to Nazi Anti-Semitism," *American Thinker*, November 19, 2007.

16. Albert Einstein, quoted in Ernst Christian Helmreich, *The German Churches under Hitler: Background, Struggle, and Epilogue* (Detroit: Wayne State University Press, 1979), 345. Some have denied that Einstein made this statement, but the fact that his words were published widely in *Time* magazine (December 23, 1940) and other media, without Einstein's refutation, would support its accuracy.

17. Romans 13:1-2, RSV.

18. Romans 13:3-5, RSV.

19. See Isaiah 14:12-17; Ezekiel 28:14-19.

20. Winston Churchill, "Fifty Years Hence, 1931," www.nationalchurchillmuseum.org/fifty-years-hence.html.

21. Kenneth W. Thompson, *Winston Churchill's World View: Statesmanship and Power* (Baton Rouge: Louisiana State University Press, 1983), 43. Thompson cites the following source for this quote from Churchill: London *Times*, September 17, 1951, 4.

22. Jim Collins, *Good to Great and the Social Sectors: A Monograph to Accompany Good to Great* (Boulder, CO: Jim Collins, 2005), 12–13. Italics in the original.

23. Authors' abridgment and paraphrase of Exodus 20:2-4, 7-8, 12-17.

CHAPTER 10: NAZISM AND THE GERMAN DISASTER

1. Mary Eberstadt, *How the West Really Lost God: A New Theory of Secularization* (West Conshohocken, PA: Templeton Press, 2013), 4. Italics in the original.

2. Samuel P. Huntington, *Who Are We? The Challenge to America's National Identity* (New York: Simon & Schuster, 2004), 107, 138.

3. Theodore Dalrymple, *Our Culture, What's Left of It: The Mandarins and the Masses* (Chicago: Ivan R. Dee, 2005), 7.

4. Ibid., x.

5. Ibid., 8.

6. Ibid., 8.

7. Margaret Thatcher, speech to the General Assembly of the Church of Scotland (Assembly Hall, Edinburgh, May 21, 1988). The full text of this speech can be found online at www.margaretthatcher.org/document/107246.

8. David Cameron, "My faith in the Church of England," *Church Times*, April 16, 2014, http://www.churchtimes.co.uk/articles/2014/17-april/comment/opinion /my-faith-in-the-church-of-england.

9. Galatians 4:4, ESV.

10. Will Durant, *Heroes of History: A Brief History of Civilization from Ancient Times to the Dawn of the Modern Age* (New York: Simon & Schuster, 2001), 19.

11. Matthew 13:7.

12. Johann Sebastian Bach, quoted in Gregory Wilbur, *Glory and Honor: The Music and Artistic Legacy of Johann Sebastian Bach* (Nashville: Cumberland House, 2005), 1.

13. Charles Burney, quoted in Richard Taruskin, *Music in the Seventeenth and Eighteenth Centuries* (Oxford: Oxford University Press, 2005), 363.

14. Ibid., 642.

15. Calvin R. Stapert, "To the Glory of God Alone," *Christian History*, issue 95, July 7, 2007, http://www.christianitytoday.com/ch/2007/issue95/1.8.html?start=5.

16. Milton S. Terry, *Biblical Hermeneutics: A Treatise on the Interpretation of the Old and New Testament* (Grand Rapids: Zondervan, 1979), 55, 62.

17. Milton S. Terry, "Exegesis of the Eighteenth Century," in *Library of Biblical and Theological Literature*, vol. 2, George R. Crooks and John F. Hurst, eds. (New York: Phillips & Hunt, 1883), 710.

18. Lord Melbourne, quoted in Charles Colson, *Kingdoms in Conflict* (Grand Rapids, Zondervan, 1989), 95. This quote is widely disseminated, and some versions have Melbourne saying "private life" rather than "public life." Whatever the case, he apparently didn't relish the "interference" of religion at either level.

19. Terry, *Biblical Hermeneutics*, 55.

20. Terry, "Exegesis of the Eighteenth Century," 710.

21. Leon Poliakov, *The Aryan Myth: A History of Racist and Nationalist Ideas in Europe*, Edmund Howard, trans. (New York: Basic Books, 1974), 310.

22. Adolf Hitler, *Mein Kampf* (New York: Reynal & Hitchcock, 1941), 23.

23. Adolf Hitler, quoted in "Hitler and Wagner," *The Telegraph*, July 25, 2011, www.telegraph.co.uk/culture/music/classicalmusic/8659814/Hitler-and-Wagner .html.

24. Poliakov, *Aryan Myth*, 311.

25. Ibid.

26. Thomas Mann, *Wagner und Unsere Zeit* (Frankfurt: S. Fischer 1963), 158.

27. Geoffrey Wheatcroft, "A Widow's Might," review of *Winifred Wagner: A Life at the Heart of Hitler's Bayreuth*, by Brigitte Hamann, *New York Times*, March 11, 2007, www.nytimes.com/2007/03/11/books/review/Wheatcroft.t.html?_r=0&page wanted=print.

28. Lucasta Miller, "At Home with the Wagners," *The Guardian*, August 19, 2005. Miller quotes the line "the seer and herald of the Third Reich" from Brigitte Hamann, *Winifred Wagner: A Life at the Heart of Hitler's Bayreuth* (Boston: Harcourt, 2005), 59. The full review can be read online at www.theguardian.com/books/2005/aug/20/featuresreviews.guardianreview8.

29. Miller, "At Home with the Wagners."

30. Larry Arnhart, "Nietzsche, Hitler, and Wagner's *Parsifal*," *Darwinian Conservatism by Larry Arnhart* (blog), November 15, 2013, http://darwinianconservatism.blogspot.com/2013/11/nietzsche-hitler-and-wagners-parsifal.html.

31. Bruce E. Benson, *Pious Nietzsche: Decadence and Dionysian Faith* (Bloomington: Indiana University Press, 2008), 31–32.

32. Friedrich Nietzsche, *The Gay Science*, trans. Walter Kaufmann (New York: Random House, 1974), 181.

33. Adolf Hitler, *Mein Kampf* (Munich: NSDAP, 1943), 144–145, as quoted in Geoffrey Cantor and Marc Swetlltz, eds., *Jewish Tradition and the Challenge of Darwinism* (Chicago: University of Chicago Press, 2006), 114.

34. This observation is found in footnote f6 on the Darwin Correspondence Project's transcription of a letter from C. R. Darwin to A. R. Wallace (5 July 1866). The full text of the letter, and the corresponding footnotes, can be found online at www.darwinproject.ac.uk/letter/entry-5145.

35. Herbert Spencer, *The Man versus the State: A Collection of Essays*, ed. Truxton Beale (New York: Mitchell Kennerley, 1916), 229.

36. Ibid., 229–230.

37. Richard Weikart, *From Darwin to Hitler: Evolutionary Ethics, Eugenics, and Racism in Germany* (New York: Palgrave Macmillan, 2004), 210.

38. Adrian Desmond, *Huxley: From Devil's Disciple to Evolution's High Priest* (Reading, MA: Addison-Wesley, 1997), 271.

39. Adolf Hitler, *Mein Kampf* (Munich: NSDAP, 1943), 316–317.

40. Konrad Heiden, quoted in Dusty Sklar, *The Nazis and the Occult* (New York: Dorset Press, 1977), 3.

CHAPTER 11: CHURCHILL'S URGENT CONCERN—AND OURS

1. Winston Churchill, chancellor's address (University of Bristol, England, July 2, 1938), in Robert Rhodes James, ed., *Winston S. Churchill: His Complete Speeches, 1897–1963*, (New York: Chelsea House, 1974), vol. 6, 5991.

2. Samuel P. Huntington, "The Erosion of American National Interest: The Disintegration of Identity," in Ernest J. Wilson III, *Diversity and US Foreign Policy: A Reader* (New York: Routledge, 2004), 101. Italics added.

3. John Maynard Keynes, "CW 10, 'My Early Beliefs' (1938)," in *The Essential Keynes* (London: Penguin Classics, 2015).

4. Winston Churchill, broadcast on the Soviet-German War, London, June 22, 1941. The full text of the speech can be read online at www.ibiblio.org/pha/policy/1941/410622d.html.

5. Richard M. Langworth, ed., *Churchill by Himself: The Definitive Collection of Quotations* (New York: Public Affairs, 2008), 137.

6. Winston Churchill, "The Defence of Freedom and Peace (The Lights Are Going Out)" (broadcast to the United States and to London, October 16, 1938). The full text of this speech can be found online at www.winstonchurchill.org/resources/speeches/1930-1938-the-wilderness/the-defence-of-freedom-and-peace.

7. The word *antinomian* is derived from the merging of two Greek terms—*anti*, meaning "against," or "in place of," and *nomos*, or "law." Antinomianism is, broadly, the idea that one need not obey the laws of God or society.

8. "Wit and Wisdom—'St. George and the Dragon,'" *Finest Hour* 145, Winter 2009–10, 19. The full text of this article can be found online at www.winstonchurchill.org/publications/finest-hour/finest-hour-145/wit-and-wisdom-st-george-and-the-dragon.

9. "Empire or Commonwealth?" *Finest Hour* 154, Spring 2012. The full text of Churchill's remarks can be found online at www.winstonchurchill.org/publications/finest-hour/finest-hour-154/wit-and-wisdom.

10. Os Guinness, *A Free People's Suicide* (Downers Grove, IL: IVP Books, 2012), 169.

11. "Christopher Dawson: His Interpretation of History," *Modern Age,* Summer 1979, 263. Cited in Charles Colson, *Kingdoms in Conflict* (Grand Rapids: Zondervan, 1987), 288.

12. Ibid.

13. Langworth, *Churchill by Himself,* 115.

14. John Lukacs, *Five Days in London: May 1940* (New Haven, CT: Yale University Press, 1999), 16–17. Italics in the original.

15. John Lukacs, *The Duel: The Eighty-Day Struggle between Churchill and Hitler* (New Haven, CT: Yale University Press, 1999), 40.

16. Mary Soames, *A Daughter's Tale: The Memoir of Winston Churchill's Youngest Child* (New York: Random House, 2011), 92–93.

17. Ibid.

18. Elizabeth Nel, *Mr. Churchill's Secretary* (New York: Coward-McCann, 1958), 78.

19. David McCullough, "Why History?" (acceptance speech at the National Book Awards ceremony, November 15, 1995). The full text of this speech can be found online at http://www.nationalbook.org/nbaacceptspeech_dmccullough.html#.VUNksPlVhBd.

20. "American Astarte," *Kairos Journal,* August 20, 2014, http://www.kairosjournal.org/document.aspx?DocumentID=5073&QuadrantID=4&CategoryID=6&TopicID=23&L=1.

21. Theodore Dalrymple, *Our Culture, What's Left of It: The Mandarins and the Masses* (Chicago: Ivan R. Dee, 2005), xi.

22. This quotation is often attributed to Mark Twain, but there is no definitive primary-source evidence that he ever actually said it.

23. Victor David Hanson, "Our Dangerous Historical Moment," *National Review,* February 19, 2015, www.nationalreview.com/node/414021/our-dangerous-historical-moment-victor-davis-hanson.

24. Graeme Wood, "What ISIS Really Wants," *The Atlantic*, March 2015, www.theatlantic.com/features/archive/2015/02/what-isis-really-wants/384980. Wood draws his ideas from George Orwell's 1940 review of *Mein Kampf.*

25. Wood, "What ISIS Really Wants."

CHAPTER 12: HOW CHURCHILL KEPT CALM AND CARRIED ON

1. Winston Churchill, chancellor's address (University of Bristol, England, July 2, 1938), in Robert Rhodes James, ed., *Winston S. Churchill: His Complete Speeches, 1897–1963*, (New York: Chelsea House, 1974), vol. 6, 5991.

2. Roger Cohen, "The Great Unraveling," *New York Times*, September 15, 2014, www .nytimes.com/2014/09/16/opinion/roger-cohen-the-great-unraveling.html?_r=0.

3. Ibid.

4. Ibid.

5. Mary Soames, *A Daughter's Tale: The Memoir of Winston Churchill's Youngest Child* (New York: Random House, 2011), 141.

6. Ibid., 142–143.

7. The history of the Keep Calm and Carry On campaign can be found online at www.keepcalmandcarryon.com/history.

8. Stuart Hughes, "The Greatest Motivational Poster Ever?" *BBC News* magazine, February 4, 2009, http://news.bbc.co.uk/2/hi/uk_news/magazine/7869458.stm.

9. Susannah Walker, *Home Front Posters of the Second World War* (Oxford: Shire Publications, 2012), 45.

10. See Proverbs 29:18.

11. "Boris Johnson discusses *The Churchill Factor*," *ChurchillCentral*, accessed May 21, 2015, www.churchillcentral.com/timeline/video/boris-johnson-discusses -the-churchill-factor.

12. Richard M. Langworth, ed., *Churchill by Himself: The Definitive Collection of Quotations* (New York: Public Affairs, 2008), 6–7.

13. Winston Churchill, "Blood, Toil, Tears and Sweat" (speech to the House of Commons, London, May 13, 1940). The full text of this speech can be found online at www.winstonchurchill.org/resources/speeches/1940-the-finest-hour /blood-toil-tears-and-sweat.

14. Winston Churchill, "Be Ye Men of Valour," BBC broadcast, May 19, 1940. The full text of this speech can be found online at www.winstonchurchill.org/resources /speeches/1940-the-finest-hour/be-ye-men-of-valour.

15. John Colville, *The Churchillians* (London: Weidenfeld and Nicolson, 1981), 157.

16. T. E. B. Howarth, ed., *Monty at Close Quarters: Recollections of the Man* (London: Leo Cooper, 1985), 86.

17. Langworth, *Churchill by Himself*, 18.

18. Ibid., 15.

19. 1 Chronicles 12:32.

20. John Lukacs, *Churchill: Visionary. Statesman. Historian.* (New Haven, CT: Yale University Press, 2002), 17–18.

21. Winston S. Churchill, acceptance speech for the Nobel Prize in Literature, 1953, in *The Nobel Prize Library* (New York: Helvetica Press, 1971), 183.

22. Langworth, *Churchill by Himself*, 20.

23. Ibid., 12.

24. Winston S. Churchill, "Air Parity Lost" (speech to the House of Commons, London, May 2, 1935). The full text of this speech can be found online at www.winston churchill.org/resources/speeches/1930-1938-the-wilderness/air-parity-lost.

25. Langworth, *Churchill by Himself*, 14.

26. Ibid., 13.

27. Ibid.

28. Lewis Broad, *Winston Churchill: The Years of Achievement* (New York: Hawthorn Books, 1963), 41.

29. Langworth, *Churchill by Himself*, 15.

30. Ibid., 18.

31. Ibid., 20.

32. Elizabeth Nel, *Mr. Churchill's Secretary* (New York: Coward-McCann, 1958), 35.

33. Winston S. Churchill, *Amid These Storms: Thoughts and Adventures* (New York: Charles Scribner's Sons, 1932), 288.

34. Ibid.

35. Steven F. Hayward, *Churchill on Leadership: Executive Success in the Face of Adversity* (New York: Gramercy Books, 2004), 152.

36. Ibid.

37. Galatians 3:24-26.

38. Hayward, *Churchill on Leadership*, 150.

39. Churchill, *Amid These Storms*, 290.

40. Charles McMoran Wilson, *Winston S. Churchill: The Struggle for Survival, 1940–1965* (London: Heron Books, 1966), 38.

41. Langworth, *Churchill by Himself*, 299.

42. Ibid., 12.

43. Churchill, *Amid These Storms*, 313.

44. Langworth, *Churchill by Himself*, 14.

45. Ibid., 18.

46. Ibid.

47. Zechariah 4:10, NIV.

48. *War Memoirs of David Lloyd George: 1916–1917* (Boston: Little, Brown, 1934), 25.

49. David Jablonsky, *Churchill, the Great Game, and Total War* (New York: Routledge, 2013), 61.

50. Langworth, *Churchill by Himself*, 15.

51. Ibid.

52. Ibid., 20.

53. Ibid., 17.

54. Ibid., 12, 13.

55. Winston S. Churchill, "Air Parity Lost," (speech to the House of Commons, London, May 2, 1935).

56. René Kraus, *Winston Churchill: A Biography* (Philadelphia: J. B. Lippincott, 1940), 102.

57. Langworth, *Churchill by Himself*, 18.

58. Ibid., 20.

59. Mary Soames, *A Daughter's Tale: The Memoir of Winston Churchill's Youngest Child* (New York: Random House, 2011), 217.

60. Langworth, *Churchill by Himself*, 13.

61. Soames, *A Daughter's Tale*, 254.

62. Ibid. Italics in the original.

63. Churchill, *Amid These Storms*, 298.

64. Ibid., 302.

65. Ibid., 307.

66. Ibid.

67. Ibid.

CHAPTER 13: CHURCHILL AND THE CHARACTER OF LEADERSHIP

1. Boris Johnson, *The Churchill Factor* (New York: Riverhead Books, 2014), 326.

2. Winston S. Churchill, *Amid These Storms: Thoughts and Adventures* (New York: Charles Scribner's Sons, 1932), 39, 45.

3. Jonathan Currier, "God's Joke Book," *Day1*, July 21, 2013. http://day1.org/5013 -gods_joke_book.

4. 1 Corinthians 1:27, NIV.

5. Maurice Hankey, cited in Steven F. Hayward, *Churchill on Leadership: Executive Success in the Face of Adversity* (New York: Gramercy Books, 2004), 115.

6. Psalm 121:1, NIV.

7. Matthew 16:21-22.

8. See Matthew 16:21-28.

9. Winston Churchill, "Blood, Toil, Tears and Sweat" (speech to the House of Commons, London, May 13, 1940). The full text of this speech can be found online at www.winstonchurchill.org/resources/speeches/1940-the-finest-hour /blood-toil-tears-and-sweat.

10. Roger Parrott, *The Longview: Lasting Strategies for Rising Leaders* (Colorado Springs: David C. Cook, 2009), 13.

11. Jeryl Bier, "Kerry on Religion: 'Not the Way I Think Most People Want to Live,'" *The Weekly Standard* (blog), May 5, 2014, www.weeklystandard.com/blogs/kerry -religion-not-way-i-think-most-people-want-live_789066.html.

12. Winston Churchill, "War of the Unknown Warriors," BBC broadcast, July 14, 1940. The full text of this speech can be found online at www.winstonchurchill.org /resources/speeches/1940-the-finest-hour/war-of-the-unknown-warriors.

13. Winston Churchill, in a speech to a joint session of the United States Congress, December 26, 1941.

14. Cited in David Faber, *Munich, 1938: Appeasement and World War II* (New York: Simon & Schuster, 2008), 190.

15. William Manchester, *The Last Lion: Winston Spencer Churchill, Alone, 1932–1940* (New York: Random House, 1988), 300.

16. Ibid.

17. Richard M. Langworth, ed., *Churchill by Himself: The Definitive Collection of Quotations* (New York: Public Affairs, 2008), 262.

18. Ibid., 484.

19. Martin Gilbert, *Churchill: A Life* (New York: Henry Holt, 1991), 82.

20. James 4:6.

21. Winston S. Churchill, *The Gathering Storm* (Boston: Houghton Mifflin, 1948), 667.

22. Proverbs 9:10.

23. Proverbs 2:7-8, NASB.

CHAPTER 14: HELP AND HOPE FOR OUR TIMES

1. Boris Johnson, *The Churchill Factor* (New York: Riverhead Books, 2014), 22–24.

2. Matthew 24:14, NIV.

3. Matthew 24:6, NIV.

4. See Romans 14:17.

5. Winston Churchill, *Thoughts and Adventures* (London: Thornton Butterworth, 1932), 294.

6. Dr. Thomas Altizer, interview with Wallace Henley.

7. Ibid., 284. Italics added.

8. Daniel 2:20-21, NIV.

9. Romans 14:17, NIV.

10. *Values regime* is a term used by William Strauss and Neil Howe in *The Fourth Turning* (Broadway, 1997) to describe the establishment elites who set cultural precedent and consensus.

11. Benjamin Franklin, *Autobiography of Benjamin Franklin* (Philadelphia: J. B. Lippincott, 1869), 253.

12. Revelation 9:11.

13. William L. Shirer, *The Rise and Fall of the Third Reich: A History of Nazi Germany* (New York: Simon & Schuster, 1960), 5.

14. 1 John 4:3, NIV.

15. 2 Thessalonians 2:8-9, NIV.

16. 1 Samuel 16:7, NIV.

17. Churchill, *Thoughts and Adventures*, 292.

18. Ibid.

19. Philip Jenkins, "The Next Christianity," *The Atlantic*, October 1, 2002. http://www.theatlantic.com/magazine/archive/2002/10/the-next-christianity/302591/.

20. Churchill, *Thoughts and Adventures*, 280.

21. Ibid.

22. 1 Peter 3:15, NIV.

23. Psalm 46:1-3, KJV.

24. Isaiah 57:15, NIV.

25. Isaiah 9:2, NIV.

26. Churchill, *Thoughts and Adventures*, 19.

ACKNOWLEDGMENTS

A BOOK OF THE MAGNITUDE of *God and Churchill* is far more demanding than our own knowledge and skills could encompass. We're grateful to the people whose efforts were essential to the completion of this project. We thank God for awakening the vision in Jonathan for this book, sowing a fascination for Churchill in Wallace decades ago, and then bringing us together. Our spouses' encouragement and forbearance as we worked long hours researching and writing deserve our deepest thanks.

Without the careful research of Sir Martin Gilbert especially, along with other Churchill scholars and writers, our task would have been impossible.

Greg Johnson, our literary agent, quickly caught the passion for *God and Churchill* and constantly encouraged us to "never give in." Jan Long Harris, publisher at Tyndale Momentum, enlarged our vision to communicate Churchill's spiritual dimension to as wide an audience as possible. Sarah Atkinson, associate acquisitions director, and Jillian VandeWege, acquisitions editor, knew the right questions to ask to bring out elements we might have otherwise overlooked. Nancy Clausen, senior marketing director, and Cassidy Gage, marketing manager, amazed us with their concepts of getting *God and Churchill* to a broad readership. Sharon Leavitt's work as senior communications manager helped us maintain links with all the Tyndale team. Senior editor Dave Lindstedt brought his professional expertise to the editing of the manuscript, and, along with associate copyeditor Kevin McLenithan, helped us hone and shape it. Art director Stephen Vosloo and his team gave great thought and creative energy to the graphic design of the book. We are also grateful to Nancy Tighe, Wallace's administrative assistant, for her behind-the-scenes contributions to the project.

INDEX

Alfred (king), 115–117

Aryanism, 66–68, 72, 138–140, 143, 176–178

authority vs. authoritarianism, 162–164

Bach, Johann Sebastian, 170

Battle of Omdurman, 19–22

Bentham, Jeremy, 140–141

Bethel Confession, 157–158

Boer War (second), 22–40

Bonhoeffer, Dietrich, 154–159

Churchill, Jennie (mother of WSC), 6

Churchill, Lord Randolph (father of WSC), 5, 11–13

Churchill, Winston Spencer
  battle of Omdurman, 20–22
  and the Bible, 8, 46–47, 74, 86–87, 108, 114, 118–121, 122
  Boer War (second), 22–40
  brushes with danger, 19–22, 24–28, 34–40, 56–57
  childhood, 3–9
  and Christian civilization, 91–94, 113–114, 115–132, 179–188
  and courage, 86–88, 200
  and destiny, 3–4, 214–215
  and the Dardanelles disaster, 48–54
  and determination, 201–202
  and Deuteronomy, 46–48
  and Elizabeth Everest, 7–9, 16, 94
  escape from prison camp, 34–40
  and faith, 196–198
  as first lord of the admiralty, 43–54
  and grace, 206–207
  at Harrow, 3–4, 8–9, 10–11, 15
  and honesty, 199–200

  and Islam, 125–126
  and King Alfred, 115–117
  and leadership, 211–225
  and the Maccabees, 86–88
  Member of Parliament, 40–42, 75–81
  military service, 15–17, 19–22, 54–57
  and moral balance, 202–203
  and Moses, 41, 108, 117, 119–121, 202
  and perspective, 204–205, 215–217
  prime minister, 82–88
  prisoner of war, 28–34
  and Providence, 196–198
  relationship with his parents, 5–7, 12
  relationship with Mrs. Everest, 7–9
  religious training, 8–9
  and rest, 207–209
  and retaliation, 109–111
  at Sandhurst, 11–12, 14, 15
  and scientism, 133–135, 139–141, 145
  and the Sermon on the Mount, 94–114
  in South Africa, 22–40
  in the Sudan, 19–22
  surrender, views on, 24, 28
  and utilitarianism, 140–141
  and vision, 198–199, 214–217
  as war correspondent, 14–15, 22–40
  and "Wilson's Death Trap," 24–27

Churchill's age and our own, 165–188, 211–225

courage, 86–88, 200
  and bravado, 127–129

cycle of nations, 232–235

Dardanelles disaster (WWI), 48–54

Darwin, Charles, 66, 136–137, 140, 176–178

destroyers and deliverers, 235–236

Einstein, Albert, and the church, 160–161
equivalency, doctrine of 180, 214–215
eugenics, 136–139, 140, 176–178
Evans, Murland de Grasse, 3–4, 11
Everest, Elizabeth, 7–9, 16, 94
Gallipoli campaign (WWI), 48–54
Gobineau, Arthur de, 67–68
Harrow, 3–4, 8–9, 10–11, 15
Heidegger, Martin, 66–67
Hildebrand, Dietrich von, 155
Hitler, Adolf
    and Aryanism, 66–68, 72, 138–140, 143,
        176–178
    and August Kubizek, 62–63
    and the Bible, 156
    and biological improvement, 137, 138–139
    brushes with danger, 61–62
    and the church, 153–164
    and civilization, 67
    and Darwin, 66, 136–137, 140, 176–178
    destiny, vision of, 62–63
    and eugenics, 136–139, 140, 176–178
    and Gobineau, 67–68
    and Heidegger, 66–67
    and Nietzsche, 66, 175
    and scientism, 133–152
    spiritual guidance, 66–68
    and Wagner, 62–63, 172–174

Kerrl, Hans, and Christianity, 160
Kubizek, August, and Adolf Hitler, 62–63
leadership, character of, 211–225
Mein Kampf (Hitler), 65, 135–136, 156–157,
    175
Moses, 41, 108, 117, 119–121, 202
Niemöller, Martin, 154–155, 158
Nietzsche, Friedrich, 66, 174–175
Nuremberg Laws (1935), 72, 138–139
Nuremberg trials, 130–132
Pastors' Emergency League, 158
rationalism, 171–172
reductionism, 142–143, 171–172
retaliation, 109–111
scientism, 133–152
    and biological improvement, 137
    and presumption, 148–151
    and reductionism, 142–143
    and transcendence, 140–141, 143,
        145–148
    and utilitarianism, 140–141
Semler, J. S., and German rationalism,
    171–172
Sermon on the Mount, 94–114
Thielicke, Helmut, 154
transcendence, 140–141, 143, 145–148
utilitarianism, 140–141
Wagner, Richard, 62–63, 172–174

ABOUT THE AUTHORS

Jonathan Sandys is an international public speaker on the life, times, and leadership of his great-grandfather, Sir Winston Churchill. Over the past ten years, he has endeavored to continue his Great-Grandpapa's legacy and bring Churchill alive for future generations.

While giving speeches throughout the United States and Europe, Jonathan became convinced of the need to recapture Churchill's "never surrender!" spirit in our day and age—the same spirit his great-grandfather instilled in Britain, Europe, and America during the Second World War.

In 2010, while reading about Winston Churchill's many near-misses and life-or-death experiences, Jonathan began to see a pattern that raised some questions in his mind: How was all this possible? How did Churchill survive? Was there something more than luck or coincidence to the events of Churchill's life? These questions became the basis of Jonathan's research with Wallace Henley for *God and Churchill: How the Great Leader's Sense of Divine Destiny Changed His Troubled World and Offers Hope for Ours.*

Jonathan has launched a blog—*Never Surrender!*—that focuses on life lessons from his great-grandfather and draws parallels between the events of yesterday and today.

Jonathan and his wife, Sara, host the "Churchill's Britain"

tours, taking visitors behind the scenes at many locations that were significant in Winston Churchill's life. They live in Houston, Texas, with their son, Jesse.

Follow Jonathan online:

Blog: http://churchillbulletin.com
Facebook: http://facebook.com/wscspeaker
Twitter: http://twitter.com/jonathansandys
LinkedIn: http://linkedin.com/in/jmesandys

For a daily quote from Sir Winston Churchill, visit http://twitter .com/churchillquote.

∞⋅∞

Wallace Henley has had a career in journalism, politics, academia, and the church. This career has given him direct engagement with many of the major events of modern times, from the 1960s civil-rights movement to Nixon-era White House upheaval to the contemporary culture wars, a frequent topic of Henley's columns in the *Christian Post*. Henley's passion for learning about Churchill began while working at the White House. Henley is senior associate pastor at Houston's 67,000-member Second Baptist Church. He has been married to Irene for fifty-three years, and they have two children, six grandchildren, and one great-grandchild.